contemporary
woodworking
projects

contemporary woodworking projects

by paul levine

Madrigal Publishing Company

We at Madrigal Publishing have tried to make this book as accurate and correct as possible. Plans, illustrations,
photographs, and text have been carefully researched by our
in-house staff. However, due to the variability of all local conditions, construction materials, personal skills, etc., Madrigal
Publishing assumes no responsibility for any injuries suffered
or damages or other losses incurred that result from material
presented herein. All instructions and plans should be carefully studied and clearly understood before beginning any construction.

Library of Congress Cataloging-in-Publication Data:

Levine, Paul, date.
    Contemporary woodworking projects.

    1. Woodwork.   I. Title.
TT180.L435   1986   684'.08   86-23622
ISBN 0-9617098-0-4 (pbk.)

Madrigal Publishing Company
517 Litchfield Road
P.O. Box 1629
New Milford, CT 06776

For Lillian, and for Sam

contents

acknowledgement

there is no adequate way to convey the enormous effort that must be expended to produce a book. The care and thought given to the design and construction of forty projects is certainly considerable, but the work required to convert this into photos, drawings, and text able to communicate the "how-to" is staggering.

To all those at Madrigal Publishing Co. involved in the production, David Peters for writing and editing, Judy Robinson, Dan Thornton, and Michael Gellatly for art and design, Jane Pratt for coordinating production, and Kim Gellatly for copy editing, a thousand thousand thanks. Thanks also to John and Jim Kane of Silver Sun Studios for photography, and to Joe Gluse and Eugene Marino III for additional technical art.

Special thanks to Tom Begnal, without whose managerial skills nothing happens, and a very special thanks to Jim McQuillan, whose generous support and encouragement made it all possible.

No sensible married man leaves out his wife. Especially if she is as capable, lovely, and supportive as Janet.

introduction

Contemporary woodworking projects is a book featuring forty designs for furniture, toys, and accessories. Although the term "contemporary" is often associated with modern or radical designs, all these projects were developed with an eye toward a harmonious blend of sensible, down-to-earth construction, attractive appearance, and functional purpose.

The book introduces two new types of joints: the knuckle joint, and the notched mitered spline joint. These joints are not only strong, but they also provide the projects on which they are used with a unique and distinctive look.

It was my intention to create furniture designs for specific living areas, and the classification of the projects into various groupings is a reflection of this. Where possible I have carried a common design element through all or most of the projects in a particular group, such as the incorporation of the knuckle joint in all the living room group pieces, and the use of the notched mitered spline joint on most of the bedroom group projects.

I believe that one of the great delights as a woodworker is making things for one's children, and the many hours I've spent in the shop building toys and furniture for my two daughters, Samantha and Jordana, bear this out. I can also state with confidence that their use of these items insures that all the children's toys and furnishings have been rigorously tested and heartily approved.

The variety of projects I present in contemporary woodworking projects is intended to appeal to a broad spectrum of woodworking skill levels. Items such as the cutting boards and jigsaw puzzle require few tools to build, and can be easily mastered by a woodworker just starting out. More ambitious projects such as the white oak credenza, while somewhat more demanding, are still well within the ability of a woodworker with an average shop and moderate experience.

Considerable planning went into the overall organization of the book and presentation of the projects. Clear, concise text complemented by accurate drawings and photographs make the project instructions easy to understand and follow. Where they are necessary or helpful, detailed step-by-step illustrations guide you through the various special techniques and operations. The Source Index in the back of the book is an important additional feature that should prove to be a valuable asset in locating materials, hardware, and general woodworking supplies.

Whether you use contemporary woodworking projects as a detailed plan book for constructing a houseful of furniture, toys, and accessories, or whether the project ideas, techniques, and unique new joinery serve mainly as a source of inspiration toward the development of your own designs, I am confident you will agree that in these pages we have broken exciting new ground in the field of woodworking. I encourage you all to share in the woodworking experience, with the hope and knowledge that your endeavors will bring you the same joy and satisfaction that I have discovered. ☐

Paul Levine

livingroom

knuckle joint

the knuckle joint is common to the five projects in the butternut living room group. As an exposed joint, it adds an attractive detail to the sturdy frame construction.

In order to look right and provide the necessary strength, the mortise and tenon parts of the knuckle joint require a good tight fit. As shown in the following step-by-step instructions, I use a router with a guide bushing, templates, and a ½ in. diameter straight bit to cut the joint to size. The ½ in. diameter straight bit (made by Freud, see source index on page 161 for address) establishes the ¼ in. radius on the inside corners, while a ¼ in. radius bearing guided round-over bit is used to apply the ¼ in. radius to all the remaining edges. After cutting out the templates, make a trial joint from scrapwood to insure accuracy.

If you do not have a ½ in. collet router, an acceptable alternative to the router and template method is to use a drill and the band saw. Lay out both parts of the joint, and with a ½ in. diameter drill bit, establish the ¼ in. radius for the inside corners. The band saw can then be used to simply cut out the waste. After the ¼ in. radius has been applied to all edges, the joint can be final sized by paring with the chisel, or if the fit is sloppy, it can be packed with veneer.

Although not quite as accurate as the router and template method, I have used the drill and band saw technique for many knuckle joint projects. After a few practice runs you should find this method both quick and reliable.

I recommend a dry "test assembly", at which time wax can be applied to the joint area. This will insure a proper fit and simplify cleanup of any glue squeeze-out around the knuckle joint after final assembly. Acetone is used to remove the wax. □

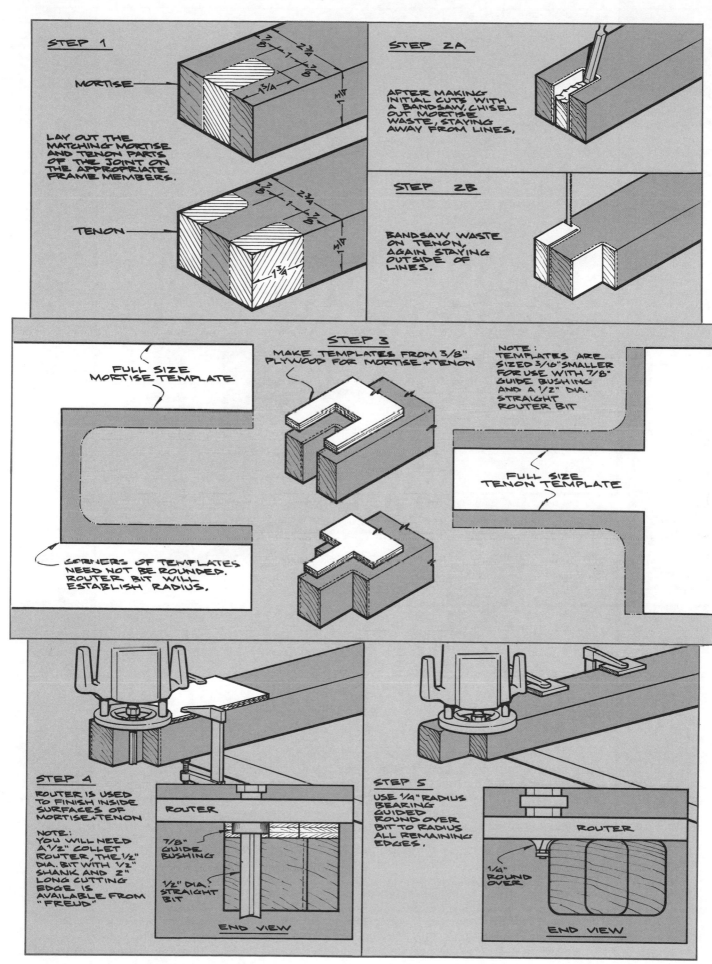

STEP 1

MORTISE

LAY OUT THE MATCHING MORTISE AND TENON PARTS OF THE JOINT ON THE APPROPRIATE FRAME MEMBERS.

TENON

STEP 2A

AFTER MAKING INITIAL CUTS WITH A BANDSAW, CHISEL OUT MORTISE WASTE, STAYING AWAY FROM LINES.

STEP 2B

BANDSAW WASTE ON TENON, AGAIN STAYING OUTSIDE OF LINES.

STEP 3

MAKE TEMPLATES FROM 3/8" PLYWOOD FOR MORTISE + TENON

FULL SIZE MORTISE TEMPLATE

NOTE: TEMPLATES ARE SIZED 3/16" SMALLER FOR USE WITH 7/8" GUIDE BUSHING AND A 1/2" DIA. STRAIGHT ROUTER BIT

FULL SIZE TENON TEMPLATE

CORNERS OF TEMPLATES NEED NOT BE ROUNDED. ROUTER BIT WILL ESTABLISH RADIUS.

STEP 4

ROUTER IS USED TO FINISH INSIDE SURFACES OF MORTISE + TENON

NOTE: YOU WILL NEED A 1/2" COLLET ROUTER, THE 1/2" DIA. BIT WITH 1/2" SHANK AND 2" LONG CUTTING EDGE IS AVAILABLE FROM "FREUD"

ROUTER

7/8" GUIDE BUSHING

1/2" DIA. STRAIGHT BIT

END VIEW

STEP 5

USE 1/4" RADIUS BEARING GUIDED ROUND OVER BIT TO RADIUS ALL REMAINING EDGES.

ROUTER

1/4" ROUND OVER

END VIEW

cabinet

I believe that most woodworkers take special pride in a project that enables them to incorporate an unusual or rare section of board displaying a striking and richly figured grain pattern. This particular project features a dramatically spalted "found" maple log that was band sawed and then slip-matched to form the door and back panels.

I had discovered the log along the roadside (a great source for spalted woods), and although the greater part of the piece had decayed so far as to be unusable, a small area was still sound. By resawing and slip matching, I was able to create lovely panels from stock that might otherwise have been relegated to the woodstove. It is a rewarding experience to discover a lovely piece such as this, and even more gratifying to see your discovery displayed prominently in a fine article of furniture.

This cabinet is an excellent opportunity for you to utilize a similar section of board that you had perhaps put aside for precisely such a use.

The cabinet carcase, the door and back frames, and the leg frame assemblies are made of butternut. If you have never worked with hardwoods, or if you have worked with them but were discouraged, I recommend that you try butternut. Butternut has a lovely light brown hue and is almost as soft as pine, although unlike pine it will not gum up your cutters. Butternut is a first cousin of black walnut and is sometimes also known as "white" walnut.

A good place to start this project is with the cabinet carcase, consisting of parts A, B, C, and D. I made the top, sides and bottom from a single 13¾ in. wide butternut board. This provides a continuous flow of the grain from the sides into the top and bottom. After ripping the sides to establish their 12¾ in. width, lay out the dovetail spacing as illustrated in the dovetail detail. The dovetails can be cut by hand, however if you have a commercial dovetail jig that will accommodate the stock width and that can be adjusted for different sizes, then the jig and router will help speed the work and insure accuracy. Accuracy is especially important in a project where the joinery is not only exposed, but is also featured prominently as a detail highlighting the construction.

Make the divider (D), using the dado head to cut the ⅜ in. by ¼ in. by 11½ in. long tenon on each end, as shown in the divider tenon detail. After mortising the cabinet top and bottom to accept the divider, dry assemble parts A, B, C, and D to check for proper fit. If all is right, glue and assemble these parts. When dry, use the router equipped with a bearing-guided ¼ in. round-over bit to apply the ¼ in. radius to the corners and edges as shown.

This cabinet uses the same type of leg/rail assembly, featuring the distinctive knuckle joint, that is common to all the living room group projects. As a design element, the knuckle joint is both an interesting sculptured detail, and an important visual device tying these projects together. Refer to the step-by-step illustrations on pages 4 and 5 for instruction on how to cut the knuckle joint on the ends of parts E and F. Note that the upper rails must be drilled and counterbored to accept the hex head bolts *before* the legs and rails are assembled.

After completing the two leg/rail assemblies, cut the stretcher (G) to length and width. Use the dado head to establish the 1½ in. long tenon on each end of the stretcher, then drill out and square the corresponding mortises in the back leg of the leg/rail assemblies. Glue and clamp the leg/rail assemblies in place on either end of the stretcher. Note that the edges of the stretcher and the shoulders where they meet the legs are all radiused with the ¼ in. bearing-guided round-over bit.

With the base assembly complete, cut the two spacers (H) to length and width. Next, drill out the ¾ in. diameter holes that will accept the hex head bolts, as shown in the base-to-cabinet assembly cross section. Drill for and insert the threaded insert into the bottom of the cabinet carcase, but do not mount the cabinet to the base yet.

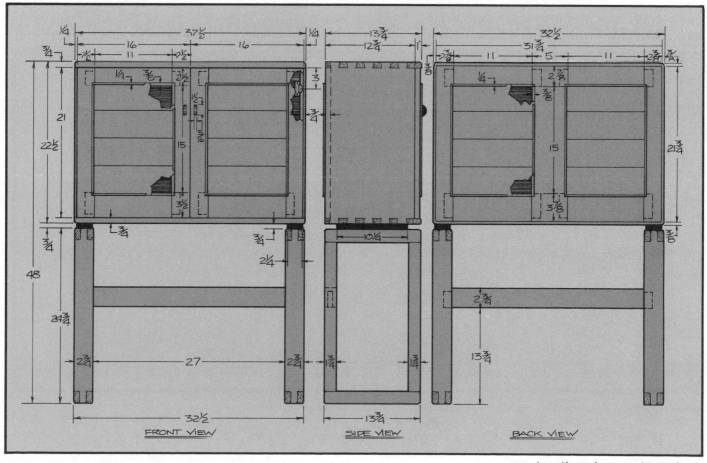

FRONT VIEW   SIDE VIEW   BACK VIEW

(continued on next page)

As you can see from the photo, the spacer is made from a dark wood. I used ebony, but if this is not readily available, you could use maple or birch stained black to achieve the same effect. Rosewood is another option if you have access to it. The importance of using a dark wood for the spacer, which separates the cabinet from the base, is strictly appearance. The dark wood provides the look of a negative space, creating an illusion in which the cabinet seems to float above the base. Both the cabinet and the sofa table make use of this visual device.

Now make the cabinet doors and the back. To make the door and back frames, first rip stock to the needed width. The various rails (parts I, J, P, and Q) are cut to length and tenoned on the ends as illustrated in the rail tenon details. The stiles (K, R, and S) are ripped to width, mortised to accept the rail tenons, and then crosscut to length. This procedure will eliminate any chance of end grain being broken out during the mortising process.

After the door and back frames have been made and assembled, use a $\frac{3}{8}$ in. rabbeting bit to rout the $\frac{3}{8}$ in. by $\frac{3}{8}$ in. rabbets that will accept the panels. Note that the corners of the door and back frame rabbets must be squared by hand with a sharp chisel.

Although I resawed and slip-matched spalted material, as noted earlier, to form the door and back panels (L and T) you may prefer an alternate panel treatment. If you use the half-lapped panels, as shown in the panel layout, each panel should be either pinned or glued on the ends to allow the

indicated $\frac{1}{16}$ in. space between. In order to permit each panel board to expand and contract with changes in humidity, apply the pin or glue only at the center point of each end. The $\frac{1}{4}$ in. by $\frac{3}{8}$ in. retainer moldings (M and U) are then tacked in place.

Rabbet the back side of the cabinet as shown to accept the back frame and panel assembly, and glue in place.

The doors are mounted with European style self-closing, full overlay cup hinges (N). A 35mm hole must be drilled in the door frames to accept the hinge cup. Special 35mm drill bits can be purchased, or if you have one, a $1\frac{3}{8}$ in. diameter Forstner bit can also be used. The hinges permit 3-way adjustment of the doors, so you should have little difficulty achieving proper alignment.

The original door pulls (O) for this cabinet were made from butternut, but the pulls shown in the photograph are ebony, a nice contrast that balances well with the dead black spalt lines of the maple panels. These pulls can be hand carved or cut out with a hole saw. When mounting the pulls, pre-drill them first and do not force the screws, lest you split the stock. Ebony is very dense, and small pieces such as these should be handled with care.

After final sanding, the cabinet and base are finished with Watco Danish Oil as the other living room group projects are. Mount the cabinet to the base with the ebony spacers in between to complete the assembly. □

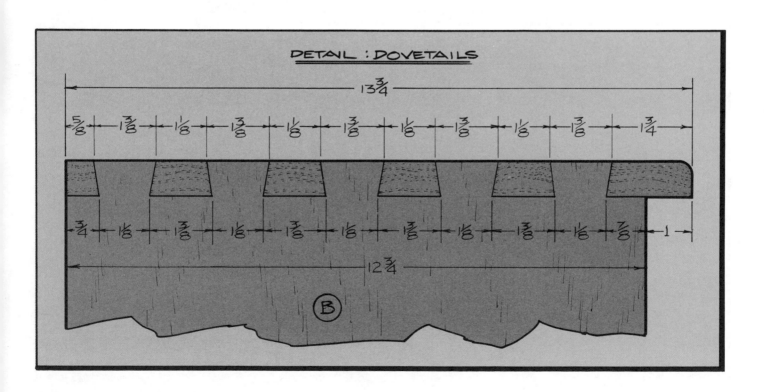

DETAIL : DOVETAILS

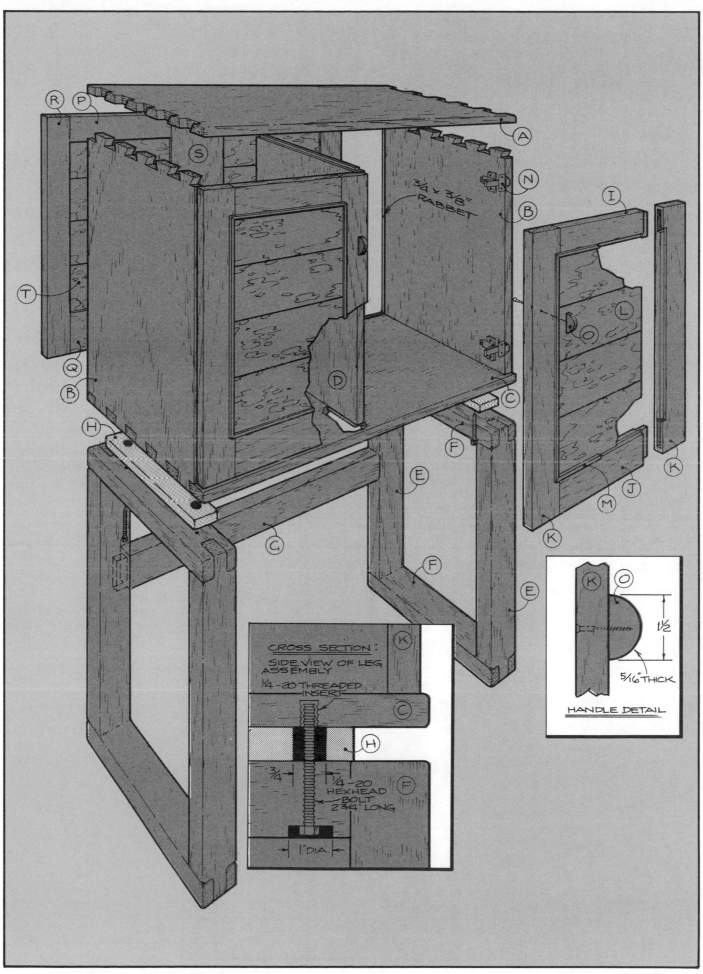

3/4 x 3/8" RABBET

HANDLE DETAIL

1 1/2

5/16" THICK

CROSS SECTION:
SIDE VIEW OF LEG ASSEMBLY

1/4 - 20 THREADED INSERT

3/4

1/4 - 20 HEXHEAD BOLT 2 3/4" LONG

1" DIA.

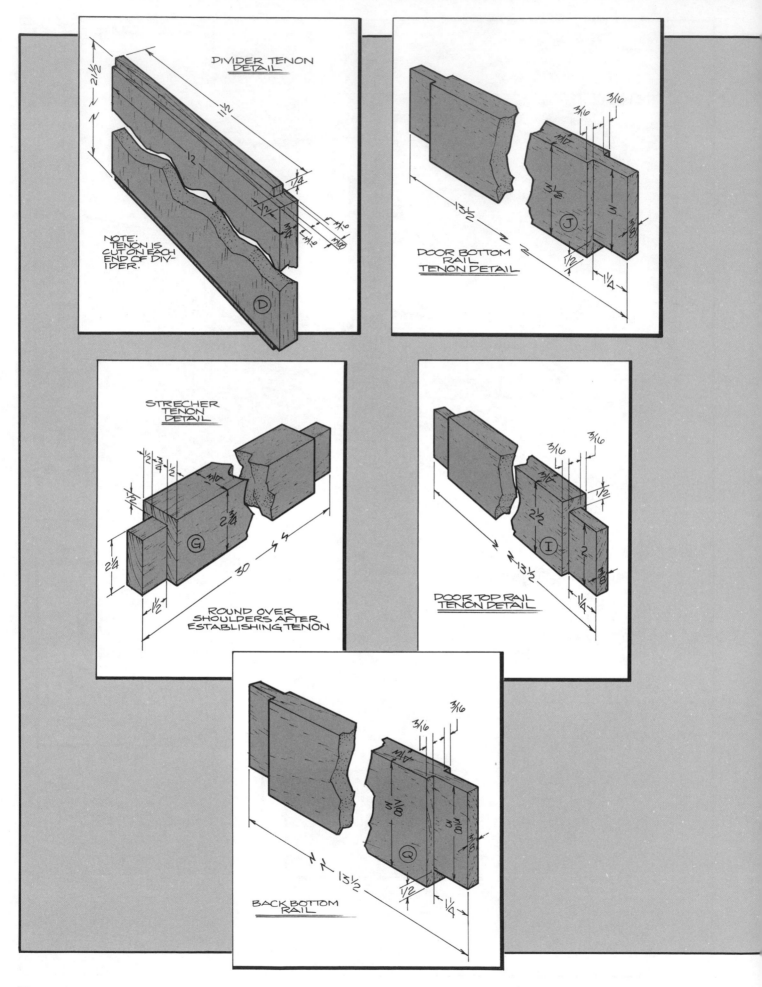

DIVIDER TENON DETAIL

NOTE: TENON IS CUT ON EACH END OF DIVIDER.

D

DOOR BOTTOM RAIL TENON DETAIL

J

STRECHER TENON DETAIL

ROUND OVER SHOULDERS AFTER ESTABLISHING TENON

G

DOOR TOP RAIL TENON DETAIL

I

BACK BOTTOM RAIL

Q

Bill of Materials
(all dimensions actual)

Part	Description	Size	No. Req'd.
A	Top	¾ × 13¾ × 32½	1
B	Side	¾ × 12¾ × 22½	2
C	Bottom	¾ × 13¾ × 32½	1
D	Divider	¾ × 12 × 21½*	1
E	Leg	1¾ × 2¾ × 24¾	4
F	Rail	1¾ × 2¾ × 13¾	4
G	Stretcher	1¾ × 2¾ × 30*	1
H	Spacer	¾ × 2¼ × 10¼	2
I	Door Top Rail	¾ × 2½ × 13½*	2
J	Door Bottom Rail	¾ × 3½ × 13½*	2
K	Door Stile	¾ × 2½ × 21	4
L	Door Panel	⅜ × 4⅛ × 11¾	8
M	Door Molding	¼ × ⅜	as req'd.
N	Door Hinge	European self close/full overlay**	4
O	Door Pull	5/16 × ¾ × 1½	2
P	Back Top Rail	¾ × 2⅞ × 13½*	2
Q	Back Bottom Rail	¾ × 3⅞ × 13½*	2
R	Back Stile	¾ × 2⅜ × 21¾	2
S	Back Center	¾ × 5 × 21¾	1
T	Back Panel	⅜ × 4⅛ × 11¾	8
U	Back Molding	¼ × ⅜	as req'd.

*Length includes tenons.

**Available from: The Woodworkers' Store, (see source index) order part no. D9632.

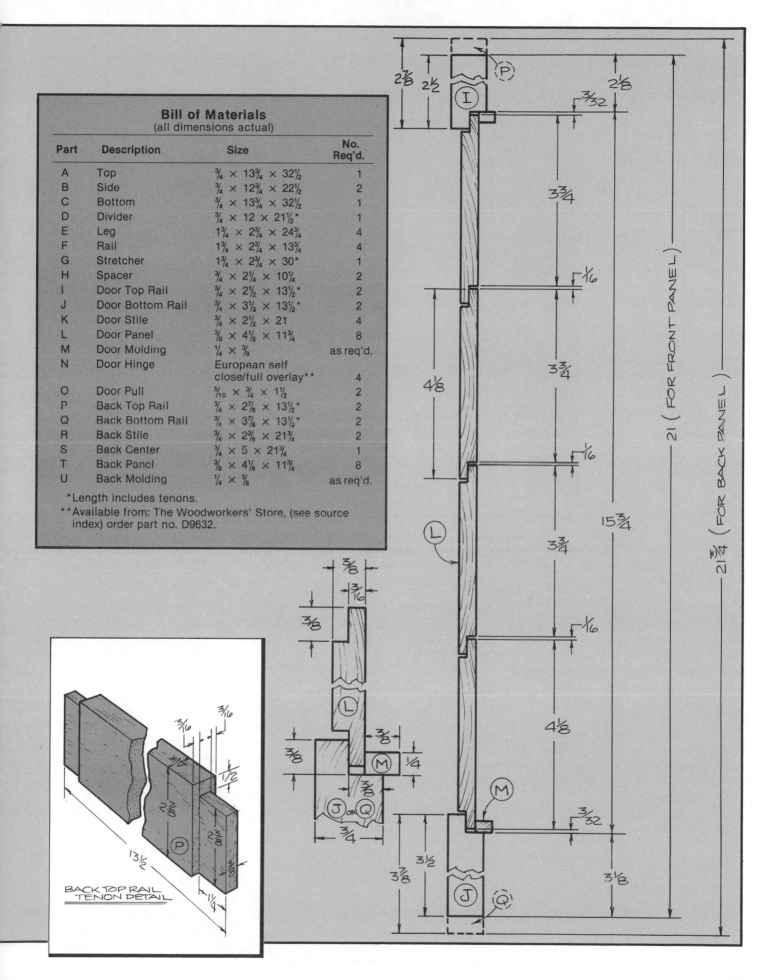

BACK TOP RAIL
TENON DETAIL

11

glass top table

this end table, crafted in butternut like the other living room pieces, is essentially a 20 in. square cube. The leg and rail frames, consisting of parts A and B, are made from the same size stock and follow the same step-by-step procedure (see instructions on pages 4 and 5) as the other knuckle-jointed projects.

Start by getting out the stock for parts A and B. Take care that your stock thickness is exactly 1¾ in. and that the width is 2¾ in. if you plan to use the full-size patterns included with the knuckle joint instructions.

An alternate to the router and template method, in the event that you do not have a ½ in. collet router or the 2 in. long trimmer bit, is to use the drill and band saw. Simply lay out the knuckle locations, use a ½ in. diameter drill bit to establish the ¼ in. radii, and clean the waste with the band saw. If you do not have a band saw, a hand saw and chisel could be used to clean the waste instead. Many of my early knuckle joint projects were crafted by this hand method and I have found it to be quite reliable.

After you have cut and assembled the rail/leg

frames, make the stretchers (C). As you will note from the stretcher cross section, the stretcher has a ¾ in. radius round-over top and bottom, and is rabbeted to accept the glass. After using the dado head to cut the ½ in. long tenons on the stretcher ends, use the router with a ¾ in. round-over bit to establish the ¾ in. radii. Cut the ¼ in. by ½ in. rabbet to accept the glass and hand sand to approximate the ¼ in. radius shown on the top edge and at the top of the stretcher shoulders where they contact the rail/leg frames.

Cut the shelf (D) and cleat (E) parts, notch the outside shelf ends to fit around the legs as shown, and after mortising the rail/leg frame to accept the stretcher tenons, assemble the table. Note that the cleats must be drilled and counterbored to accept the 1½ in. long shelf mounting screws as shown in the side view.

After final sanding, finish the table with Watco Danish Oil. The ¼ in. thick plate glass top (F) can be custom-cut at your local glass shop. Check the measurements before ordering the glass to insure an accurate fit. □

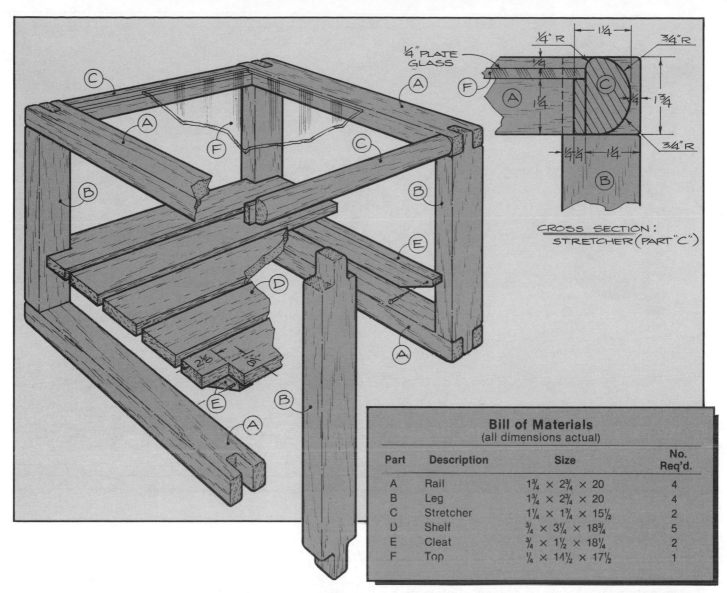

¼" PLATE GLASS

¼" R   1¼

¾" R

¼

F

A

C

¾

1¾

¼

⅛ ¼   1¼

¾" R

B

CROSS SECTION:
STRETCHER (PART "C")

Bill of Materials
(all dimensions actual)

Part	Description	Size	No. Req'd.
A	Rail	1¾ × 2¾ × 20	4
B	Leg	1¾ × 2¾ × 20	4
C	Stretcher	1¼ × 1¾ × 15½	2
D	Shelf	¾ × 3¼ × 18¾	5
E	Cleat	¾ × 1½ × 18¼	2
F	Top	¼ × 14½ × 17½	1

2⅛   ¾

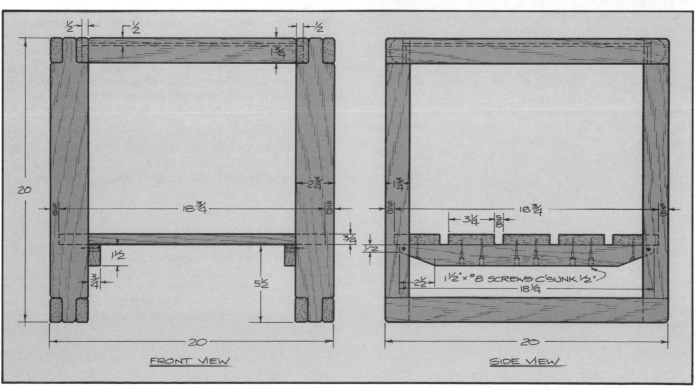

½   ½   ½

1¾

20

⅝   18¾   ⅝

2¾

1½

¾

5½

20

FRONT VIEW

1¾

⅝   ¾   18¾   ⅝

¾
½

3¼   ⅝

2½   1½" × #8 SCREWS C'SUNK ½"

18¼

20

SIDE VIEW

13

sofa table

this piece is a handsome combination of simple, straightforward design and visually interesting wood surfaces. The design features exposed and sculptured joints, softened edges and the ability to dismantle the unit without damage. Construction is not difficult, but as with most contemporary projects, great care should be given to the joinery and finishing.

Although the table shown here measures six feet in length, which will fit well in most rooms, an earlier version was built on commission to a length of eleven feet and rested on four frames instead of three. Obviously, the dimensions can be altered considerably to suit your particular needs without losing the basic character of the piece.

I'm lucky enough to live near a rural sawmill where it is possible to obtain interesting and unusual native woods at reasonable cost. The top of this piece was made from two consecutive 1¾ in. slices ripped from a seasoned butternut log. These boards (A) were arranged to form a bookmatch in which the grain patterns of both boards are nearly identical and are matched as mirror images. With interesting grain patterns, crotch figures, wormholes, etc., the top becomes almost a piece of artwork.

If you do not have access to a sawmill, you can

forego the book-matching and build this table from almost any seasoned hardwood.

The top boards are laid side by side to achieve the most attractive arrangement, then trimmed to length and width. Turn the boards on edge, face sides out and make five marks 17 in. on center, starting 2 in. from each end. Using a marking gauge and working from the face sides, score across these lines to establish the centers for the five spacer discs (B).

With a doweling jig or pre-drilled block of wood as a guide, bore the five holes in each edge with a ⁵⁄₁₆ in. diameter drill. The holes are drilled to a depth of 2 in. and you should use a depth gauge to insure accuracy.

The spacer discs are cut from a contrasting hardwood (I used Brazilian rosewood) with a 1¼ in. diameter plug cutter. Bore into the face of a ½ in. or ¾ in. by 2 in. by 8 in. piece of wood, stopping just short of cutting all the way through. After cutting five plugs, drill a ⁵⁄₁₆ in. diameter hole in the center of each, then turn the board on edge and resaw it ⅜ in. thick, thus freeing the plugs which then resemble little doughnuts.

Round off the edges of the two top boards. On what will be the front and back edges of the unit, use a router and a ¾ in. round-over bit. All other edges are rounded with a ¼ in. bit. The top boards are then given a complete sanding.

Cut ¼ in. threaded rod into five 4¼ in. lengths. Use a thin stick to spread epoxy in the holes in one board, and push the threaded rods (C) in so that they all protrude an equal length. Then add the hardwood spacer discs and, after spreading epoxy in the holes of the other board, join and squeeze them together with pipe clamps until the spacer discs are held firmly. When clamping up, use scrap wood under the clamp jaws to avoid marring the top.

To make the supporting frames, I chose clear 2 in. stock planed to 1¾ in. Rip the pieces of all frames (parts D and E) to a width of 2¾ in. Then refer to the step-by-step illustrations on page 4 for instructions on making the "knuckle joint." Take care that the joints are well fitted with good contact at all adjoining surfaces. You should be able to force the joints together by hand. If you goof and a joint turns out a bit loose, glue one or more slips of veneer to the sides of the rail notch to tighten it up.

Before assembling the joints, counterbore the three top rails to a depth of ½ in. and drill pilot holes for the lag screws. Sand the parts and assemble with glue on a flat surface. Make sure that the assembled frames are perfectly square before the glue sets.

The 1 in. by 1½ in. by 10 in. top cleats (F) located between the top and the supporting frames can be cut from a contrasting hardwood or any scrap hardwood painted flat black. Drill these spacers to align with the pilot holes in the top rails. After this is done, the frames and top may be assembled. The shelf cleats (G) to support the lower shelf are then cut and fastened and the shelf boards (H) are fitted

as shown in the plan. These boards are ripped from ¾ in. thick hardwood to match the top and legs. The front and back boards are notched to fit around the legs. Note that there are eight shelf boards in all, meeting between the center cleats. The boards are secured with one screw at each end.

I finished the unit with Watco Danish Oil, applying as many coats as necessary to saturate the wood. End grain will require additional coats. When the wood absorbed no more oil, all surfaces were wiped down and allowed to dry in a heated room for one week, after which a coat of furniture wax was applied and buffed. □   (continued on next page)

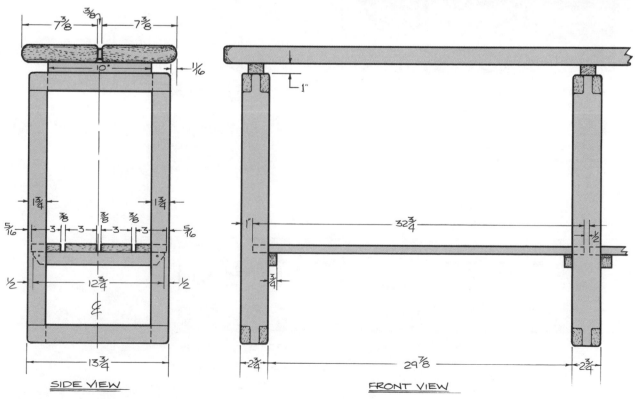

SIDE VIEW

FRONT VIEW

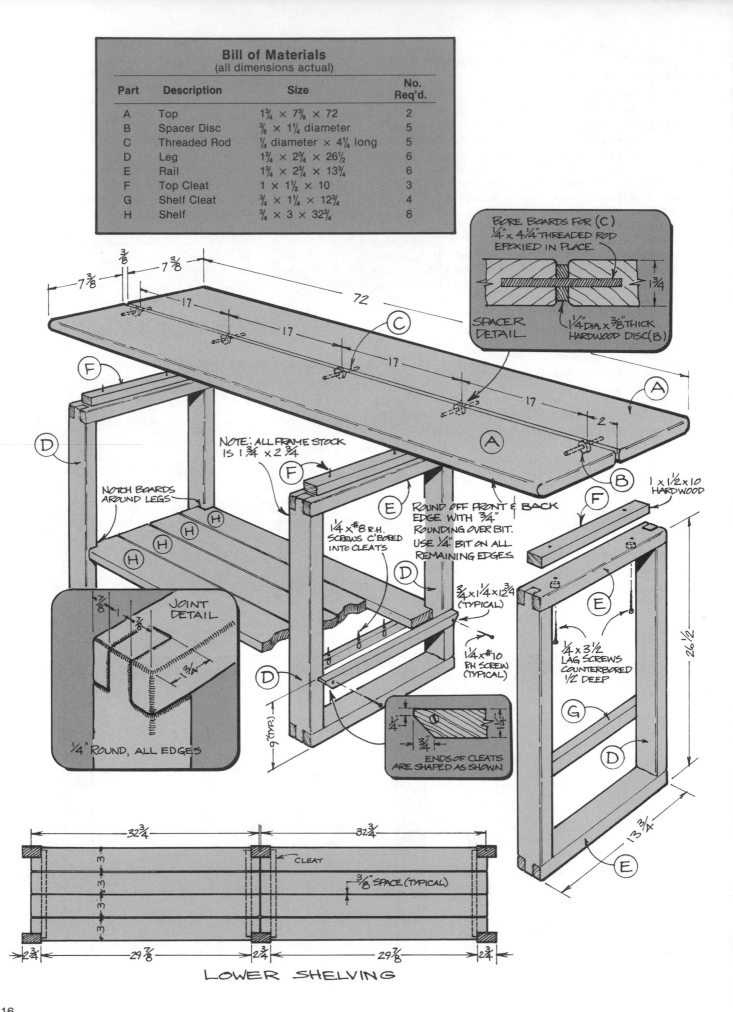

Bill of Materials
(all dimensions actual)

Part	Description	Size	No. Req'd.
A	Top	$1\frac{3}{4} \times 7\frac{3}{8} \times 72$	2
B	Spacer Disc	$\frac{3}{8} \times 1\frac{1}{4}$ diameter	5
C	Threaded Rod	$\frac{1}{4}$ diameter $\times 4\frac{1}{4}$ long	5
D	Leg	$1\frac{3}{4} \times 2\frac{3}{4} \times 26\frac{1}{2}$	6
E	Rail	$1\frac{3}{4} \times 2\frac{3}{4} \times 13\frac{3}{4}$	6
F	Top Cleat	$1 \times 1\frac{1}{2} \times 10$	3
G	Shelf Cleat	$\frac{3}{4} \times 1\frac{1}{4} \times 12\frac{3}{4}$	4
H	Shelf	$\frac{3}{4} \times 3 \times 32\frac{3}{4}$	8

BORE BOARDS FOR (C)
$\frac{1}{4}$" $\times 4\frac{1}{4}$" THREADED ROD
EPOXIED IN PLACE

$1\frac{3}{4}$

SPACER DETAIL

$\frac{1}{4}$" DIA $\times \frac{3}{8}$" THICK HARDWOOD DISC (B)

$\frac{3}{8}$

$7\frac{3}{8}$

$7\frac{3}{8}$

17 17 17 17 17

72

C

A

A

B

F

D

NOTE: ALL FRAME STOCK IS $1\frac{3}{4} \times 2\frac{3}{4}$

F

E

$\frac{1}{4} \times$ #8 R.H. SCREWS C'BORED INTO CLEATS

ROUND OFF FRONT & BACK EDGE WITH $\frac{3}{4}$" ROUNDING OVER BIT. USE $\frac{1}{4}$" BIT ON ALL REMAINING EDGES.

$1 \times 1\frac{1}{2} \times 10$ HARDWOOD

F

B

2

NOTCH BOARDS AROUND LEGS

H H

H H

H

D

$\frac{3}{4} \times 1\frac{1}{4} \times 12\frac{3}{4}$ (TYPICAL)

D

E

$\frac{1}{4} \times$ #10 R.H. SCREW (TYPICAL)

$\frac{1}{4} \times 3\frac{1}{2}$ LAG SCREWS COUNTERBORED $\frac{1}{2}$" DEEP

$26\frac{1}{2}$

G

D

JOINT DETAIL

$\frac{7}{8}$ 1

$\frac{7}{8}$

$\frac{7}{8}$

$1\frac{3}{4}$

$\frac{1}{4}$" ROUND, ALL EDGES

6" (TYP.)

$\frac{1}{4}$" $\frac{1}{4}$"

$\frac{3}{4}$"

ENDS OF CLEATS ARE SHAPED AS SHOWN

$13\frac{3}{4}$

E

LOWER SHELVING

$32\frac{3}{4}$ $32\frac{3}{4}$

3 3 3 3

CLEAT

$\frac{3}{8}$" SPACE (TYPICAL)

$2\frac{3}{4}$ $29\frac{7}{8}$ $2\frac{3}{4}$ $29\frac{7}{8}$ $2\frac{3}{4}$

bookmatch butternut tabletop (detail)

chair

the chair, love seat, ottoman, glass top table, sofa table, and cabinet were constructed as a set. All these pieces feature the handsome and uncomplicated knuckle joint.

When I set about designing these pieces, I was seeking to combine a variety of elements, several of which were seemingly inconsistent. On one hand, I wanted the construction to be basic enough so that anyone, even a novice woodworker, could build them. On the other hand, the design had to be such that the pieces were contemporary yet sensible. I needed to develop a motif that would place these pieces in the "fine furniture" class, while maintaining the balance between the appearance of the projects and the ease of construction.

The leg/rail frames common to all the living room pieces are an idea that can be traced back to the basic "2 × 4" furniture of the 1970's. Yet the knuckle joint motif is an element that transforms

these projects into distinctive "designer" pieces that look great in most any setting. As an exposed sculpted joint, the knuckle joint detail highlights the construction and provides both beauty and strength. Naturally, as with much contemporary work, the selection of material is a vital element contributing heavily to the overall impact and success of a piece. This particular set is crafted in butternut, though cherry is a fine alternative. The cover photo shows a detail of a sofa table made in cherry.

Start by constructing the leg/rail frames, consisting of parts A and B. The step-by-step instructions on pages 4 and 5 will enable you to accurately and quickly reproduce the knuckle joint. I strongly recommend this router method because it will guarantee accuracy. If you prefer, however, the joint can also be crafted by first drilling to establish the various $\frac{1}{4}$ in. radii, then sawing and chopping out

18

the waste, and rounding over finally with the router and the ¼ in. round-over bit. Should you use the hand method of cutting the joint and the fit of the mortise and tenon parts is a little sloppy, you can always pack the difference out with a slip of veneer. I have made many of these pieces using the hand method of making the joint, and the results have always been very acceptable. If you use the hand method, I recommend making your cuts on the waste side of the line. The joint can then be trimmed back with a chisel as necessary until the legs and rails fit up snugly. It is better to work this way, rather than having to pack out a loose fitting joint with veneer.

Dry assemble the leg frames, and spread a thin layer of wax over the rounded edges of the joint area, taking care to not get any wax on the surfaces to be glued. This application of wax will simplify cleaning after the glue-up, since any glue squeeze-out onto the inaccessible radiused edges would be most difficult to clean up. After the glue has dried, the wax is removed with acetone. When clamping the leg/rail assemblies, check for squareness.

Next, make the seat frame, consisting of parts C and D. Use the dado head to tenon the ends of parts C and D as shown in the seat frame detail. Mortise C to accept D, and use the table saw with the blade angled at 20 degrees to cut the 9/16 in. deep kerf (see seat frame cross section) to accept the metal

webbing clips (F). A slight fence adjustment will probably be needed to establish the 5/32 in. kerf width if you do not have a blade with that width.

(continued on next page)

Bill of Materials
(all dimensions actual)

Part	Description	Size	No. Req'd.
A	Leg	1¾ × 2¾ × 22½	4
B	Rail	1¾ × 2¾ × 31½	4
C	Seat Frame Front/Back	1½ × 2½ × 25½*	2
D	Seat Frame Stretcher	1½ × 2½ × 29½*	2
E	Face	¾ × 3½ × 23	1
F	Metal Clip	2 in. long**	10
G	Webbing	2 in. wide reinforced rubber**	13 ft.
H	Back Stile	1½ × 2½ × 19*	2
I	Back Rail	1½ × 2½ × 23	1
J	Back Stretcher	1½ × 2½ × 20½*	1
K	Seat Cushion	6 × 23 × 26***	1
L	Back Cushion	6 × 16 × 23***	1

  * Length includes tenons.

 ** Both metal clips and webbing are available from The Woodworkers' Store, (see source index) order part no. H1101 for the clip, and part no. H1100 for the webbing.

*** The seat and back cushions are available as a set from: Sears Roebuck and Company, (see source Index) order part no. 24G19174NH for set.

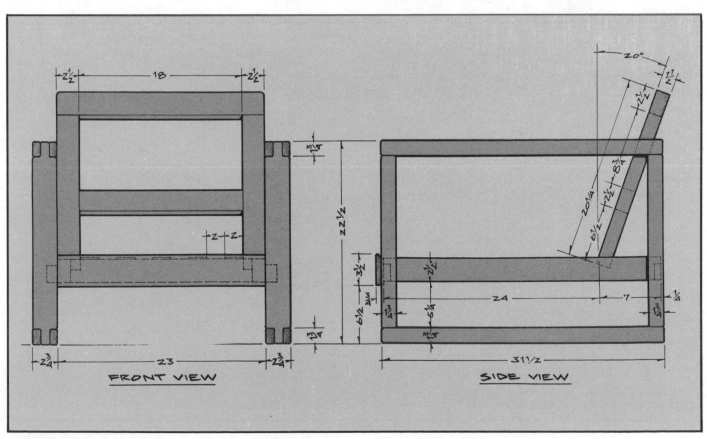

FRONT VIEW

SIDE VIEW

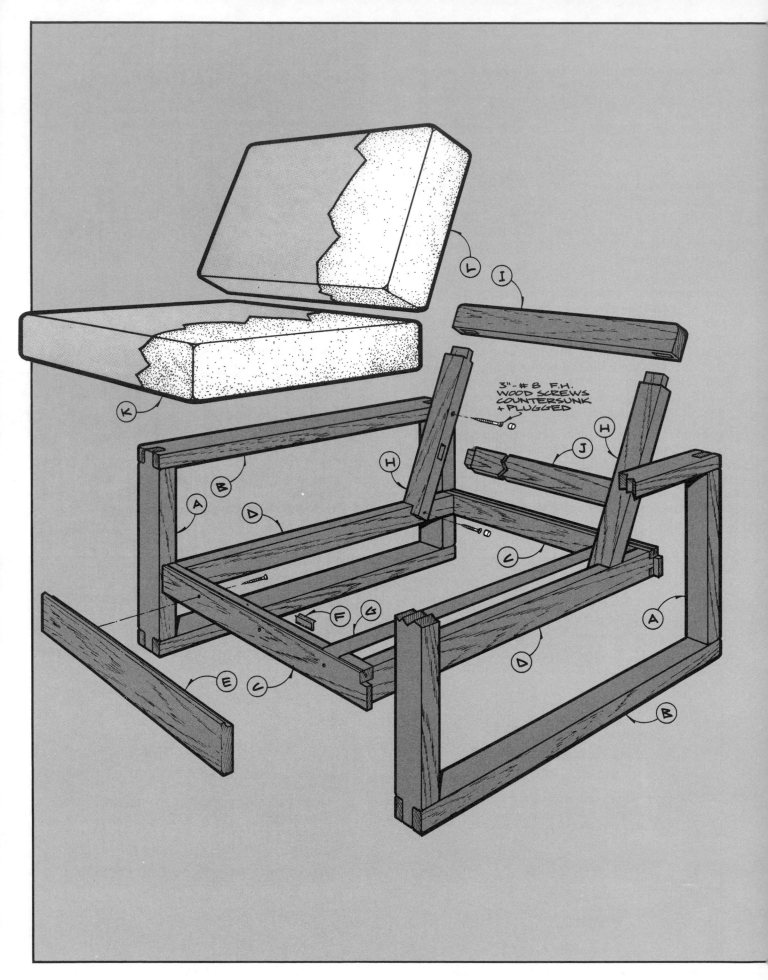

3"-#8 F.H.
WOOD SCREWS
COUNTERSUNK
+ PLUGGED

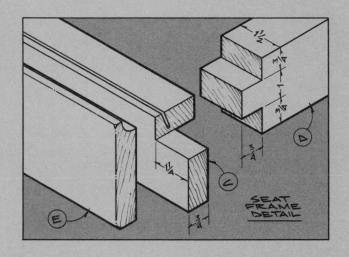

SEAT FRAME DETAIL

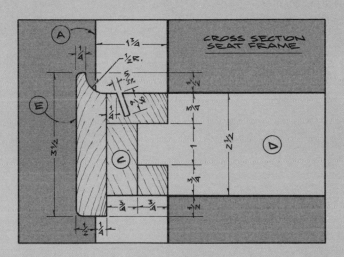

CROSS SECTION SEAT FRAME

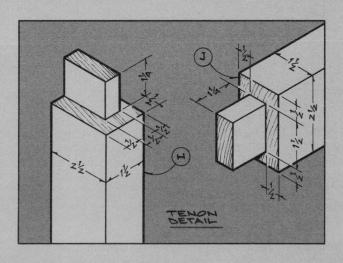

TENON DETAIL

Assemble the seat frame, mark out the mortise locations on the legs to accept the 1¼ in. long tenons, and then drill and square the mortises. Note that these mortises are located 7 in. up from the floor, and are inset ¼ in. from the front and back edges of the leg/rail frame (see side view).

Now cut the individual lengths of rubber webbing (G) to support the seat cushion. As with the other living room projects that utilize this webbing, I prefer a medium tension, and therefore the webbing lengths should be 30 in. each. For firmer seating decrease the length to 29 in. and for softer seating increase the length to 31 in. Press the metal clips onto the ends of the webbing, tap the clip into the kerf, stretch to the other side, and tap the opposite end in place. There are five lengths of webbing spaced two in. apart, as shown in the front view. Glue and mount the leg/rail assemblies on either side of the seat frame. Make the face piece (E) using a ½ in. cove cutter and the router to establish the ½ in. radius cove. Then glue and screw part E in place on the front end of the seat frame. Note that all front edges of the face piece are quarter rounded.

Next, make the back frame. Tenon the ends of parts J and H (see tenon detail) and mortise parts H and I correspondingly. Use the miter gauge set at 20 degrees and the dado head to notch the ends of H where they fit over the seat frame. Assemble the back frame, consisting of parts H, I, and J, round the corners of I and the outside edges of H, and then mount to the seat frame and leg/rail assemblies with screws, as illustrated. Note that these screws are counterbored and plugged.

After sanding with 100, 150, 180 and finally 220 grit paper, apply the final finish.

My preferred finish is Watco Danish Oil. Start by applying as many coats as are needed to saturate the wood, keeping in mind that end grain will require additional coats. Once the wood will absorb no more oil, wipe all surfaces down and allow to dry in a heated room for about one week. Apply a generous coat of furniture wax and buff to a soft sheen.

The seat and back cushions (parts K and L) may be ordered as a set from Sears. Slip covers to fit these cushions are also available in a variety of materials from Sears. If you prefer, you can make the cushions and slipcovers yourself. Both the foam rubber for the cushions and the material for the slip covers can be purchased from an upholstery store.

The cushions can either be tied to the seat frame, or velcro strips on the bottom side of the seat cushion can be used to anchor it and prevent slippage. □

ottoman

a n ottoman provides perfect accompaniment to the seating in the butternut living room group. The frame assemblies, consisting of the rails (A) and legs (B), are made as shown in the step-by-step knuckle joint illustrations on pages 4 and 5. When getting out stock for these parts, make certain that the thickness is exactly 1¾ in. If your stock is planed to 1¾ in. thickness, and you have a ½ in. diameter straight cutter and a ⅞ in. diameter guide bushing, then use the full size template illustrations as a pattern for making the knuckle joint. If your stock thickness is slightly different, or if you intend to use a different guide bushing and bit combination, then the mortise and tenon templates will have to be sized accordingly.

After making and assembling the frames, cut the 1½ in. deep mortises into the legs, as shown in the mortise detail, to accept the stretcher tenons. Note that these mortises are located 7½ in. up from the frame bottoms. Next, make the two stretchers (C). Use the dado head to cut the tenons on each of the ends, and the ½ in. cove cutter to establish the ½ in. radius cove along the top inside edge, as shown in the cross-sectional view.

Also cut the cleats (D) and ends (E). Using the table saw with the blade set at 20 degrees to cut a ⁹⁄₁₆ in. deep slot, cut the ⁵⁄₃₂ in. wide kerf which will accept the metal webbing clips (F). A slight fence adjustment will be needed if your blade is not ⁵⁄₃₂ in.

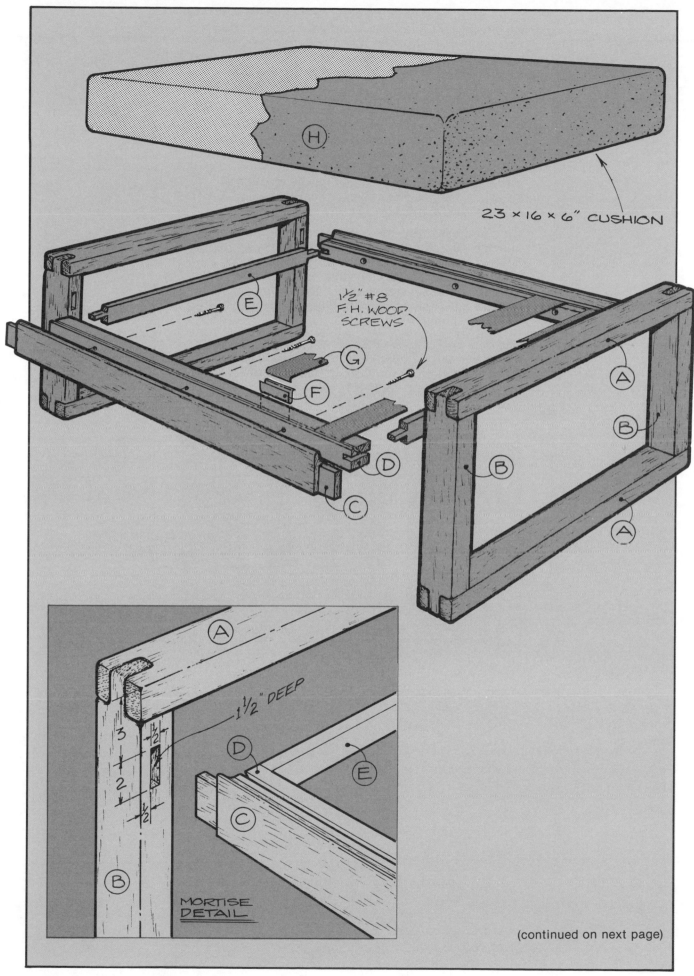

23 × 16 × 6" CUSHION

H

E

1½" #8
F.H. WOOD
SCREWS

G

F

A

B

B

D

C

B

A

MORTISE DETAIL

A

1½" DEEP

D

E

C

B

3

1½/2

2

½/2

(continued on next page)

wide. As indicated in the cross-sectional view, the kerf is located ¼ in. from the cleat edge. Cut the corresponding slip joint tenon and mortise on the ends of parts E and D respectively, glue and assemble these parts, then add the stretchers.

Now cut the strips of webbing (G) to length. I recommend a length of 14 in. which will result in a medium tension. The webbing strips could be made longer for a softer effect and shorter for a firmer effect, if you prefer. Use a vise to press the clips onto the ends of the webbing, then insert the clips into the ⁵⁄₃₂ in. wide kerfs cut into the cleats. As shown in the top view, six lengths of webbing are spaced 2 in. apart.

Glue and assemble the completed seat frame to the knuckle jointed end frames and finish. If you are making the ottoman with the other living room projects as a set, use the same finish for all the pieces. I used several coats of Watco Danish Oil, with a final application of furniture paste-wax buffed to a satin sheen.

The 6 in. by 16 in. by 23 in. foam rubber cushion and slip cover can be ordered from a furniture or upholstery store or from Sears Roebuck and Co. (see source index, page 161). □

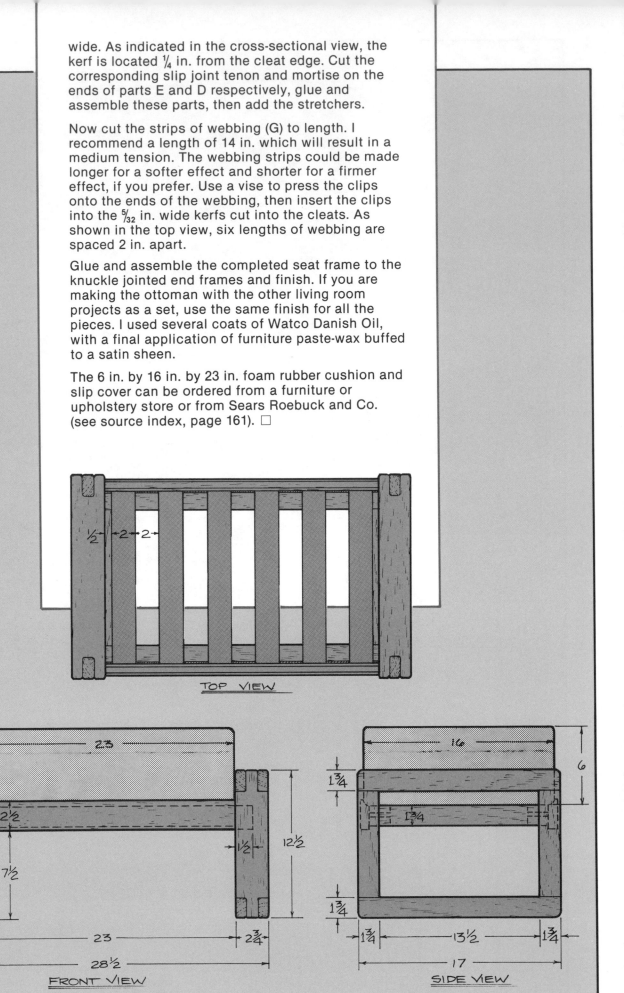

TOP VIEW

FRONT VIEW

SIDE VIEW

Bill of Materials
(all dimensions actual)

Part	Description	Size	No. Req'd.
A	Rail	$1\frac{3}{4} \times 2\frac{3}{4} \times 17$	4
B	Leg	$1\frac{3}{4} \times 2\frac{3}{4} \times 12\frac{1}{2}$	4
C	Stretcher	$\frac{3}{4} \times 2\frac{1}{2} \times 26$	2
D	Cleat	$1\frac{3}{4} \times 1\frac{3}{4} \times 23$	2
E	End	$\frac{3}{4} \times 1\frac{3}{4} \times 15$	2
F	Metal Clip	2 in. long*	12
G	Webbing	2 in. wide reinforced rubber*	7 ft.
H	Cushion	$6 \times 16 \times 23$**	1

* Both metal clips and webbing are available from The Woodworkers' Store, (see source index).

** The cushion can be ordered from Sears Roebuck and Company.

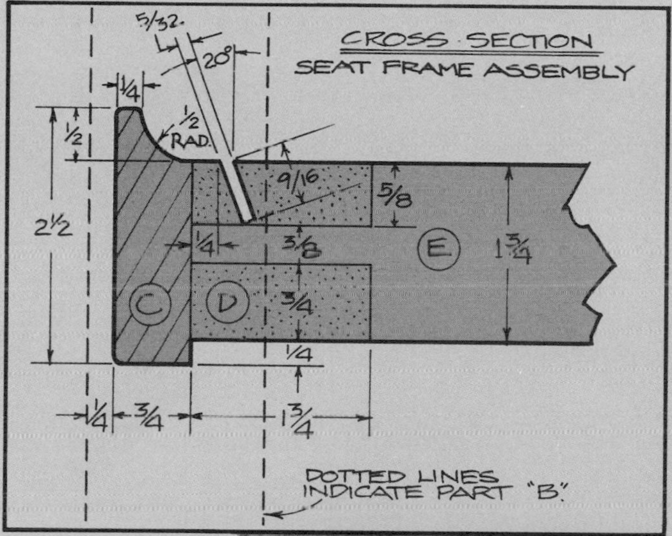
CROSS SECTION
SEAT FRAME ASSEMBLY
5/32
20°
1/4
1/2
1/2 RAD.
9/16
5/8
2 1/2
1/4
3/8
E
1 3/4
C
D
3/4
1/4
3/4
1 3/4
DOTTED LINES INDICATE PART "B"

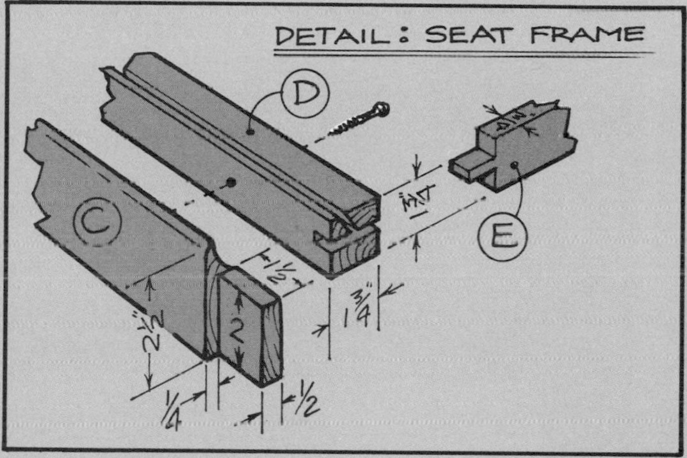
DETAIL: SEAT FRAME
D
C
E
1/2
2 1/2
2
1 3/4
1/4
1/2

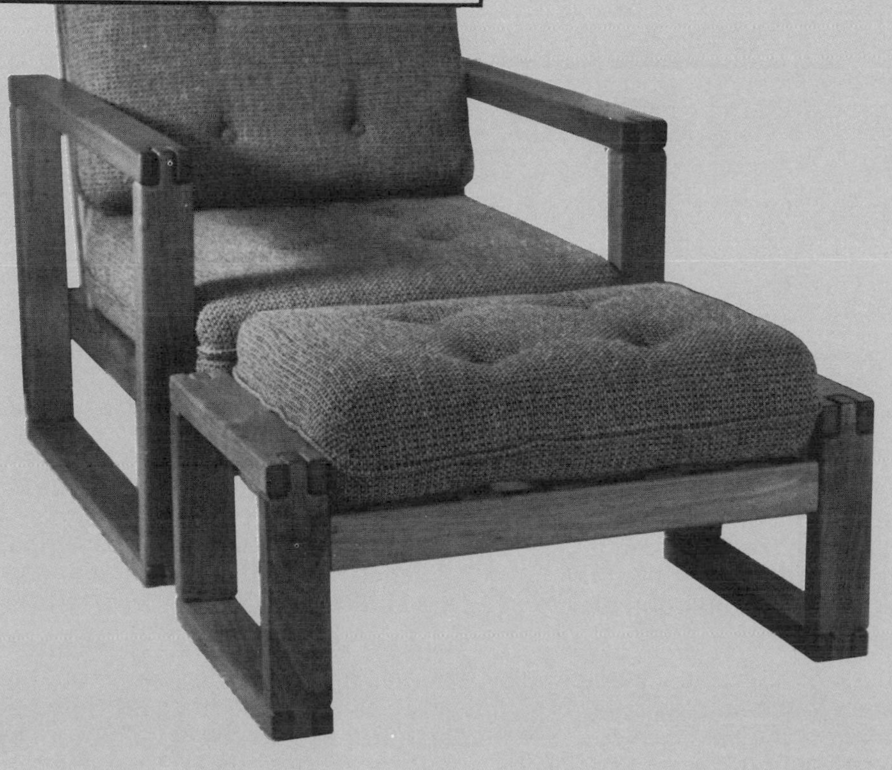

love seat

the love seat is a companion piece to the chair, and although these pieces were intended as a set, one could of course simply make the love seat and not the chair, or vice versa.

The construction of the love seat is identical to the chair in nearly every respect, the only difference being the addition of a brace in the back and an extra seat frame stretcher. The love seat features the same cushion set as the chair, although two of these sets will be required.

Begin by constructing the leg/rail frames, made up of parts A and B. As shown in the step-by-step illustrations on pages 4 and 5, the best way to accurately and consistently reproduce the knuckle joint is by using the router and template method.

Take note that the full-size template we show requires that your stock be exactly 1¾ in. thick, and that you have a ⅞ in. diameter guide bushing.

The knuckle joint can also be cut by hand. After drilling through with a ½ in. diameter drill bit to establish the various ¼ in. inside corner radii, use a backsaw and chisel to clean out the waste. Test fit, adjust as needed, and then glue and assemble the legs and rails.

The seat frame, consisting of parts C and D, is constructed next. Cut the tenons on the ends of parts C and D, as shown in the seat frame detail. Mortise parts C to accept the ¾ in. by 1 in. by 1½ in. tenons on the ends of parts D. Then use the table saw, with the blade set at a 20-degree tilt to cut the ⁵⁄₃₂ in. wide by $^9/_{16}$ in. deep kerf in parts C that will serve as the anchor slot for the webbing retainer clips (F).

After assembling the seat frame, scribe the mortise locations on the legs to accommodate the $^3/_4$ by $1^3/_4$ by $1^1/_4$ in. tenons on the ends of the seat frame front and back, and chop these mortises out.

Cut the reinforced rubber webbing (G) into ten sections, each 30 in. long, then crimp the metal retainer clips over the ends of the webbing, and tap the clips into the kerf cut to accept them. The webbing is spaced out at 2 in. intervals, as shown in the front view. Glue up the leg/rail assemblies on each side of the seat frame, then counterbore through the front of the seat frame to accept the face piece (E), which is both glued and screwed in place. Note that all front edges of part E are quarter rounded.

Now make the back frame. Cut the tenons on the ends of the back stiles (H), back stretcher (J), and back brace (K). Dimensions for these tenons and the corresponding mortises are shown in the tenon detail. Notch the bottom end of the stiles so they lap over the seat frame, as shown in the exploded view. Note that the shoulder of this lap is cut at 20 degrees to establish the 20-degree angle of the back. Assemble the back, and round the corners of the back rail (I) and the outside edges of the back stiles. Then mount the back as shown with 3 in. long flathead wood screws, countersunk and plugged.

I ordered the seat and back cushions (L and M) and the seat covers from Sears Roebuck and Company. The cushions and seat covers could be made from furniture grade foam rubber and upholstery fabric, but I prefer the convenience of the ready-made product.

Velcro strips or tie straps should be used to secure the seat cushions against movement, as they tend to slide rather easily out of place without some form of restraint.

The piece is finished using the same technique as the other living room group projects with Watco Danish Oil. □

(continued on next page)

Bill of Materials
(all dimensions actual)

Part	Description	Size	No. Req'd.
A	Leg	$1^3/_4 \times 2^3/_4 \times 22^1/_2$	4
B	Rail	$1^3/_4 \times 2^3/_4 \times 31^1/_2$	4
C	Seat Frame Front/Back	$1^1/_2 \times 2^1/_2 \times 48^1/_2$*	2
D	Seat Frame Stretcher	$1^1/_2 \times 2^1/_2 \times 29^1/_2$*	3
E	Face	$^3/_4 \times 3^1/_2 \times 46$	1
F	Metal Clip	2 in. long**	20
G	Webbing	2 in. wide reinforced rubber**	25 ft.
H	Back Stile	$1^1/_2 \times 2^1/_2 \times 19$*	2
I	Back Rail	$1^1/_2 \times 2^1/_2 \times 46$	1
J	Back Stretcher	$1^1/_2 \times 2^1/_2 \times 43^1/_2$*	1
K	Back Brace	$1^1/_2 \times 2^1/_2 \times 11^1/_4$*	1
L	Seat Cushion	$6 \times 23 \times 26$***	2
M	Back Cushion	$6 \times 16 \times 23$***	2

* Length includes tenons.

** Both metal clips and webbing are available from The Woodworkers' Store (see source index). Order part no. H1101 for the clip, and part no. H1100 for the webbing.

*** The seat and back cushions are available as a set from Sears Roebuck and Company (see source index). Order part no. 24G19174NH for the set. Note that two sets are required for the love seat.

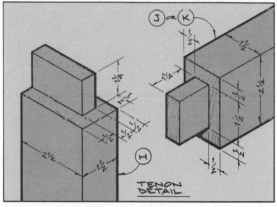

TENON DETAIL

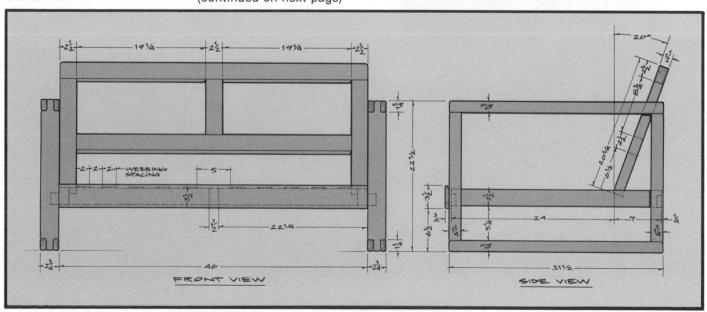

FRONT VIEW

SIDE VIEW

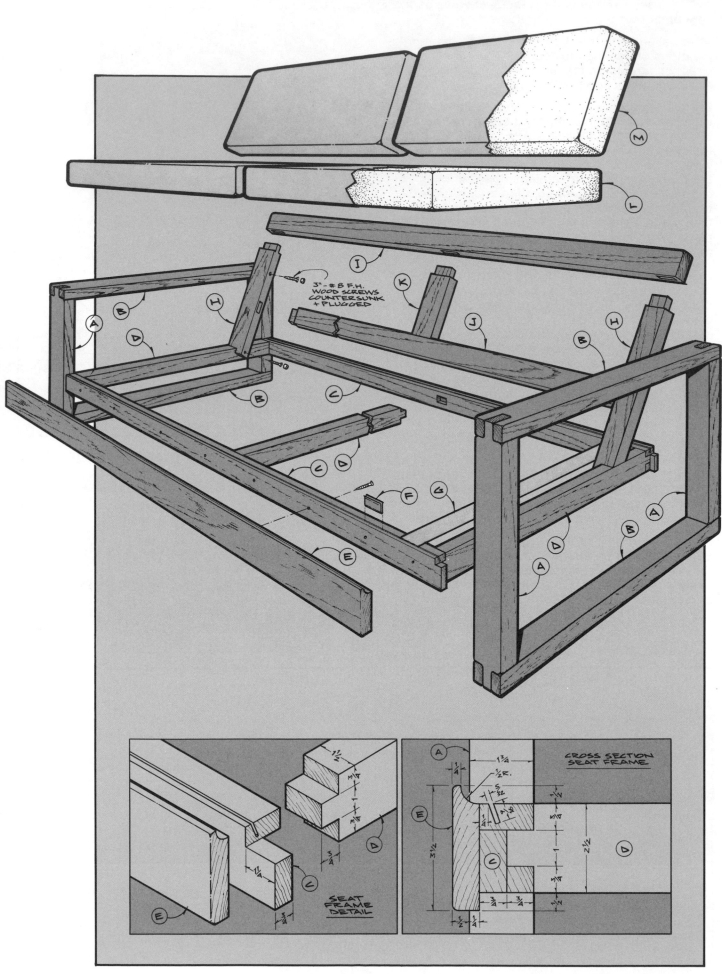

M

L

I

3"-#8 F.H.
WOOD SCREWS
COUNTERSUNK
+ PLUGGED

K

J

H

B

H

A

B

D

B

C

C

D

F

G

A

D

B

A

E

A

SEAT FRAME DETAIL

E

C

D

1½

¾

1

¾

¼

¾

CROSS SECTION
SEAT FRAME

A

E

C

D

3½

1¾

½R.

5/32

¼

½

½

¾

1

¾

2½

½

¼

¾

¾

¼

dining room

Design by Martin Bloomenthal, AIA, Princeton, NJ

oak & laminate dining table

this oak and laminate dining table is an especially handsome piece. The dramatic contrast of the light colored oak with the jet black laminate provides a truly distinctive contemporary look.

Start by ripping 2¼ in. square stock for parts A, B, and C. Refer to the leg and rail tenon details, and cut the tenons on the ends of parts A and B as illustrated. Note that the part A tenons extend through to the floor to provide a bearing surface. Also cut the corresponding mortises on the upper ends of the legs to accept the rail tenons, and on the ends of the stretchers to accept the leg tenons. After test-fitting your joinery, glue and assemble the legs and rails. Do not add the stretchers, since these are not assembled until later.

Now cut parts D, E, F, and G to length and width from ¾ in. thick stock. Cut the ¾ in. by ⅜ in. deep dadoes in parts D to accept parts F, in parts F to accept parts G, and rabbet the ends of parts E to accept the ends of F. Use the table saw dado head to establish the tenons on the ends of parts D and E (see tenon detail). After mortising the two leg/rail assemblies to accept these tenons (use parts D and E to check for mortise and tenon fit), glue up and screw the apron/frame assembly, consisting of parts D, E, F, and G. Add the cleats (K) and the glue blocks as shown, and then join the leg/rail assemblies on either side of the apron/frame assembly.

At this point you can also glue and assemble the stretchers (C). Next, cut the top core (H) and the end core (I) to length and width from ¾ in. thick plywood or particleboard. Apply the laminate (J) to both sides and to the drawer end of the top core, and to the back side of the end core. Also, polyurethane the side edges of the top and end core parts where they will butt to the leg/rail assembly to seal against moisture.

32

Mount both the top and end core to the frame assembly with screws, and apply the laminate, covering both the outside face and lower edge of the end core and the exposed end of the top core. This may sound like it is complicated, but as you actually follow the assembly process, you will discover that these operations are quite simple.

All that remains is to construct the drawer. Cut the sides (L), front (M), and back (N) to size. Rabbet the front and back and dado the sides as shown in the drawer corner detail. Then use the dado head to cut the $\frac{1}{4}$ in. by $\frac{1}{4}$ in. groove in the sides and front to accept the drawer bottom (O). After the drawer box is assembled, the bottom is slid into these grooves from the rear and then tacked up into the back with several small brads.

Now make the drawer face. Start by cutting the drawer face core (P) to length and width. Then laminate all around using the same laminate (J) that you used over the top and end core parts. Drill and counterbore through the drawer front, and mount the drawer box using the 18 in. long Accuride brand full extension drawer slides (Q). Position and mount the laminated drawer face to complete the construction.

All the wood surfaces of the project are finished with several coats of Watco Danish Oil. □

(continued on next page)

Bill of Materials
(all dimensions actual)

Part	Description	Size	No. Req'd.
A	Leg	$2\frac{1}{4} \times 2\frac{1}{4} \times 30$	4
B	Rail	$2\frac{1}{4} \times 2\frac{1}{4} \times 60$	2
C	Stretcher	$2\frac{1}{4} \times 2\frac{1}{4} \times 36$	2
D	Apron	$\frac{3}{4} \times 3\frac{3}{4} \times 33$	1
E	Drawer End Apron	$\frac{3}{4} \times 3\frac{3}{4} \times 8\frac{1}{4}$	2
F	Long Frame	$\frac{3}{4} \times 3\frac{3}{4} \times 56\frac{1}{4}$	2
G	Short Frame	$\frac{3}{4} \times 3\frac{3}{4} \times 17\frac{1}{4}$	2
H	Top Core	$\frac{3}{4} \times 31\frac{1}{2} \times 58\frac{1}{2}$	1
I	End Core	$\frac{3}{4} \times 3\frac{3}{4} \times 31\frac{1}{2}$	1
J	Laminate	for Top, End, and Drawer Face	as needed
K	Cleat	$\frac{3}{4} \times \frac{3}{4} \times 55\frac{1}{2}$	4
L	Drawer Side	$\frac{5}{8} \times 3\frac{3}{4} \times 18$	2
M	Drawer Front	$\frac{5}{8} \times 3\frac{3}{4} \times 14\frac{7}{8}$	1
N	Drawer Back	$\frac{5}{8} \times 3\frac{1}{4} \times 14\frac{7}{8}$	1
O	Drawer Bottom	$\frac{1}{4} \times 14\frac{3}{4} \times 17\frac{5}{8}$	1
P	Drawer Face Core	$\frac{3}{4} \times 3\frac{5}{8} \times 31\frac{3}{8}$	1
Q	Drawer Slides	18 in. Accuride full-extension*	1 pair

*Available from: The Woodworkers' Store, (see source index) order part no. D7570 for 18 in. model.

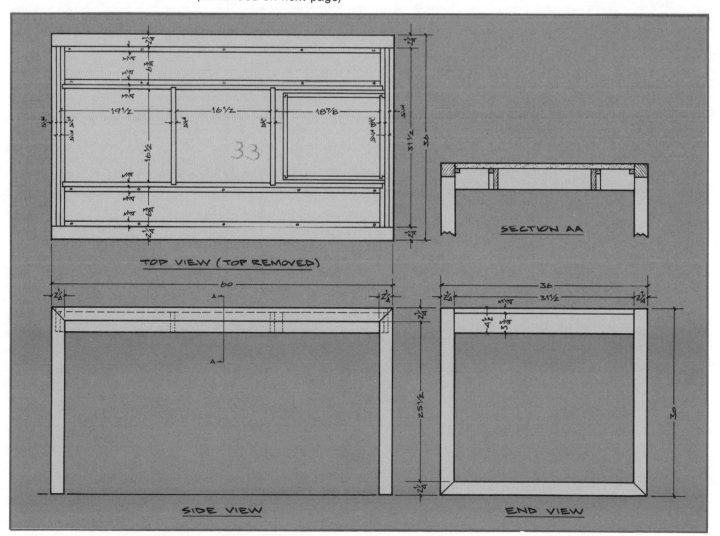

TOP VIEW (TOP REMOVED)

SECTION AA

SIDE VIEW

END VIEW

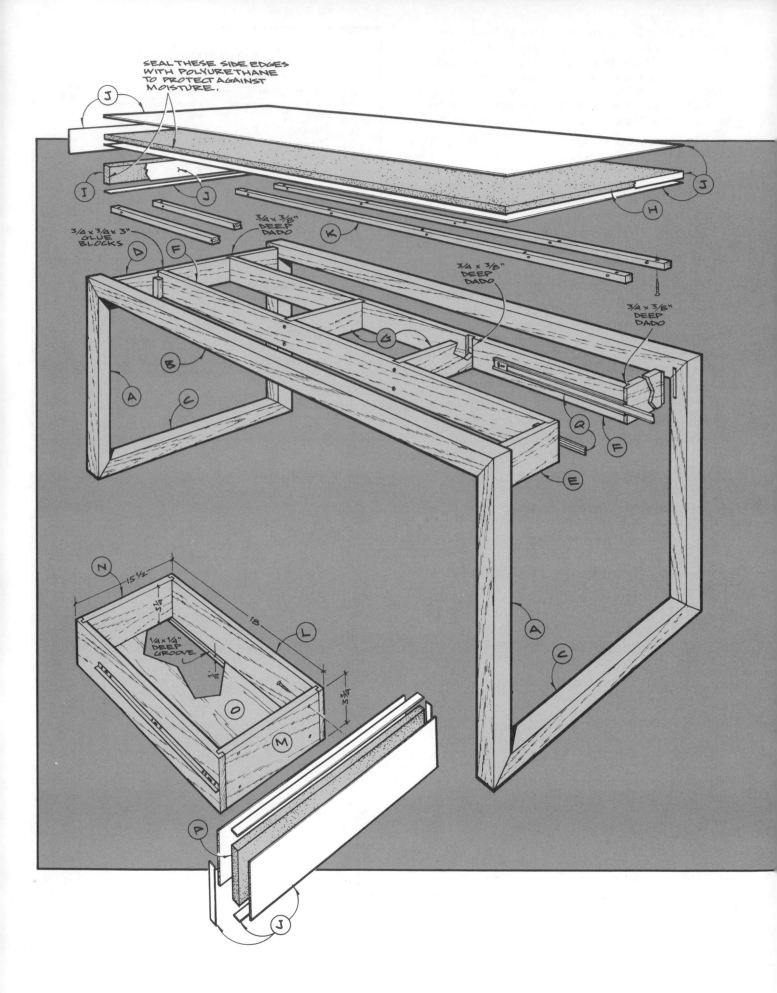

SEAL THESE SIDE EDGES
WITH POLYURETHANE
TO PROTECT AGAINST
MOISTURE.

3/4 x 3/4 x 3" GLUE BLOCKS

3/4 x 3/8" DEEP DADO

3/4 x 3/8" DEEP DADO

3/4 x 3/8" DEEP DADO

1/4 x 1/4" DEEP GROOVE

15 1/2

LEG + RAIL TENON DETAIL

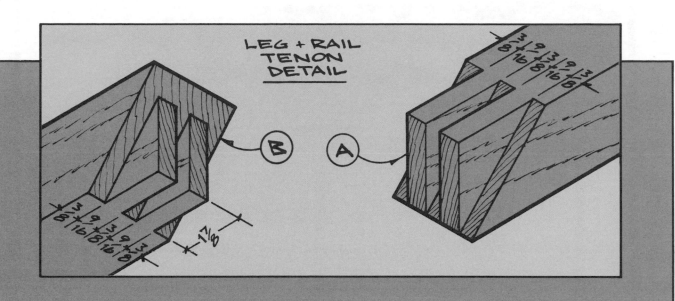

B — A

3/8 · 9/16 · 3/8 · 9/16 · 3/8

1 7/8

3/8 · 9/16 · 3/8 · 9/16 · 3/8

TENON DETAIL

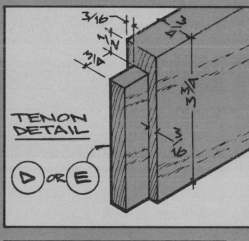

3/16
1/2
3/4
3/4
3 3/4
1/2

D or E

DRAWER CORNER DETAIL

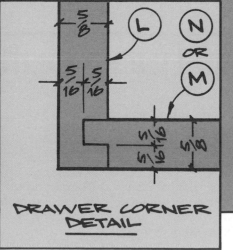

5/8

L   N
     or
5/16 | 5/16   M

5/16 | 5/8

Design by Martin Bloomenthal, AIA, Princeton, NJ

wall-hung buffet

t o build this sleek wall-hung cabinet, I teamed up satin black ⅟₁₆ in. plastic laminate with ¾ in. birch plywood. Use it as a buffet or storage cabinet for silverware, dishes, liquor or stereo components. If you have a long wall, two of these cabinets can be joined as shown in the photo on page 39 to form an impressive eight-foot unit.

The cabinet top, bottom, shelf and sides are cut from ¾ in. birch plywood. Rails, dividers and hinge posts are of ¾ in. solid birch. Care should be used in cutting all parts perfectly square. When the unit is assembled, it will square itself if the parts have been properly cut.

Start by cutting the sides (A), bottom (B), shelf (C), top (L), back rail (I) and top rails (H) first. Add a ⅛ in. solid stock edging to the front edge of the bottom and shelf. Use a router to run ¼ in. by ⅜ in. rabbets on the ends of the bottom to fit the corresponding grooves in the case sides. Note that the lower grooves on the case sides stop ¾ in. from the front edges. Also drill holes in the sides as shown for the shelf supports.

Lay out and chisel notches in the sides to receive the tongues of the back rail and the ends of the two top rails (H). Notch the bottom (B) and the front top rail (H) for a flush fit of the door stop (F).

36

At this point the cabinet can be glued and clamped. Check for squareness, then add the bottom rail (D), door stop (F), and center divider (J) which is fastened by screwing down through parts H. Next add the door stile (E) and hinge posts (G) which are set back ¾ in. to allow for the doors.

Now apply the laminate. Using contact cement, laminate the two horizontal front edges first. Use 1 in. wide strips and apply two coats of cement to the cabinet and one coat on the strips. Align the strips with an overhang on each side, and bring into contact with the edges.

Cut the strips to fit the three vertical edges of the door stile and case ends so they butt snugly against the strips previously laid (these strips will be shorter than the parts they cover). Again use two coats of cement on the wood and one coat on the laminate. A router with a ⅜ in. straight laminate trimming bit and pilot bearing is used to trim overhangs. Intersections between the horizontal and vertical strips are trimmed square with a file.

Next, apply the laminate to the case sides, using one heavy coat of adhesive and after rolling, trim off excess. Protect previously laminated surfaces with strips of tape. The top is covered last and trimmed

flush with the sides and front edges. Trimmed edges will look better if given a slight (10 degrees) bevel with a file.

Next, make the doors (M) which are ¾ in. birch plywood with a ⅛ in. thick birch edging all around. The doors are hinged with Stanley #332 cabinet hinges (see source index, page 161) as shown in the detail. Mount the unit with lag screws through the back rail (I) into wall studs. For additional security, a metal angle or hardwood strip is lagged to the wall studs and into the mounting cleat (K) that is screwed into the bottom of the unit. Finish all wood surfaces with Deft Spray Finish. ☐

(continued on next page)

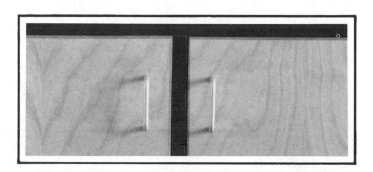

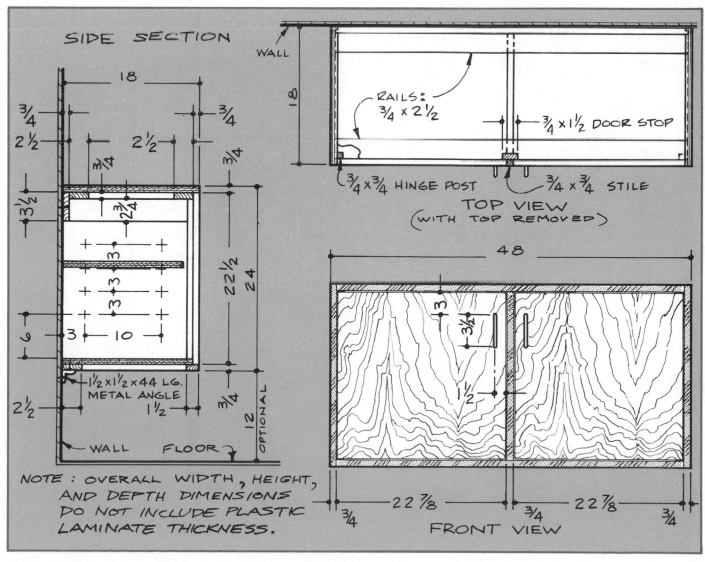

Bill of Materials
(all dimensions actual)

Part	Description	Size	No. Req'd.
A	Side	¾ × 18 × 24	2
B	Bottom	¾ × 17¼ × 47*	1
C	Shelf	¾ × 15½ × 46½*	1
D	Bottom Rail	¾ × 1½ × 46½	1
E	Door Stile	¾ × ¾ × 22½	1
F	Door Stop	¾ × 1½ × 22½	1
G	Hinge Post	¾ × ¾ × 21	2
H	Top Rail	¾ × 2½ × 47	2
I	Back Rail	¾ × 3½ × 47	1
J	Center Divider	¾ × 2¾ × 15¾	1
K	Mounting Cleat	¾ × 2½ × 46½	1
L	Top	¾ × 18 × 47	1
M	Door	¾ × 22⅞ × 22½**	2
N	Mounting Angle Iron	1½ × 1½ × 44	1
O	Door Pull	3 in. long	2

* Width dimension includes ⅛ in. edging on front.
** Length and width dimensions include ⅛ in. edging all around.

PLASTIC LAMINATE OVERLAPS TO COVER SIDES

SIDE · TOP

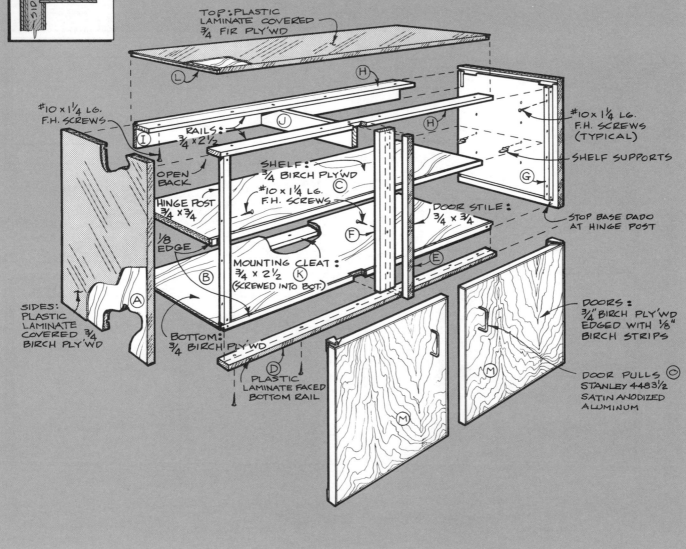

TOP: PLASTIC LAMINATE COVERED ¾ FIR PLY'WD

#10 × 1¼ LG. F.H. SCREWS

RAILS: ¾ × 2½

#10 × 1¼ LG. F.H. SCREWS (TYPICAL)

SHELF SUPPORTS

OPEN BACK

SHELF: ¾ BIRCH PLY'WD

#10 × 1¼ LG. F.H. SCREWS

DOOR STILE: ¾ × ¾

HINGE POST ¾ × ¾

⅛ EDGE

STOP BASE DADO AT HINGE POST

MOUNTING CLEAT: ¾ × 2½ (SCREWED INTO BOT.)

SIDES: PLASTIC LAMINATE COVERED ¾ BIRCH PLY'WD

BOTTOM: ¾ BIRCH PLY'WD

PLASTIC LAMINATE FACED BOTTOM RAIL

DOORS: ¾" BIRCH PLY'WD EDGED WITH ⅛" BIRCH STRIPS

DOOR PULLS Ⓞ STANLEY 4483½ SATIN ANODIZED ALUMINUM

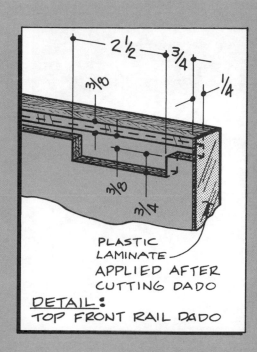

2½   ¾
¾₈   ¼
¾₈
¾

PLASTIC
LAMINATE
APPLIED AFTER
CUTTING DADO

DETAIL:
TOP FRONT RAIL DADO

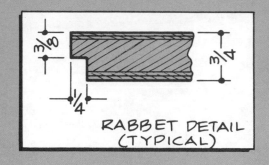

¾₈   ¾

¼

RABBET DETAIL
(TYPICAL)

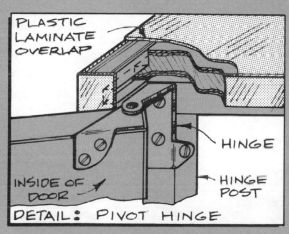

PLASTIC
LAMINATE
OVERLAP

HINGE

INSIDE OF
DOOR

HINGE
POST

DETAIL: PIVOT HINGE

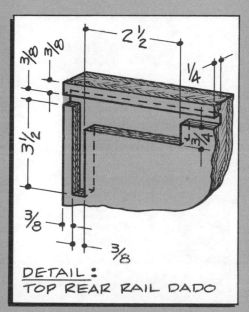

3/8 3/8   2½
¼
3½
3/8   ¾

3/8   3/8

DETAIL:
TOP REAR RAIL DADO

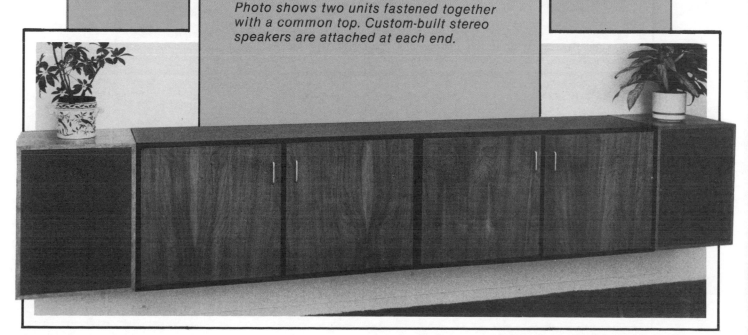

Photo shows two units fastened together
with a common top. Custom-built stereo
speakers are attached at each end.

credenza

this project and the dresser, which is featured in the bedroom grouping, utilize similar construction. Veneers and solids are carefully matched to create a dramatic yet refined look. Like much contemporary work and many of the projects in this book, the choice of material is every bit as important as the care you take in cutting, machining and assembly.

The credenza, like the dresser, features matched oak veneer and oak solids. As you can see, the door panel veneer and the side panel veneer all show the same pattern. There are two ways to achieve this effect. You can either lay up the veneer yourself over plywood or other core material, or you may purchase pre-veneered hardwood plywood sheets and obtain the matched faces from these sheets. Most commercial veneers are "straight cut" and consecutive faces appear side-by-side. Of course, whether you are laying up the veneer yourself or using pre-veneered plywood, selecting the most attractive part or face will contribute significantly to the overall success of the piece.

Other woods such as walnut, figured maple, cherry, and the exotics are alternatives you may also consider. If you desire an especially bold or dramatic effect, you could use a combination of woods or even colored core laminate and wood. One point you should consider with this project, however, is that the interior or reverse sides of the various doors, panels and sides are also exposed and visible when the doors are open. Top grade veneers are not needed here, but you would not want the interior surfaces to demean the rest of the piece. You may not want to go to the extent I did, matching the drawer bottom veneers and using rare olive ash burl on the under side, but this piece offers the serious woodworker an opportunity to truly showcase his skills.

If your budget permits, by all means opt for the marble top, as shown in the photo. The edges of the marble show the same 1/4 in. radius common to the piece, and the rich look of genuine marble is a splendid compliment to the wood. Marble can be ordered through your local monument dealer. You may wish to place the order well before you start this project since, as I discovered, delivery may take a while. The colored core laminate top shown in the illustration is a reasonable alternative to the marble

top, however, and one that is particularly nice should you decide to substitute the same color laminate for the various exterior veneered surfaces.

Start by cutting the interior sides (A), top and bottom (B) and back (C) to size. Cut the 1/4 in. by 3/8 in. deep grooves in A to accept the corresponding tongue cut with the dado head on the ends of B. When cutting the 1/4 in. thick plywood back, make certain it is square since the back serves to help square the case during the assembly process. Next, cut sufficient case edging (D). To save time later, you may also wish to rip enough edging for parts K, P, U and AA at the same time. I always make this edging slightly wider than required, usually 7/8 in. to 1 in., since this enables me to then flush trim the edging with a laminate trimmer bit after it has been applied.

Cut the base sides (E) and base front and back (F), mitering the ends. After gluing and assembling the base, use a 1/4 in. radius bearing-guided round-over bit to round the outside edges. If you choose the laminated top instead of the marble, cut the top core (G) to size from 3/4 in. thick plywood and apply the black plastic laminate (H).

Colored core laminate is essentially like all other laminates, with the added feature that the color extends through the full thickness of the material. Although I use Wilson Art's "Solicor" brand, Formica's "Colorcore" is also acceptable. Start by applying the laminate to the bottom side of the plywood substrate. Cut the laminate slightly oversize, use contact cement adhesive, and trim the laminate flush with the sides using a laminate trimmer bit in the router. Next, apply the edge laminate, flush it with the laminate trimmer, and finally apply the top laminate, once again flushing with the trimmer bit. A laminate edge beveling router bit is now used to apply a 45-degree bevel all around. Since the color extends through the

(continued on next page)

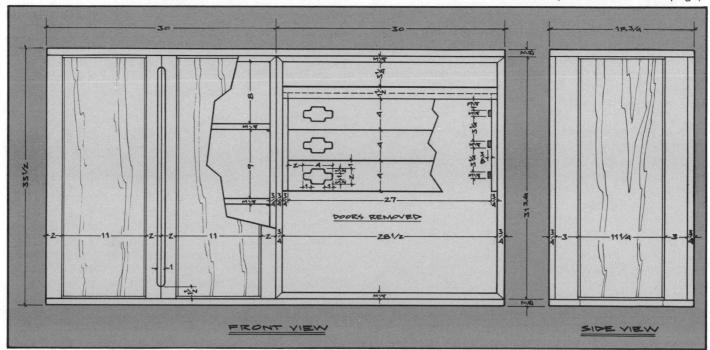

FRONT VIEW

SIDE VIEW

laminate, none of the lines that characterize common laminates will be visible. If you have a laminate trimmer, this tool is much lighter and consequently easier to use than a full-size router.

Before assembly of the case, you must construct the sides which consist of parts I, J, K, L, and M. After applying veneer (J) to both sides of the side panel core (I), add the side panel edging (K). Remember that with all veneering, what is done to one side must also be done to the other in order to equalize stresses on the substrate. To save time, you can lay up several of the panels and doors at one time.

I have a little system that simplifies the veneering and edging process for both the sides and doors on this project. Start by making the panel and door core (I and N) about ½ to 1 in. oversize all around. Lay up the veneer (J and O) on both sides of the substrate (I and N). Then run the veneered door and side panels through the table saw to establish the final panel *width.* Now edge the two sides. The veneered and side-edged door and side panels are now cut to length. By cutting a little off one end and making the final cut to length on the opposite end, you will simultaneously flush the side edging. The top and bottom edging is now applied, and all edges are rounded with the ¼ in. radius bearing-guided router bit. You will note that the above process is feasible only on projects where the edging can be butted and where end grain will be unobtrusive. On the dresser, I chose to miter the edging, making this process impossible for that project.

After cutting the side stiles (L) and the side ends (M) to length and width, rabbet parts M as shown to accept the back. Part M is a separate strip that serves to visually balance the doors on the front, in case you are wondering about the importance of this seemingly "extra" strip. Again utilizing the ¼ in. radiusing bit, round the outside edges of parts L and M. The laminated and edged side panels and parts L and M can now be assembled to complete the sides. Since these mating edges are all long grain-to-long grain, and given that these side assemblies will be mounted to the top and bottom, no splines are necessary. The splines are used on the door assemblies since the stress of opening and closing does require supplemental mechanical strength where the parts meet.

After the glued and clamped side assemblies have dried thoroughly, you may cut the ¼ in. wide by ⅜ in. deep grooves to accept the top and bottom. Note that these grooves are stopped one full inch from the front edge of the side assemblies, although they can run out the back edge where the rabbet to accept the back has been cut.

The interior sides, the top and bottom, the side assemblies, and the back can now be glued and assembled. Try a dry fitting first, just to be sure. As noted earlier, if you have cut the back square it will serve as a guide in squaring the two separate cases. The cases are joined with ¼ in. T nuts, as shown in the exploded view. Now add the case edging (D), mitering the corners as shown and butting it against the side assemblies. If you have erred slightly in the location of the side assemblies relative to the top and bottom, simply adjust the thickness of the edging as needed to bring it out flush. Remember it is important that the case front presents a flush surface all around for the doors to close tightly and neatly.

Now, make and assemble the doors consisting of parts N, O, P, Q, R, and S. The door panel core (N),

Bill of Materials
(all dimensions actual)

Part	Description	Size	No. Req'd.
A	Interior Side	¾ × 17½ × 31¾	2
B	Top/Bottom	¾ × 17½ × 29¼	4
C	Back	¼ × 31¾ × 59¼	1
D	Case Edging	¼ × ¾	as needed
E	Base Side	⅞ × 4 × 18¾	2
F	Base Front/Back	⅞ × 4 × 60	2
G	Top Core	¾ × 18⅝ × 59⅞	1
H	Top Laminate	black plastic Colorcore	as needed
I	Side Panel Core	¾ × 10¾ × 31¼	2
J	Side Panel Veneer	as required	
K	Side Panel Edging	¼ × ¾	as needed
L	Side Stile	¾ × 3 × 31¾	4
M	Side End	¾ × ¾ × 31¾	2
N	Door Panel Core	¾ × 10½ × 31¼	4
O	Door Panel Veneer	as required	
P	Door Panel Edging	¼ × ¾	as needed
Q	Door Stile	¾ × 2 × 31¾	8
R	Spline	¼ × 1 × 29¾	8
S	Pull Backing	⅛ × 2 × 30	4
T	Drawer Case Side	¾ × 16 × 12½	2
U	Drawer Case Edging (bottom)	¼ × ¾	as needed
V	Drawer Case Top	¾ × 16 × 28½	1
W	Drawer Case Edging (side)	¾ × ¾ × 12	2
X	Drawer Case Edging (top)	¾ × 1½ × 28½	1
Y	Drawer Guide	⅜ × ¾ × 15¼	6
Z	Shelf Core	¾ × 15 × 28	2
AA	Shelf Edging	¼ × ¾	as needed
BB	Shelf Pin	common	8
CC	Drawer Side	½ × 3¼ × 16	6
DD	Drawer Front/Back	½ × 3¼ × 26¾	6
EE	Drawer Bottom	¼ × 15½ × 26¼	3
FF	Drawer Face	¾ × 4 × 27	3
GG	Door Hinge	European self-close/ full overlay*	8

* Available from: The Woodworkers' Store, (see source index) order part no. D9632.

door panel veneer (O), and door panel edging (P) are handled in the same manner as the side panel assemblies. Cut the door stiles (Q) to length and width, machine the door pull detail as shown in the step-by-step illustrations following this project, and join the stiles to the door panel with ¼ in. by 1 in. by 29¾ in. long plywood splines (R). Use the router and a wing cutter to cut these spline grooves. To complete the door assembly, add the ⅛ in. thick by 2 in. wide by 30 in. long pull backing strips (S), which are simply glued in place, centered ⅞ in. from the

(continued on next page)

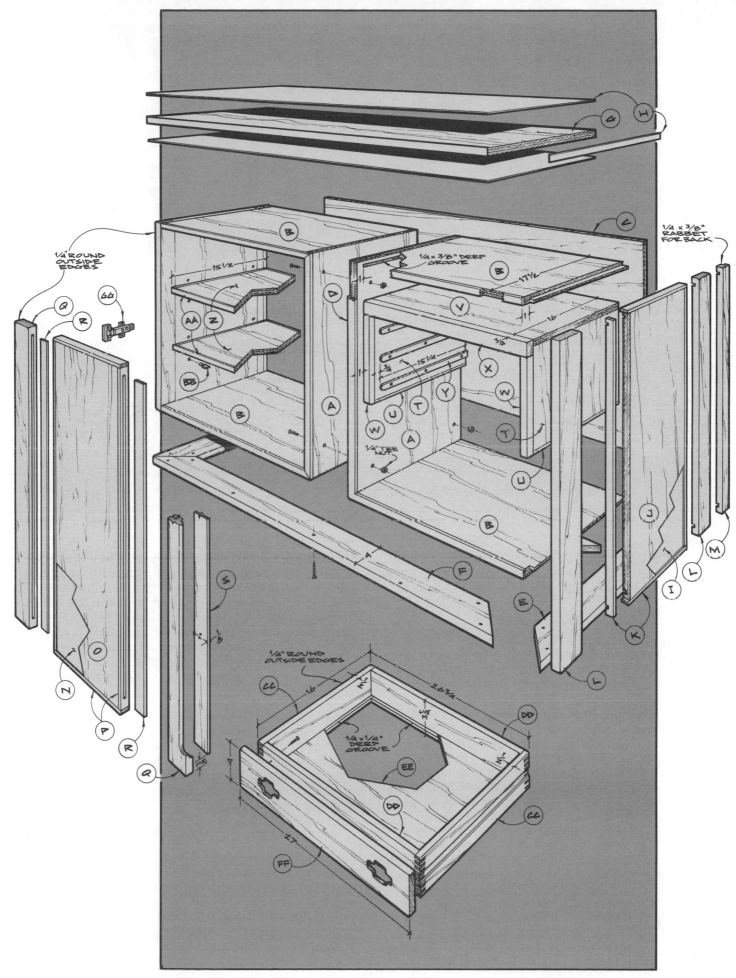

¼" ROUND OUTSIDE EDGES

¼ x ⅜" RABBET FOR BACK

15½

¼ x ⅜" DEEP GROOVE

17½

16

15¼

¾

¼" TEE NUT

¼" ROUND OUTSIDE EDGES

26¾

¼ x ¼" DEEP GROOVE

27

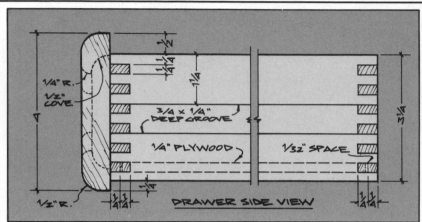

DRAWER SIDE VIEW

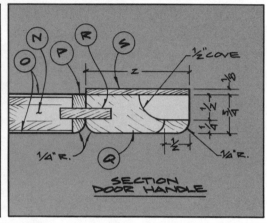

SECTION DOOR HANDLE

top and bottom. The pull backing strips are needed to provide a visual backing for the routed pull detail; without them one would see clear through to the inside of the credenza. Do not mount the doors at this time.

The drawer case assembly is made next. Cut the drawer case sides (T) to the 12½ in. length, apply the bottom edging (U) and cut to a width of 16 in. This cut will neatly flush parts T and U. Now apply the ¾ in. square side edging (W). Position the edged drawer case sides four inches down from the inside case top and screw in place. Pre-drill and counterbore for the 1¼ in. long screws. Cut the drawer case top (V) and drawer case edging (X) to size. Round the top and bottom edges of part X with the ¼ in. round-over bit and apply this edging to the front of the case top. The edging will be flush at the top and overlap ¾ in. at the bottom. Test fit the drawer case top and edging assembly, and then glue in place with a bead of glue along the top of both drawer case sides. Note that, if necessary, the case top edging can be trimmed back with the hand plane should it interfere with part S. The drawer guides (Y) can be made and mounted at this time. Take care that their location is exactly as shown in the front view. Countersink the drawer guide mounting screws so their heads are recessed about ⅛ in.

The shelves can also be made now. The procedure is the same as detailed earlier for the side and door panels. You will note, however, that we have not indicated an applied veneer here in either the bill of materials or the artwork. Since these shelves are interior surfaces, a pre-veneered matching plywood can be used. If you prefer, the shelves could be veneered both sides with a selected face veneer for the top and a lesser veneer for the reverse or underside.

Cut the shelves (Z) to length, apply the side shelf edging (AA) and, after cutting to width, apply the front and back shelf edging (AA). Drill the case sides to accept the shelf pins (BB) which are available from various mail-order sources, including The Woodworkers' Store (see source index), or from your local hardware store.

The drawers feature a basic box joint construction. Set up the table saw and dado head to cut the ¼ in. box joint fingers. The dado head with the same ¼ in. width setting is also used to cut the ¼ in. deep grooves in the drawer sides (CC) to accept the ¼ in. thick plywood drawer bottom (EE). The ¼ in. by ¼ in. grooves in the drawer front and back (DD) are stopped and must be cut with the router. Size the drawer bottom just under (about ¹⁄₃₂ in. all around) the length and width dimensions specified in the bill of materials. If the drawer bottoms are cut square and accurate, they will serve to square the drawers during assembly.

After the drawers have been assembled, use the dado head or the router with a straight bit to cut the ¼ in. deep by ¾ in. wide grooves to accept the drawer guides.

The drawer faces (FF) are made last. After cutting stock to length and width, refer to the step-by-step credenza drawer pull detail on pages 48 and 49 for instructions on making the routed drawer pulls. Remember to apply the ¼ in. radius round-over to the drawer face perimeter.

The completed drawer faces are centered and mounted one at a time on the drawer boxes. Note that the countersunk screw holes through the drawer fronts must be positioned away from the routed drawer pull recess. The drawer faces are mounted so they extend ½ in. past the drawer box top and ¼ in. below the drawer box bottom, as shown in the drawer side view.

At this point in the assembly process, you should final finish the various parts of the credenza. My sanding sequence starts with 100 grit, proceeding to 150, 180, and ultimately 220 grit paper. I prefer a sprayed lacquer finish for this piece. A sprayed-on finish is exceptionally even with no brush marks,

and when applied properly, will be completely drip and run free. If your shop is not set up for spraying, cans of Deft spray finish will provide a similar look, though a project of this size will require a number of cans. Both spray-on lacquer and Deft Clear Semi-Gloss aerosol spray cans are available from The Woodworkers' Store.

To complete the credenza assembly, mount the base, the top, and the doors to the case. The base and top are mounted with countersunk wood screws. I use self-closing full overlay European style hinges (GG) to mount the doors, although you may prefer some other system. The European style hinges require that a 35 mm (1⅜ in.) diameter hole be bored into the doors. Both the hinges and the special 35 mm bits to bore these holes are available from The Woodworkers' Store. A 1⅜ in. diameter Forstner bit can be used as well, if you have one. The beauty of European style hinges is that they are fully concealed, provide 3-way adjustment of the door to give you a perfect fit, and they allow maximum access to the interior by moving the door out and away from the carcase. You may be unfamiliar with them and therefore reluctant to use them, but their strength, adjustability and ease of installation make the European hinges far superior to conventional hinges. Once you try them, I'm sure you'll agree. □

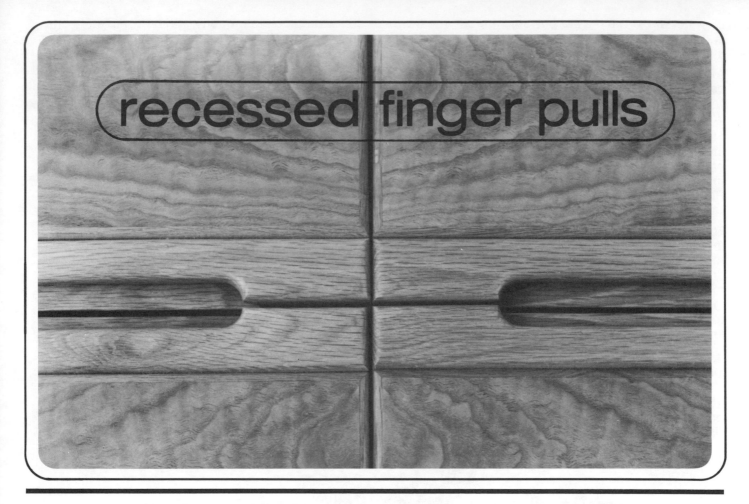

recessed finger pulls

credenza door, dresser drawer, and bed drawer pulls

recessed finger pulls are an element often associated with fine furniture. The inherent beauty and function of a pull that is built in, and not added on, is widely recognized by the best craftsmen as a most desirable and practical feature.

Recessed finger pulls eliminate the need for expensive or hard-to-find hardware, and on the credenza, dresser and bed projects, the pulls contribute significantly to the overall design and impact of the piece.

As you will note, for the credenza doors and the dresser drawers (see page 47), the stock must first be ripped down the middle (step 1). For the bed drawers, however, the stock is left in one piece, and is crosscut in half only *after* all shaping is complete (see step 6). In both cases the plan is for the grain pattern to present a continuous visual element. For those who prefer an even more dramatic effect with the credenza doors and dresser drawers, I recommend resawing and surfacing 1¾ in. thick stock to provide bookmatched halves. If you don't mind the additional work, the bookmatched effect is

an added detail that will truly label your project as distinctive.

There are several options you may use to drill the 1 in. diameter holes in step 2. Although a hole saw, fly cutter or even a spade or regular drill bit will get the job done, I prefer using a Forstner bit, which cuts an exceptionally clean and even hole. Note that the fly cutter is the best method for cutting the 2⅛ in. diameter holes in the bed drawers.

When saber sawing the waste between the holes (step 3), remember to stay on the inside or waste side of the line.

In step 6, although the ½ in. cove cutter bearing must ride on the previously rounded-over portion of the pulls, I have found that this does not present a problem. If a small indentation is left around the pull perimeter where the ball bearing makes contact, simply hand sand this indentation out.

A final sanding of the pulls to remove router marks and to soften sharp edges is recommended before the final finish is applied. □

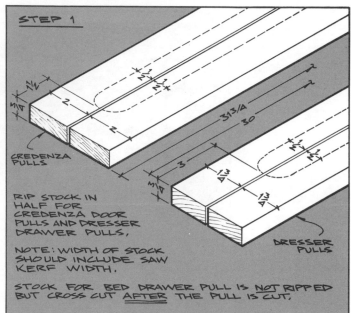

CREDENZA
PULLS

DRESSER
PULLS

RIP STOCK IN
HALF FOR
CREDENZA DOOR
PULLS AND DRESSER
DRAWER PULLS.

NOTE: WIDTH OF STOCK
SHOULD INCLUDE SAW
KERF WIDTH.

STOCK FOR BED DRAWER PULL IS NOT RIPPED
BUT CROSS CUT AFTER THE PULL IS CUT.

STEP 2

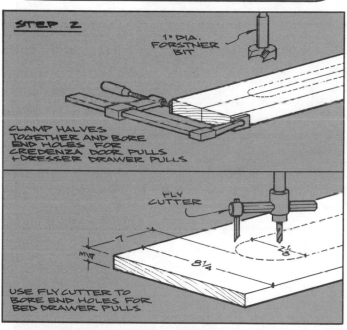

1" DIA.
FORSTNER
BIT

CLAMP HALVES
TOGETHER AND BORE
END HOLES FOR
CREDENZA DOOR PULLS
+ DRESSER DRAWER PULLS

FLY
CUTTER

USE FLY CUTTER TO
BORE END HOLES FOR
BED DRAWER PULLS

STEP 3

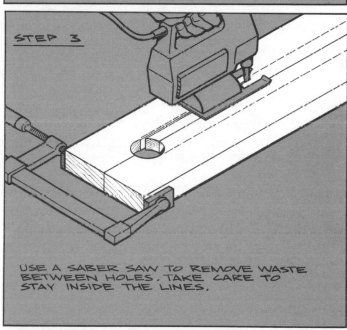

USE A SABER SAW TO REMOVE WASTE
BETWEEN HOLES. TAKE CARE TO
STAY INSIDE THE LINES.

STEP 4

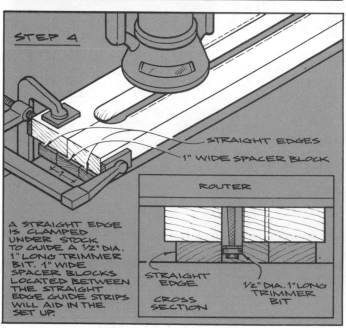

STRAIGHT EDGES

1" WIDE SPACER BLOCK

ROUTER

A STRAIGHT EDGE
IS CLAMPED
UNDER STOCK
TO GUIDE A 1/2" DIA.
1" LONG TRIMMER
BIT. 1" WIDE
SPACER BLOCKS
LOCATED BETWEEN
THE STRAIGHT
EDGE GUIDE STRIPS
WILL AID IN THE
SET UP.

STRAIGHT
EDGE

CROSS
SECTION

1/2" DIA. 1" LONG
TRIMMER BIT

STEP 5

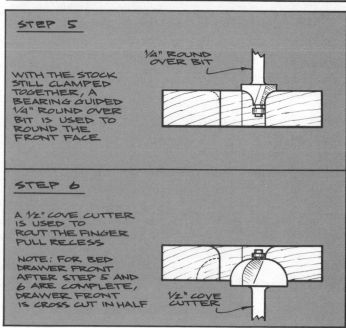

1/4" ROUND
OVER BIT

WITH THE STOCK
STILL CLAMPED
TOGETHER, A
BEARING GUIDED
1/4" ROUND OVER
BIT IS USED TO
ROUND THE
FRONT FACE

STEP 6

A 1/2" COVE CUTTER
IS USED TO
ROUT THE FINGER
PULL RECESS

NOTE: FOR BED
DRAWER FRONT
AFTER STEP 5 AND
6 ARE COMPLETE,
DRAWER FRONT
IS CROSS CUT IN HALF

1/2" COVE
CUTTER

credenza drawer pull

the credenza drawer pulls, like the other recessed pulls I feature in my work, are made using a technique that involves laying out, roughing in, and final shaping with the router. It differs from the previous pull technique though, in that a template is used to reproduce identical pulls. The template serves as a guide for locating the drill bit in step 2, and for the 1 in. long trimmer bit bearing in step 4. Make the template the same width as the drawer faces and center the pull to simplify positioning and clamp-up.

The final appearance of these pulls will depend on the accuracy with which you make the template. Lay out the $\frac{1}{2}$ in. diameters carefully, then drill, jigsaw and smooth the template to eliminate any irregularities that could be transferred to the pulls. When using the $\frac{1}{2}$ in. cove cutter in step 6, I recommend several passes with the router, rather than attempting to hog out all the material in a single pass. Removing the material gradually will result in a smoother cut with decreased chip out and reduce the need for final sanding.

It is important that the rounding-over (step 5) be done before the coving (step 6), since the coving operation effectively removes the material on which the ¼ in. radius round-over bit's bearing will ride.

Since the drawer faces are mounted to the drawer boxes, the box fronts serve as a pull backing, eliminating the need for an additional applied backing.

The technique used to craft these recessed finger pulls can be applied to other pulls of your own layout and design. Recessed finger pulls can be used in a broad variety of projects, from jewelry boxes to chests of drawers to cabinet work. Remember that careful stock selection, well thought out pull design, and an accurate template are the keys to a good looking, attractive recessed finger pull. □

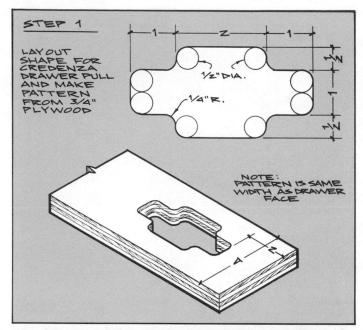

STEP 1

LAYOUT SHAPE FOR CREDENZA DRAWER PULL AND MAKE PATTERN FROM 3/4" PLYWOOD

½" DIA.

¼" R.

NOTE: PATTERN IS SAME WIDTH AS DRAWER FACE

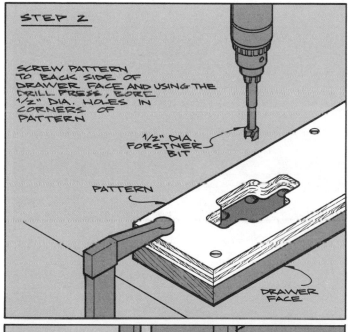

STEP 2

SCREW PATTERN TO BACK SIDE OF DRAWER FACE AND USING THE DRILL PRESS, BORE ½" DIA. HOLES IN CORNERS OF PATTERN

½" DIA. FORSTNER BIT

PATTERN

DRAWER FACE

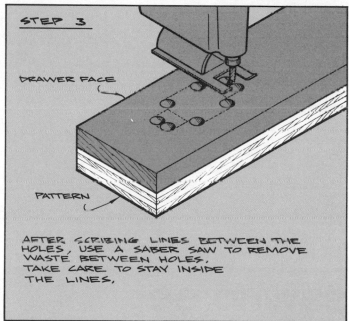

STEP 3

DRAWER FACE

PATTERN

AFTER SCRIBING LINES BETWEEN THE HOLES, USE A SABER SAW TO REMOVE WASTE BETWEEN HOLES. TAKE CARE TO STAY INSIDE THE LINES.

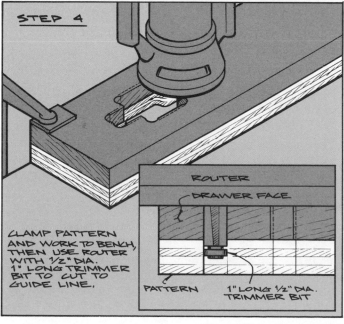

STEP 4

ROUTER

DRAWER FACE

CLAMP PATTERN AND WORK TO BENCH, THEN USE ROUTER WITH ½" DIA. 1" LONG TRIMMER BIT TO CUT TO GUIDE LINE.

PATTERN

1" LONG ½" DIA. TRIMMER BIT

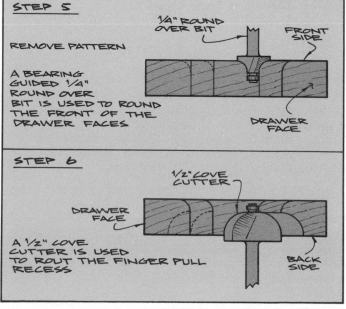

STEP 5

¼" ROUND OVER BIT

FRONT SIDE

REMOVE PATTERN

A BEARING GUIDED ¼" ROUND OVER BIT IS USED TO ROUND THE FRONT OF THE DRAWER FACES

DRAWER FACE

STEP 6

½" COVE CUTTER

DRAWER FACE

A ½" COVE CUTTER IS USED TO ROUT THE FINGER PULL RECESS

BACK SIDE

sawhorse
dining table

the sawhorses shown here were originally built
to be used in my workshop. Knowing how
difficult it can be to transport a pair of sawhorses,
especially if they must be squeezed into a car, I
wanted them to be portable, and that meant they
had to fold flat. Of course, it was also important that
they be sturdy.

I was so pleased with the appearance of the
finished pair, the idea stuck me that the sawhorses
could be teamed up with a nicely finished oak top to
make a handsome dining room table. Since it can be
stored away, it is the perfect extra table for those
holidays and special occasions when there are more
guests than the regular dining table can
accommodate.

Readers have the option of making just a good pair
of portable sawhorses or, by adding the top, an
attractive contemporary dining table.

The tabletop shown measures 36 in. wide by 72 in.
long, but it can be made larger or smaller depending
on your needs. A pair of cleats on the underside of
the top keeps it from sliding.

I used solid oak for the sawhorses and ¾ in. thick
oak veneer plywood for the top, although other
combinations of hardwood and ply can be used.

To make the sawhorses you will need stock that
measures ¾ in. thick by 5 in. wide. The rails (A) and
the spreaders (D) can be cut to the final lengths
shown in the bill of materials (30 in. and 4 in.

respectively). The legs (B) and stretchers (C), however, should be cut slightly longer than the indicated final lengths to allow for mitering and tenoning.

Use the table saw or radial arm saw with the miter gauge set at 5 degrees to cut off the legs at one end. With this same miter angle setting, now cut the $1\frac{1}{2}$ in. long tenons on the top end of the legs. As shown in Fig. 1, these tenons are made so that the corresponding rail mortises need not be angled. Do not cut the rail mortises yet. Referring to Fig. 2, tenon the stretcher ends and mortise the legs to accept these tenons; check with a dry fitting. If the fit is correct, glue and clamp the four leg and stretcher assemblies. When dry, lay these assemblies out against the rails in order to locate the rail mortises that will accept the leg tenons. Cut the mortises, check for fit, and then glue and clamp the rails in place. Round the sawhorse corners as shown. I used a spray can cover as a template to scribe these arcs. Use a jigsaw to remove the waste; sand the arc. The edges are rounded over using a router equipped with a $\frac{1}{4}$ in. round-over bit.

Next, mark for the upper hinges, which are located about $2\frac{3}{4}$ in. from the rail ends. Position these hinges so they are flush with the top of the rails. After mortising for the hinge plates, use the router and a $\frac{1}{2}$ in. core box bit to rout a cove that will accept the barrel of the hinge (see Fig. 3). Either hold the router base against a straight edge, or use the router edge guide.

The spreaders (D) are hinged together in much the same fashion, the only difference being that the hinge is positioned so the barrel will protrude above the edge. The spreaders can now be hinged to the stretchers. Note that these hinges are mounted in reverse (Fig. 5). Lay out and mark for one hinge first. Mortise for that hinge, then rout along the stock edge for the hinge barrel (Fig. 4),

Horses fold flat for easy storage and handling.

and assemble. Place the horse in the open position and mark where the spreader falls out on the opposing stretcher. Mark, mortise and rout for the other hinge, then complete assembly.

To make the top, select an attractive piece of $\frac{3}{4}$ in. thick lumber core red or white oak plywood, and cut it to size. Then, using the rabbet and dado method (see Fig. 6), apply a $\frac{3}{4} \times 1\frac{1}{2}$ in. edging (H and I) all around, carefully mitering the corners. When making the edging, allow a little extra width so that, when applied, the edging will protrude about $\frac{1}{16}$ in. above the plywood surface. This protruding lip is later planed back flush with the plywood. (continued on next page)

Hinged flaps shown from underneath.

Round over the top and bottom of the molded edge, using the router equipped with a 3/8 in. bearing-guided round-over bit. Final sand and apply Watco oil or the finish of your choice. If you use Watco, wait ten minutes, then sand with an orbital sander using 500 grit wet or dry silicone carbide paper. This will provide a very smooth finish.

To complete the project, screw the cleat assembly (parts E and F) to the underside of the top (see Figs. 7 and 8). □

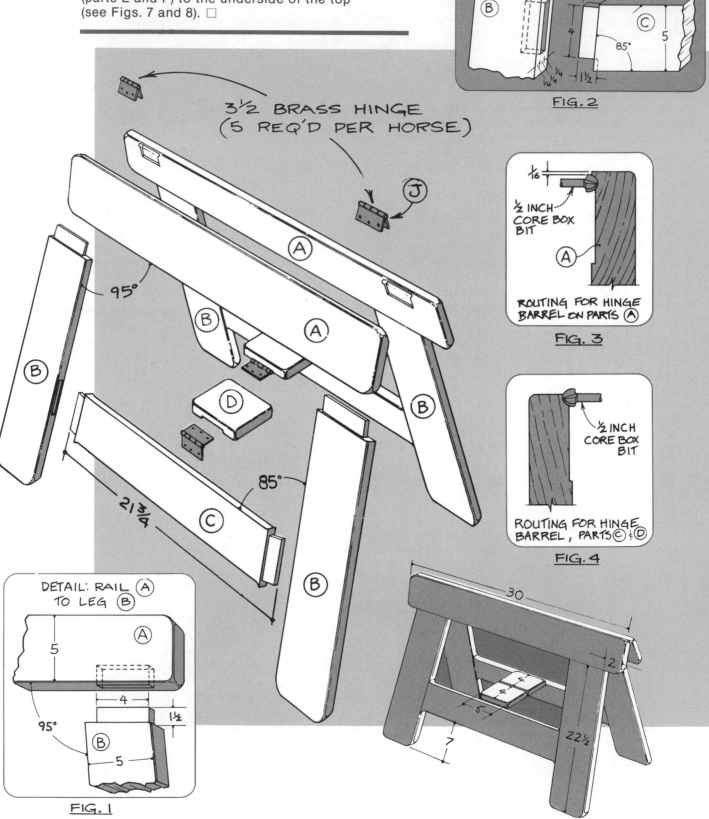

DETAIL: STRETCHER Ⓒ
TO LEG Ⓑ

FIG. 2

3½ BRASS HINGE
(5 REQ'D PER HORSE)

Ⓙ

95°

Ⓐ

Ⓑ

Ⓐ

Ⓑ

Ⓑ

Ⓓ

21¾

Ⓒ

85°

Ⓑ

½ INCH
CORE BOX
BIT

Ⓐ

ROUTING FOR HINGE
BARREL ON PARTS Ⓐ

FIG. 3

½ INCH
CORE BOX
BIT

ROUTING FOR HINGE
BARREL, PARTS Ⓒ & Ⓓ

FIG. 4

DETAIL: RAIL Ⓐ
TO LEG Ⓑ

Ⓐ

5

95°

4

1½

Ⓑ

5

FIG. 1

30

2

4
4

5

7

22½

52

Bill of Materials
(all dimensions actual)

Part	Description	Size	No. Req'd.
A	Rail	¾ × 5 × 30	4
B	Leg	¾ × 5 × 24	8
C	Stretcher	¾ × 5 × 21¾	4
D	Spreader	¾ × 5 × 4	4
E	Cleat Side	¾ × 1¼ × 32½	4
F	Cleat End	¾ × 1¼ × 2¼	4
G	Top	¾ × 35½ × 71½	1
H	Edge Side	¾ × 1½ × 72	2
I	Edge End	¾ × 1½ × 36	2
J	Hinge	3½ in. butt hinge	10

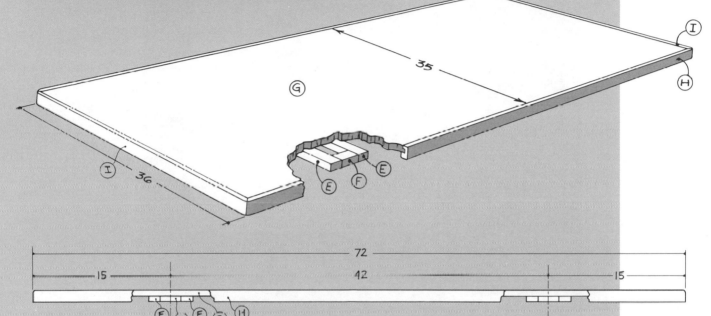

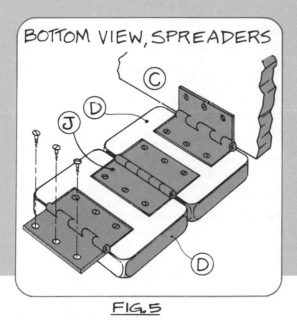

BOTTOM VIEW, SPREADERS

FIG. 5

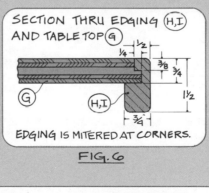

SECTION THRU EDGING (H,I) AND TABLE TOP (G)

EDGING IS MITERED AT CORNERS.

FIG. 6

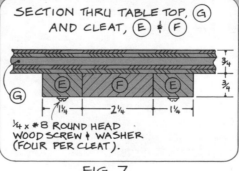

SECTION THRU TABLE TOP, (G) AND CLEAT, (E) & (F)

¼ × #8 ROUND HEAD WOOD SCREW & WASHER (FOUR PER CLEAT).

FIG. 7

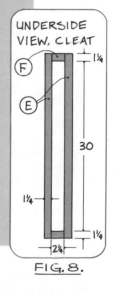

UNDERSIDE VIEW, CLEAT

FIG. 8.

clock

this handsome clock utilizes a simple table saw technique to achieve a beveled frame look. While appearing to be cut at a bevel from heavy stock, the frame is actually made with compound miters from standard ¾ in. thick material.

In order to achieve this compound miter cut, the table saw blade is tilted 21 degrees, while the miter gauge angle is set at 49 degrees. These settings will result in the frame being angled at 60 degrees, as illustrated in the cross-sectional view. The illustrations show a table saw that tilts to the left.

Begin by cutting the four walnut frame pieces (A) to length, using the 21-degree blade tilt and 49-degree miter gauge settings. Make the compound miter cut on one end of each of the four frame pieces by setting up the miter gauge in the left hand slot, as shown in Fig. 1A. Then, without touching the blade or miter angle settings, switch the miter gauge to the right side slot, butt the frame piece against a stopblock cut to the same compound angle, and miter the opposite end (see Fig. 1B). The stopblock will insure that the four frame pieces are all identical in length. This is essential if the frame is to fit up right. Note that the *back* side of the frame parts will be facing *up* for the first cut (Fig. 1A), while the pieces must be flipped over so the *front* side is facing *up* for the second cut (Fig. 1B). A section of sandpaper glued to the miter gauge extension and a clamp will prevent the frame pieces from "walking" during the first cut, as also shown in Fig. 1A. If your table saw is not absolutely precise, I recommend making four test frame parts in pine in order to check the accuracy of the angle settings.

Next, with the dado head set to ¼ in. width and inclined at a 30-degree angle (Fig. 2), cut the rabbet into which the clock face will fit. Also cut to thickness and width sufficient stock for the walnut retainer pieces (B).

The clockface is made by veneering both sides of a ¼ in. thick by 10 in. square section of plywood. Start with the plywood for part C oversize since it is trimmed to final size only after the frame has been assembled. I used the cutoffs from an olive ash burl veneer flitch for the face veneer (D) in this project. Keep the veneer pieces in the same consecutive order as they were in the flitch. Yellow glue is used to apply both the face and the reverse veneer (E). Although any veneer will do on the reverse side, remember that it is important to veneer both sides of the plywood to balance the stresses of the veneer on the plywood substrate. Finally, drill through the center of the clockface to accept the movement handshaft. I selected a mini quartz movement from Mason and Sullivan (see source index on page 163). Order part no. 3609X-14 for the movement and part no 4880X for the hands.

Assemble the four frame pieces, gluing along the miters, and then add the clockface and the four retainer pieces which are also glued in place. Both the veneered clockface and these retainer strips are cut to fit snugly within the assembled frame.

I finished this project with several coats of Watco Danish Oil. Note that the veneered clockface should be final sanded and oiled before assembly for best results. □ (continued on next page)

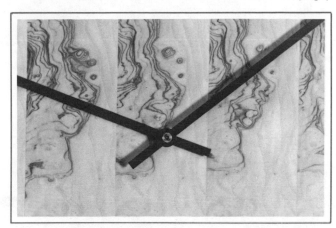

Bill of Materials
(all dimensions actual)

Part	Description	Size	No. Req'd.
A	Frame	¾ × 3 × 14½	4
B	Retainer	¼ × ⅜ × 9½	4
C	Face	¼ × 9½ × 9½	1
D	Face Veneer	as required	
E	Reverse Veneer	as required	
F	Movement	Quartz	1
G	Hands	Black	1 pair

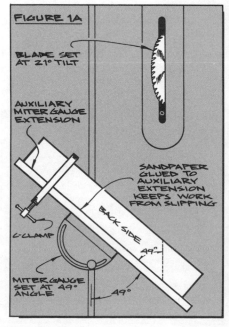

FIGURE 1A

BLADE SET AT 21° TILT

AUXILIARY MITER GAUGE EXTENSION

SANDPAPER GLUED TO AUXILIARY EXTENSION KEEPS WORK FROM SLIPPING

C-CLAMP

BACK SIDE

MITER GAUGE SET AT 49° ANGLE

49°

49°

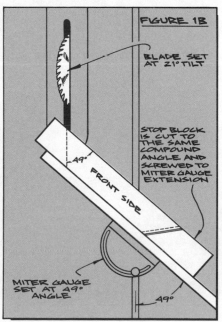

FIGURE 1B

BLADE SET AT 21° TILT

STOP BLOCK IS CUT TO THE SAME COMPOUND ANGLE AND SCREWED TO MITER GAUGE EXTENSION

FRONT SIDE

49°

MITER GAUGE SET AT 49° ANGLE

49°

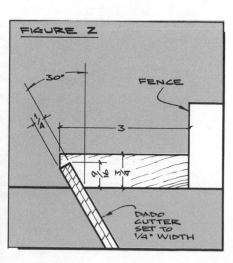

FIGURE 2

30°

¼

FENCE

3

9½

DADO CUTTER SET TO ¼" WIDTH

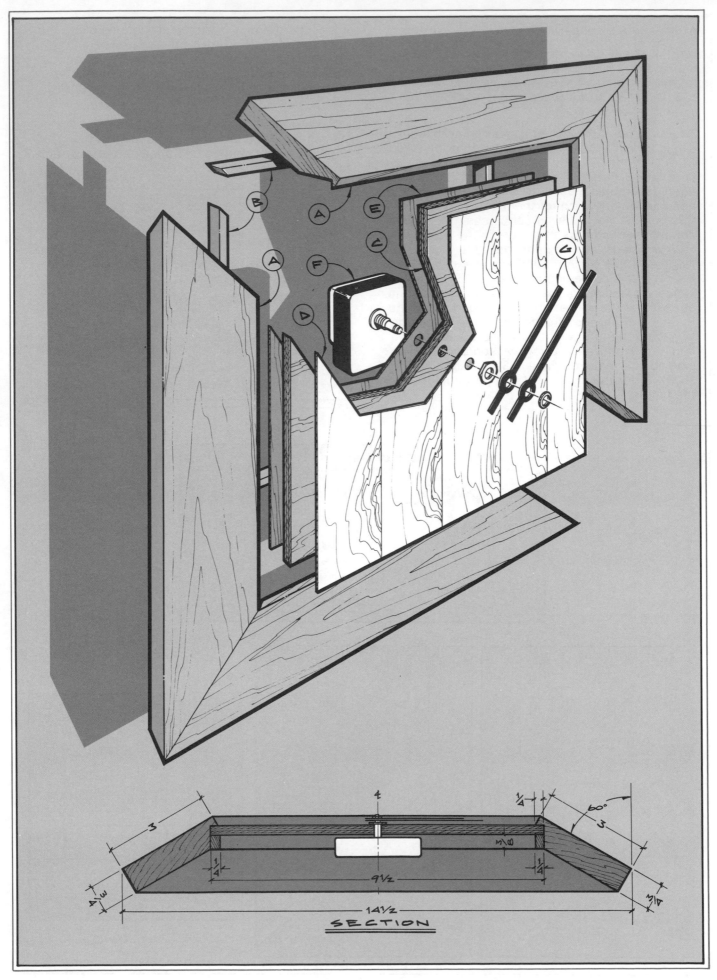

SECTION

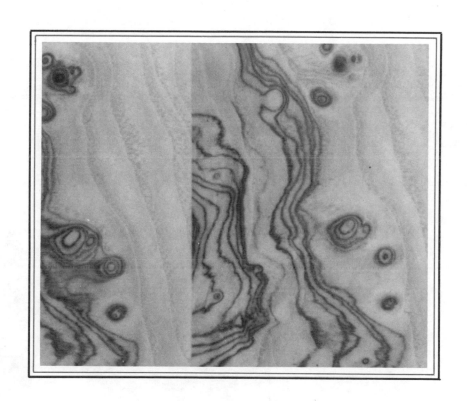

bedroom

the notched mitered spline joint

t he notched mitered spline joint is common to all the projects in the bedroom group except the dresser and wall shelf. As its name implies, the joint is basically a spline joint with a notch that creates a "stepped" appearance. Remember to cut the plywood splines so the outside grain is parallel to the joint. This will mean that the inner plywood grain runs perpendicular, or across the joint, providing maximum strength. □

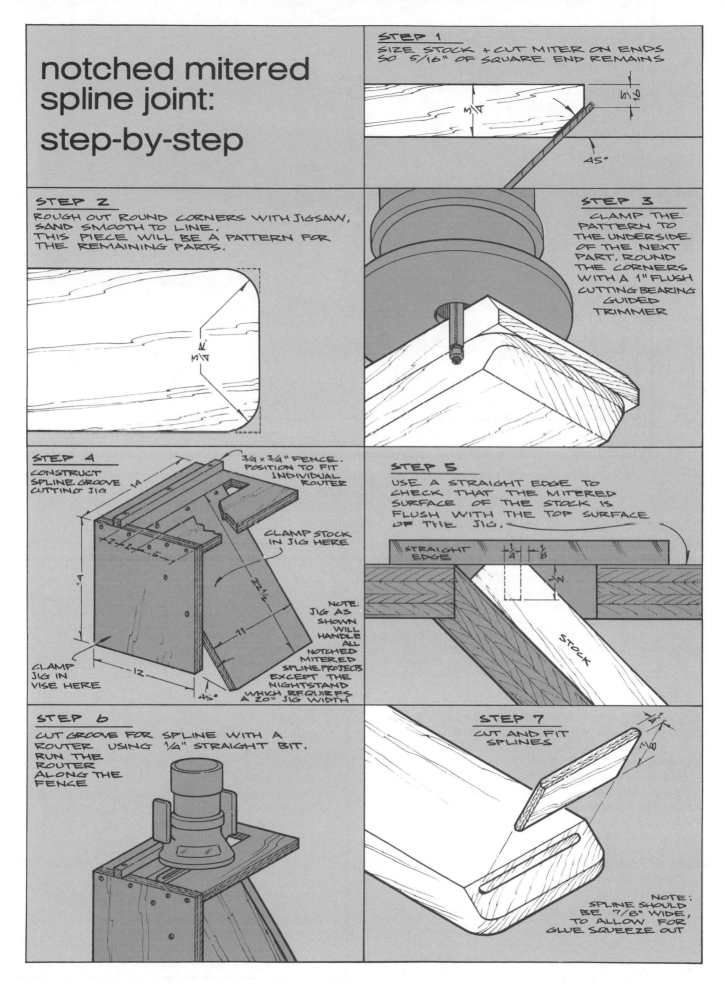

notched mitered spline joint:
step-by-step

STEP 1
SIZE STOCK + CUT MITER ON ENDS SO 5/16" OF SQUARE END REMAINS

3/4

5/16

45°

STEP 2
ROUGH OUT ROUND CORNERS WITH JIGSAW, SAND SMOOTH TO LINE. THIS PIECE WILL BE A PATTERN FOR THE REMAINING PARTS.

3/4 R.

STEP 3
CLAMP THE PATTERN TO THE UNDERSIDE OF THE NEXT PART, ROUND THE CORNERS WITH A 1" FLUSH CUTTING BEARING GUIDED TRIMMER

STEP 4
CONSTRUCT SPLINE GROOVE CUTTING JIG

3/4 x 3/4" FENCE. POSITION TO FIT INDIVIDUAL ROUTER

CLAMP STOCK IN JIG HERE

22 1/2

11

CLAMP JIG IN VISE HERE

12

45°

NOTE: JIG AS SHOWN WILL HANDLE ALL NOTCHED MITERED SPLINE PROJECTS EXCEPT THE NIGHTSTAND WHICH REQUIRES A 20" JIG WIDTH

STEP 5
USE A STRAIGHT EDGE TO CHECK THAT THE MITERED SURFACE OF THE STOCK IS FLUSH WITH THE TOP SURFACE OF THE JIG.

STRAIGHT EDGE

1/4 1/8

STOCK

STEP 6
CUT GROOVE FOR SPLINE WITH A ROUTER USING 1/4" STRAIGHT BIT. RUN THE ROUTER ALONG THE FENCE

STEP 7
CUT AND FIT SPLINES

1/4

1/8

NOTE: SPLINE SHOULD BE 7/8" WIDE, TO ALLOW FOR GLUE SQUEEZE OUT

bed

platform beds are relatively easy to make and provide an attractive alternative to conventional style beds, particularly if you prefer a contemporary look. This bed, which features the notched mitered spline joint, provides the added advantage of two storage drawers located in the base section. I use a 3 in. thick layer of foam beneath the mattress, which makes this bed exceptionally comfortable.

Although I show a standard size twin bed designed to accept a mattress that is 75 in. long by 39 in. wide, you may prefer a different size mattress. The standard mattress size chart below shows the actual standard mattress dimensions. As you will note, the interior dimensions across the frame allow approximately 1 in. extra in both length and width. This extra space is important to accommodate the additional thickness of sheets and blankets. The various bed parts will have to be sized up as needed to accommodate a larger mattress, however I recommend retaining the overall proportions of the piece. If you opt for a larger size mattress, you might also consider locating two additional drawers on the opposite side of the bed.

standard mattress size chart

Twin	39 × 75
Double	54 × 75
Queen	60 × 80
King	76 × 80

Bill of Materials
(all dimensions actual)

Part	Description	Size	No. Req'd.
A	Side	¾ × 6½ × 76¾	2
B	End	¾ × 6½ × 40¾	2
C	Bottom	¾ × 40⅝ × 76⅝	1
D	Short Spacer	¾ × 3 × 34⅛	3
E	Long Spacer	¾ × 3 × 73⅛	1
F	Base Side	¾ × 8½ × 71	1
G	Base End	¾ × 8½ × 35	2
H	Divider	¾ × 8½ × 33⅞	1
I	Cleat	¾ × ¾ stock	as needed
J	Corner Block	¾ × ¾ × 7¾	2
K	Base Bottom	⅜ × 35⅛ × 71⅛	1
L	Drawer Side	½ × 7 × 28	4
M	Drawer Front/Back	½ × 7 × 33¹¹⁄₁₆	4
N	Drawer Bottom	¼ × 27½ × 33³⁄₁₆	2
O	Drawer Face	¾ × 8³⁄₁₆ × 35½*	2
P	Drawer Face Backing	¼ × 7 × 35**	2
Q	Drawer Slides	28 in. Accuride full extension***	2 pair

   * Drawer faces are crosscut from a single board. See recessed pull step-by-step instructions on pages 46 and 47.

  ** Length dimension allows ¹⁄₃₂ in. either side of drawer face backing for clearance.

*** Available from: The Woodworkers' Store (see source index). Order part no. D7575 for 28 in. long model.

Begin by constructing the upper bed frame assembly, consisting of the sides (A), ends (B), and bottom (C). Refer to pages 60 and 61 for step-by-step instructions on how to make the notched mitered spline joint. Note that the spline grooves are located ½ in. down from the top edge and 2 in. up from the lower edge of this upper frame. Next, use the dado head to cut the ¾ in. wide by ⅜ in. deep groove in parts A and B to accept the ¾ in. thick bottom. As shown, this groove is located ¾ in. up from the lower edge. The bottom can be either plywood or particleboard, though a good-one-side hardwood plywood is your best choice.

Cut the splines from ¼ in. plywood, and then glue and assemble parts A and B around part C. Cut the short and long spacers (D and E) to size from ¾ in. plywood, and glue these in place under the bottom. Since I cut the bottom from a 4 ft. by 8 ft. sheet of plywood, the waste provided ample stock for parts D and E.

Next construct the base frame, consisting of parts F, G, H, I, J, and K. The base side (F) and ends (G) are made and assembled with the same notched mitered spline joint used on the upper frame construction. Make the divider (H), the cleats (I), and the corner blocks (J), and then glue up, screw as necessary and assemble these parts. Cut two temporary spacers to locate across the drawer openings between the divider and ends to insure that the ends and divider remain parallel, then cut the base bottom to size from ⅜ in. thick plywood and screw it up into the base assembly. Note that this base bottom is sized ¼ in. smaller all around, and must be notched at the corners to

accommodate the stepped corner treatment of the base assembly. Now screw down through parts C, D, and E to joint the upper and lower sections.

Make the finger-jointed drawer box assemblies, consisting of parts L, M, and N, and after assembling these parts refer to the step-by-step pull illustrations on pages 46 and 47 for instruction on machining the recessed finger pull. The fact that the two drawer faces (O) are cut from the same board contributes substantially to the appearance of the bed. When making these recessed pulls I always take extra time with stock selection. An attractive board with unusual, dramatic, or highly figured grain will enhance the recessed pull, especially in this project, where the pull detail is an important element in the design. Note that the front ends of the base ends and the outside ends of the drawer faces are notched and rounded exactly the same as the notched mitered spline corner construction, but *without* the spline groove.

Apply the drawer face backing strip (P) which is also crosscut from a single board, and mount the drawer boxes using the 28 in. long Accuride full extension drawer slides (Q). After the drawer boxes are mounted, position and mount the drawer faces, drilling and countersinking through the drawer box as illustrated.

I used Watco Danish Oil on this project, as with the other pieces in the bedroom group. Whatever finish you select, I recommend staying with a natural look, which best displays natural wood color and grain. The finish must be thoroughly dry, of course, before you insert the mattress. □

(continued on next page)

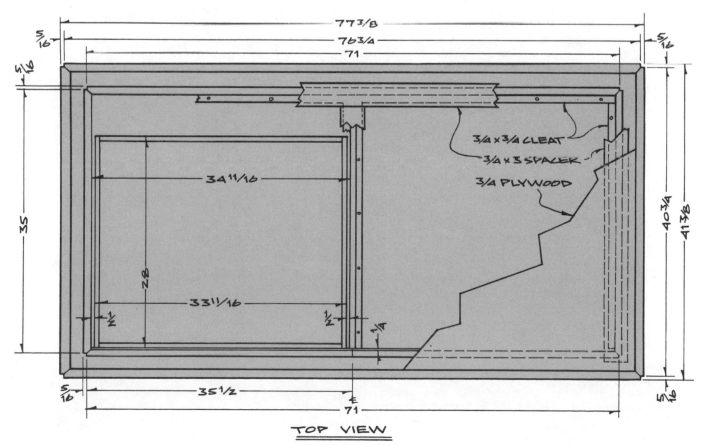

TOP VIEW

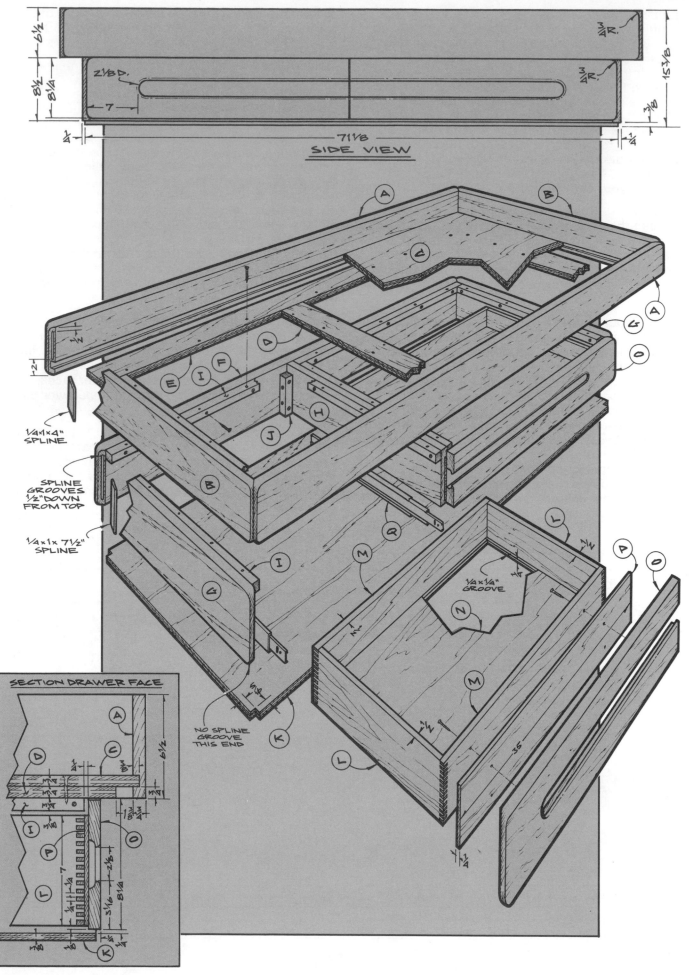

6½
8½
8¼
2⅛ D.
7
¼
71⅛
⅜
¾ R.
¾ R.
15⅜
⅜
¼

SIDE VIEW

A
B
C
A
G
O
D
E
I
F
H
J
B
I
G
Q
M
L
P
O
N
M
L
K
N
L
K

¼
½
2

¼ x 1 x 4"
SPLINE

SPLINE
GROOVES
½" DOWN
FROM TOP

¼ x 1 x 7½"
SPLINE

NO SPLINE
GROOVE
THIS END

¼ x ¼"
GROOVE

35

¼

SECTION DRAWER FACE

A
C
D
I
P
L
O
K

6½
7
2⅛
8¼
3/16
⅜
½

64

dresser

t he beauty of this project lies in the fact that simple construction and careful stock selection are combined for a striking effect. There is no exposed hardware. Cleverly machined recessed pulls integrate with matched hardwoods and veneer for a classic contemporary style.

I have crafted the dresser in oak, although walnut, figured maple, and cherry are other alternatives you may wish to consider. A colored laminate could be substituted for the veneered surfaces, if you prefer. Although the dresser in the photo has a genuine marble top, the illustrations show black laminate, which has a similar appearance at a far lower cost.

The general construction of the dresser may seem involved at first glance. However, when broken down into its separate elements it becomes evident that following a logical sequence vastly simplifies the project. The dresser is essentially two plywood

boxes that are joined together and edged at the front, with a plywood back, sides, drawers, and top.

Start by making the plywood boxes, which are composed of the sides (A) and top and bottom (B). Cut the ⅜ in. wide by ½ in. deep rabbet in the ends of the top and bottom, and the ¼ in. wide by ⅜ in. deep corresponding groove in the sides. Glue and assemble the two boxes, using ¼ in. T nuts to join the boxes together. Next cut the ¼ in. thick plywood back (C) to length and width, making certain that it is square. The back is now glued and screwed to the boxes. If the back has been cut accurately, it will serve to square up the boxes. Remember, it is important that the boxes be square for the rest of the project to fit together right.

Now mill the ¼ in. thick by ¾ in. wide edging (D) that will be applied around the front edges of the case. You might note that the same size edging is also

(continued on next page)

needed for parts J and N. If you wish to save set-up time later, mill sufficient edging for all these parts now. Make about 110 feet total, which will allow for some waste. After fitting, mitering, and gluing up the case edging, use a laminate trimmer or a sharp hand plane to flush it with the plywood sides. In practice I always rip edgings such as these slightly wider than the final required dimension, in this case $\frac{7}{8}$ in. instead of $\frac{3}{4}$ in. The additional width is vital for the edgings (parts J and N) as they will have to cover the $\frac{3}{4}$ in. plywood core (parts I and M) plus the face and reverse veneers (parts K and O) which measure about $\frac{1}{32}$ in. thick each.

Cut and miter the base sides (E) and front and back (F). Assemble the base with glue, and use a $\frac{1}{4}$ in. radius bearing-guided round-over bit to apply the $\frac{1}{4}$ in. radius to the perimeter edges, as illustrated. When gluing up the miters, remember that sizing the joint first will result in a much stronger glue joint. Now drill through, counterbore, and screw the base assembly to the case bottom. Note that the case must be centered on the base which, at this point in the construction, will extend $\frac{3}{4}$ in. proud of the case at both the sides and the front.

The top assembly can also be made at this time. If you opt for the marble, it can be ordered through monument dealers. The black plastic solid color laminate (H) I specify is simply a laminate with the color extending through the entire thickness of the material. Wilson Art's "Solicor" and Formica's "Colorcore" are two of the more popular brand names. The solid color laminate is applied over the plywood or particleboard core (G). The recommended procedure here is to apply the lower or reverse side laminate first, gluing it in place with contact cement. Start with the laminate about $\frac{1}{4}$ in.

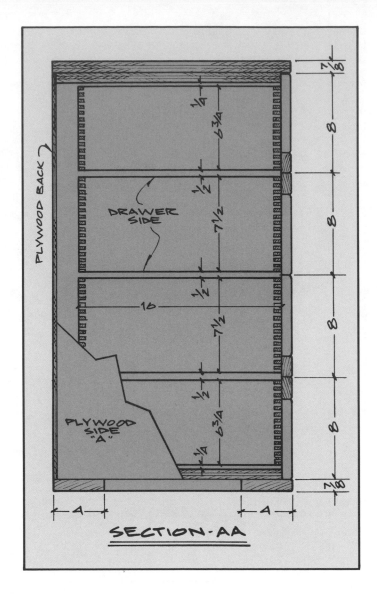

SECTION-AA

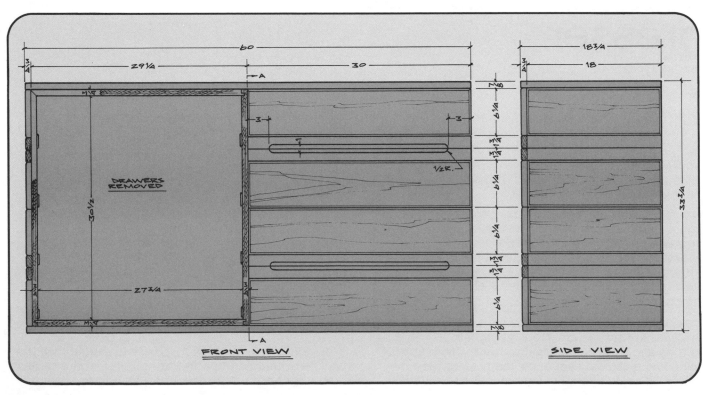

FRONT VIEW   SIDE VIEW

oversize all around and use a laminate trimmer to flush the edge. Next, following the same technique, apply the laminate edging and finally the top laminate.

A laminate bevel cutter bit can be used to bevel the laminate edge, or you can achieve the same result by hand using a fine flat file. Drill and counterbore up through the case to accept the top mounting flathead wood screws. As with the base assembly, the top will extend ¾ in. proud of the case on both the sides and at the front.

Now set about constructing the side and drawer face panels. As you can see from the exploded view, these panels are simply plywood sections laminated both sides with veneer and edged in solid stock. Select the veneers for these panels and the matching solid stock parts of the project with great care. If you take the time to use matching consecutive veneers as I have done, the effect can be quite dramatic, as the photo illustrates. Should you wish to save time, however, an acceptable alternative is to use pre-veneered hardwood plywood. Again, select the plywood sheets carefully in order to obtain the matched veneer faces. Other alternatives to the painstaking process of veneering are the use of plastic laminates or veneered faces. The veneered faces are usually available in exotic burls, crotch, and other precious woods. The advantage here is that although these veneered faces must still be laminated onto the plywood substrate, they are pre-flattened to simplify the procedure. Remember that with all veneers, as with any other laminations, you must veneer both sides of the substrate to equalize stresses. Of course there is no need to waste valuable and expensive veneer faces on the reverse side which will not be visible.

Apply the veneer (K) over the side panel core (I). For convenience, you might want to lay up four panels at a time and use a shop built press to clamp them in a single operation. Again, as a construction tip, I find that it is best to start with both the plywood panels and the veneer about ½ in. to 1 in. oversize all around. This enables one to simply cut the veneered panels to final size on the table saw. Now add the side panel edging, mitering the corners as shown. Then use the ¼ in. bearing-guided round-over bit to apply the ¼ in. radius around the outside face perimeter. Cut the side rails (L) to length and width, and apply the same ¼ in. radius round-over as shown. Note that the solid stock for parts L should be selected to compliment your choice of veneer. The side panel assemblies, consisting of parts I, J, and K, and the side rails are now mounted to the carcase. Drill and counterbore through the case to accept the flathead mounting screws. Use screws no longer than 1¼ in. so there will be no danger of the screw tip penetrating the face veneer.

Now make the drawer face assemblies, consisting of parts M, N, and O, following the same process you used for the side panel assemblies. The drawer rail pulls are machined into the drawer rails (P) using the recessed pull technique described in the white oak credenza project on pages 46 and 47.

Note that the routed pull detail is centered 3 in. from either end of the drawer rails. Apply the ¼ in. radius around the drawer face assemblies and drawer rails, again using the ¼ in. bearing-guided round-over bit.

You must now join the drawer face assemblies and the drawer rails. Use the router and a ¼ in. wing cutter to rout the ½ in. deep by 28 in. long spline grooves in each member. Make the splines (Q) from ¼ in. thick plywood. Glue and assemble the drawer face assemblies and drawer rails.

Next, make all the drawers. As noted in the bill of materials, although the drawer face assemblies are

Bill of Materials
(all dimensions actual)

Part	Description	Size	No. Req'd.
A	Side	¾ × 17½ × 32	4
B	Top/Bottom	¾ × 17½ × 28½	4
C	Back	¼ × 32 × 58½	1
D	Case Edging	¼ × ¾	as needed
E	Base Side	⅞ × 4 × 18¾	2
F	Base Front/Back	⅞ × 4 × 60	2
G	Top Core	¾ × 18⅝ × 59⅞	1
H	Top Laminate	black plastic solid color	as needed
I	Side Panel Core	¾ × 5¾ × 17½	8
J	Side Panel Edging	¼ × ¾	as needed
K	Side Panel Veneer	as required	
L	Side Rail	¾ × 1¾ × 18	8
M	Drawer Face Core	¾ × 5¾ × 29½	8
N	Drawer Face Edging	¼ × ¾	as needed
O	Drawer Face Veneer	as required	
P	Drawer Rail	¾ × 1¾ × 30	8
Q	Spline	¼ × 1 × 28	8
R	Pull Backing	⅛ × 1 × 25⅝	8
S	Drawer Front/Back	½ × (see below*) × 26⅝	16
T	Drawer Side	½ × (see below*) × 16	16
U	Drawer Bottom	¼ × 15⅜ × 26	8
V	Drawer Slide	16 in. black Accuride® full extension**	8 pair

* Note that the top and bottom drawers are 6¾ in. high, while the middle drawers are 7½ in. high.

** Accuride® drawer slides are available from: The Woodworkers' Store, (see source index).

all identical, there are two drawer box heights. The drawer front and back (S) and sides (T) of the top and bottom drawers are 6¾ in. high, requiring that you machine twenty-seven ¼ in. wide finger joint pins and slots in each member. The four middle drawers are 7½ in. high and require thirty ¼ in. wide pins and slots in each member.

Cut the ¼ in. by ¼ in. groove in parts S and T to accept the ¼ in. thick plywood drawer bottoms (U). Note that these bottom panels are sized 1/16 in. smaller all around than the actual groove-to-groove dimensions so they will not interfere with the drawer assembly. Glue up the drawer front, back and sides around the plywood bottom, making certain that the boxes are square. Now use the router and a straight cutter to machine the ⅛ in. deep recess in the

(continued on next page)

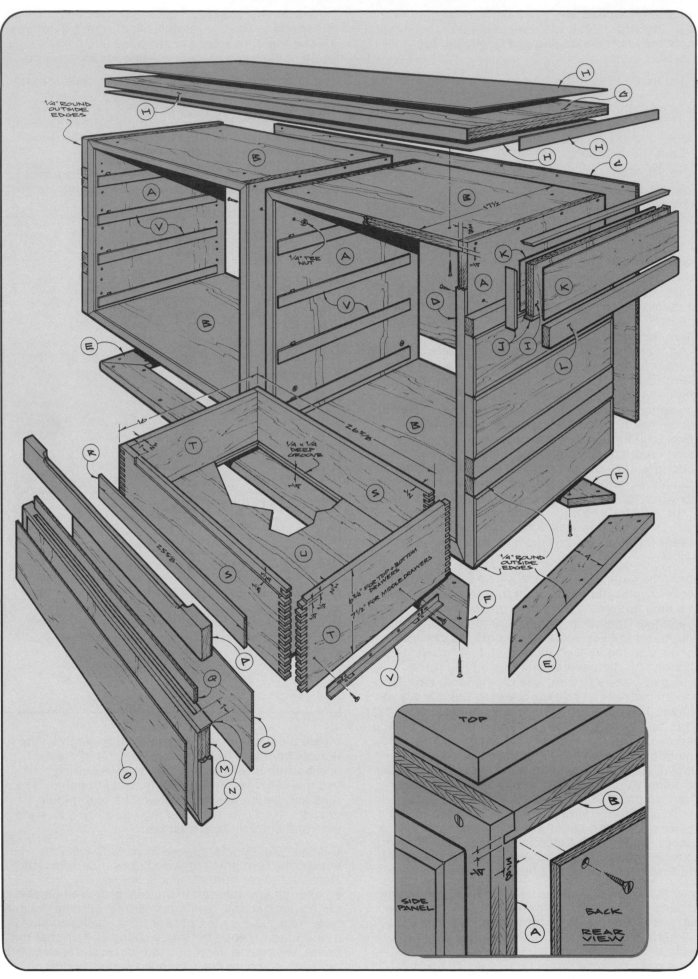

1/4" ROUND OUTSIDE EDGES

H
H
G
H
H
J

B

A
V

A

1/4" TEE NUT

V

B

B

17½

B

K

K

A

D

L

J I

E

16

R

T

1/4 × 1/4 DEEP GROOVE

1/4

26⅝

S

U

½

B

F

S

25⅝

6¾" FOR TOP & BOTTOM DRAWERS

7½" FOR MIDDLE DRAWERS

T

F

1/4" ROUND OUTSIDE EDGES

E

P

Q

O

M

N

O

V

TOP

B

SIDE PANEL

3/8

A

BACK

REAR VIEW

drawer fronts to accept the pull backing strips (R). Note that these recesses are off-center. On the right side drawer front (illustrated), the recess starts 1 in. from the left side of the drawer box. For the left side drawers, these recesses must start 1 in. from the right side of the drawer box. Glue the pull backing strips in place and then mount all the drawers, using black, full-extension Accuride® slides (V). As shown in the drawer location detail, the top and bottom drawers are spaced ¼ in. from both the top and the bottom, and the drawers are all spaced ½ in. apart.

The drawer face and rail assemblies are now mounted to the drawers. Although the illustrations and bill of materials all show the drawer face and rail members sized full width, you should actually have a little clearance between the drawers. The best way to accomplish this is to size the drawer face assemblies slightly under (³⁄₃₂ in.) the indicated width. The faces can also be final adjusted by taking several passes with the hand plane along the drawer face edging. Removing between ¹⁄₁₆ in. and ¹⁄₃₂ in. should provide the necessary clearance. I recommend using a section of plastic laminate as a spacer when mounting the completed drawer front assemblies. Place the strip on the base, butt the bottom drawer front assembly onto it, and mount the assembly to the drawer. Drill and countersink for the 1 in. long mounting screws. Next, place the laminate strip atop the bottom drawer front assembly as a location aid for positioning the next drawer front assembly, and so on until all the drawer front assemblies are mounted. Note that a shorter plastic laminate spacer strip should also be used to provide similar clearance between the left side and right side drawer front assemblies.

To finish the dresser, I rubbed in two coats of Watco Danish Oil. The first coat acts as a kind of a sealer and should be applied generously as the unfinished wood will be thirsty. The second coat is applied after the first has dried, and after buffing, will provide the wood surface with a low luster satin sheen. Thorough sanding before final finish is applied is always the key to a quality, professional appearance. I start with 100 grit, and progress through 150 to 180 and finally 220. The laminated and edged panels and drawer faces, and all the other component parts should be final sanded *before* assembly. When sanding the veneered surfaces, keep in mind that veneers will usually be ¹⁄₃₂ in. or less in thickness. Care should be exercised to avoid sanding through or in any way damaging the face veneers. □

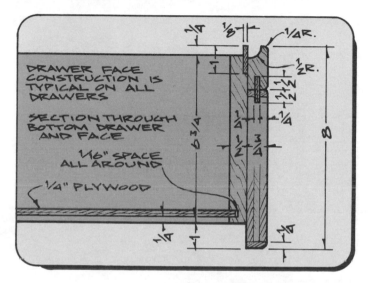

nightstand

the nightstand makes a perfect companion piece to the bed. The construction features the notched mitered spline joinery common to most of the bedroom group projects, and the casters allow the nightstand to be rolled aside for access to the bed drawer.

Start by getting out stock for the sides (A) and top and bottom (B). I used two pieces of 7½ in. wide stock to obtain the 15 in. width required for the parts.

When the edge-glued pieces are dry, sand and then trim to the final 18 in. length. The notched mitered spline joint is formed using the technique detailed on pages 60 and 61. Take note, however, that the jig for this project must be wider than the jig shown in the step-by-step instructions. If you plan to make the nightstand project, make a jig 20 in. wide instead of the indicated 14 in. width.

All final sanding should be done before assembly, since the exposed end grain of the joint will be difficult to sand after. Pre-drill the sides to accept the shelf pins (I), as illustrated. I use a pre-drilled pattern piece with seven evenly spaced holes, clamping the pattern to the sides and using a drill bit fit with a stop collar to insure a consistent ½ in. hole depth. Assemble parts A and B, using two band clamps or eight pipe clamps. If you use the pipe clamp method, protect the case with ¾ in. square by 15 in. long clamp strips. Note the use of several ¼ in. thick plywood splines, which are better able to accommodate wood movement across the width of the material, instead of a single long spline for the joint.

Now cut the stretcher (C) to fit snugly. Also cut the ¾ in. square long and short cleats (D and E), drilling and countersinking for 1¼ in. long no. 8 flathead wood screws. After sanding, install the stretcher and cleats.

Make the shelf (F) and shelf back (G) next, edge-gluing stock to achieve the 13¾ in. total width needed for the shelf. Round the front corners of the shelf and the top corners of the shelf back, and assemble.

The router and a mortising bit are used to notch the bottom of the shelf to accept the shelf supports. These notches are important since they serve to prevent the shelf from sliding off the shelf pins.

The nightstand is now given two coats of Watco Danish Oil, and is waxed thoroughly once the oil has penetrated and completely dried. The plate mount casters (H) are screwed in place to complete this project. □

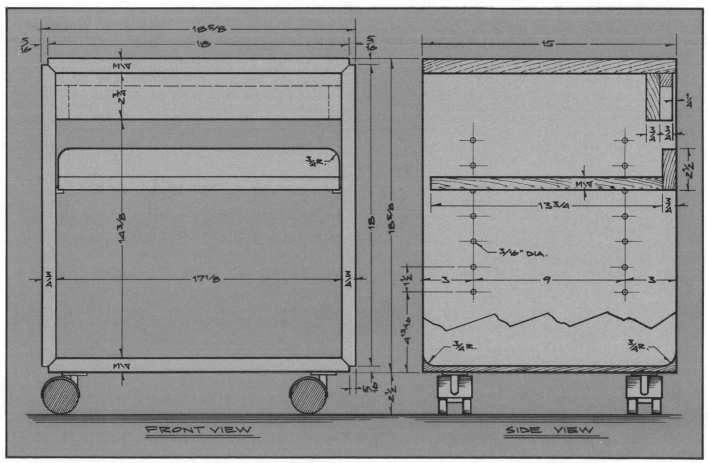

FRONT VIEW   SIDE VIEW

(continued on next page)

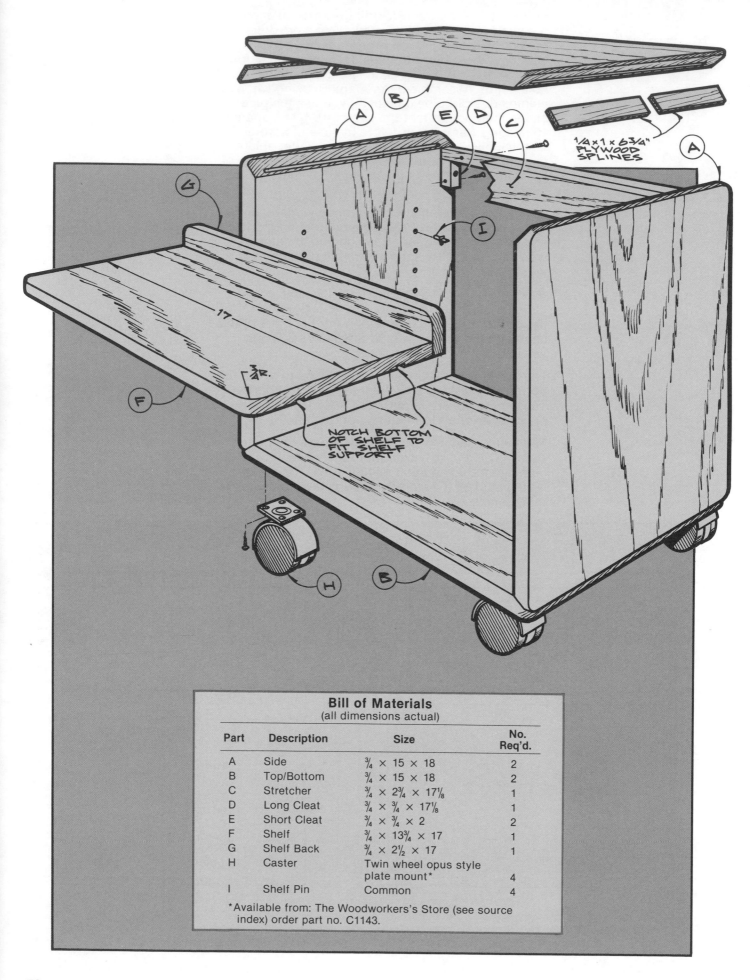

**¼ × 1 × 6¾"
PLYWOOD
SPLINES**

17

¾ R.

NOTCH BOTTOM
OF SHELF TO
FIT SHELF
SUPPORT

Bill of Materials
(all dimensions actual)

Part	Description	Size	No. Req'd.
A	Side	¾ × 15 × 18	2
B	Top/Bottom	¾ × 15 × 18	2
C	Stretcher	¾ × 2¾ × 17⅛	1
D	Long Cleat	¾ × ¾ × 17⅛	1
E	Short Cleat	¾ × ¾ × 2	2
F	Shelf	¾ × 13¾ × 17	1
G	Shelf Back	¾ × 2½ × 17	1
H	Caster	Twin wheel opus style plate mount*	4
I	Shelf Pin	Common	4

*Available from: The Woodworkers's Store (see source index) order part no. C1143.

mirror

t his attractive mirror features the stepped spline joint that is common to several of the bedroom group projects. I placed this project first in the grouping, since its simplicity affords an ideal opportunity for you to make and become familiar with the notched mitered spline joint.

Begin by cutting the sides (A) and the top and bottom (B) to length and width from ¾ in. thick oak stock. Now refer to page 60 for a step-by-step explanation of how the notched mitered spline joint is made. The spline grooves, which are 1⅜ in. long, start ½ in. back from the front edge of the frame, and the splines are ¼ in. plywood. Note that the spline grooves are stopped short so they will not interfere with the rabbet that is cut next. Use the table saw dado head to cut this ¼ by 1 in. rabbet around the sides, top, and bottom to accept the plywood back (C), mirror (D), and retainer (E and F). After applying the ¾ in. radius (see side view) to the ends of parts A and B, assemble the frame, making certain that it is perfectly square. To avoid scratching the mirror glass, the frame should be final sanded and finished *before* the mirror glass and back are mounted.

Now measure for the ⅜ in. thick plywood back and the ⅛ in. thick mirror. Have the mirror glass cut ¹⁄₁₆ in. smaller all around, but size the plywood for a snug fit. Mount the mirror and plywood and secure them both with the ¼ in. × ½ in. retainer strips. This retainer is mitered at the ends, and must be pre-

bored and countersunk to accept the ½ in. long no. 8 mounting screws. The retainer strips are not glued in place to facilitate replacement of the mirror glass should the need ever occur.

The mirror is hung by means of a simple locking cleat system, as shown in the cleat detail. Cut both cleats (G) to size, using the table saw blade set at 45 degrees to establish the long bevels. Glue one cleat as shown to the plywood back and screw the other securely to the wall, preferably into several studs, which in most wood frame homes are typically spaced 16 in. on center.

Like the other projects in this group, I finished the mirror frame with Watco Danish Oil. □

Bill of Materials (all dimensions actual)			
Part	Description	Size	No. Req'd.
A	Side	¾ × 2⅞ × 24	2
B	Top/Bottom	¾ × 2⅞ × 36	2
C	Back	⅜ × 23⅝ × 35⅝*	1
D	Mirror	⅛ × 23⅝ × 35⅝*	1
E	Short Retainer	¼ × ½ × 23⅝	2
F	Long Retainer	¼ × ½ × 35⅝	2
G	Cleat	½ × 2½ × 35	2

*Mirror and back are sized to fit assembled frame. Actual mirror size should be ¹⁄₁₆ in. smaller all around. Mirror glass is available at local glass shops.

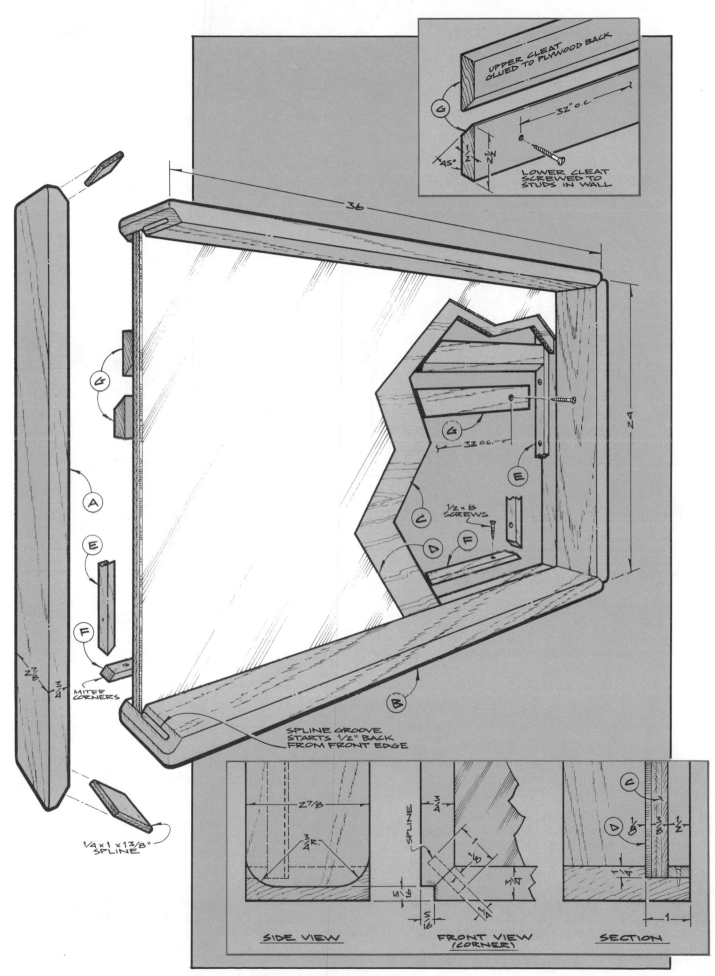

UPPER CLEAT
GLUED TO PLYWOOD BACK

Ⓖ

32" o.c.

LOWER CLEAT
SCREWED TO
STUDS IN WALL

45°

1/2"

2"W

36

24

Ⓖ

Ⓖ

32 o.c.

Ⓔ

1/2 x 8
SCREWS

Ⓒ

Ⓓ

Ⓕ

Ⓐ

Ⓔ

Ⓕ

2 7/8

3/4

MITER
CORNERS

SPLINE GROOVE
STARTS 1/2" BACK
FROM FRONT EDGE

Ⓑ

1/4 x 1 x 1 3/8"
SPLINE

2 7/8

3/4 R.

5/16

SIDE VIEW

SPLINE

1/4

1/8

1/4

5/16

FRONT VIEW
(CORNER)

Ⓒ

Ⓓ

1/8

3/8

1/2

1/4

1

SECTION

75

oak wall shelf

this oak wall shelf is a nice accessory piece to the bedroom group. I use it above the bed to hold books and a clip-on lamp, but it is also handy over a desk.

Begin by getting out stock for the shelves (A), divider (B), and back (C). Select good, clear, well-seasoned material that is not likely to cup, bow, or twist. Cut the shelves to length and width, rabbet the back edge as indicated to accept the shelf back, and round the corners to a 1 in. radius. Clamp a temporary fence (a length of ¾ in. by 1½ in. scrap stock will do) to the shelves to act as a guide for the router and, using a ¼ in. straight bit, rout the 7 in. long spline grooves. Several passes will be needed

to achieve the ⅜ in. groove depth. Rout the corresponding spline grooves in the divider on the router table, and make the splines from the same oak stock you used for the other parts. Note that the grain direction of the splines is parallel to that of the shelves and divider. Thickness plane the back stock to the indicated ⅝ in. dimension and, after cutting to length and width, apply the ½ in. radius to both ends.

Assemble the shelf with white or yellow glue and clamp securely. For added strength I countersunk three 1¼ in. flathead screws through the back and into the divider. When dry, final sand and finish with two coats of Watco Oil. □

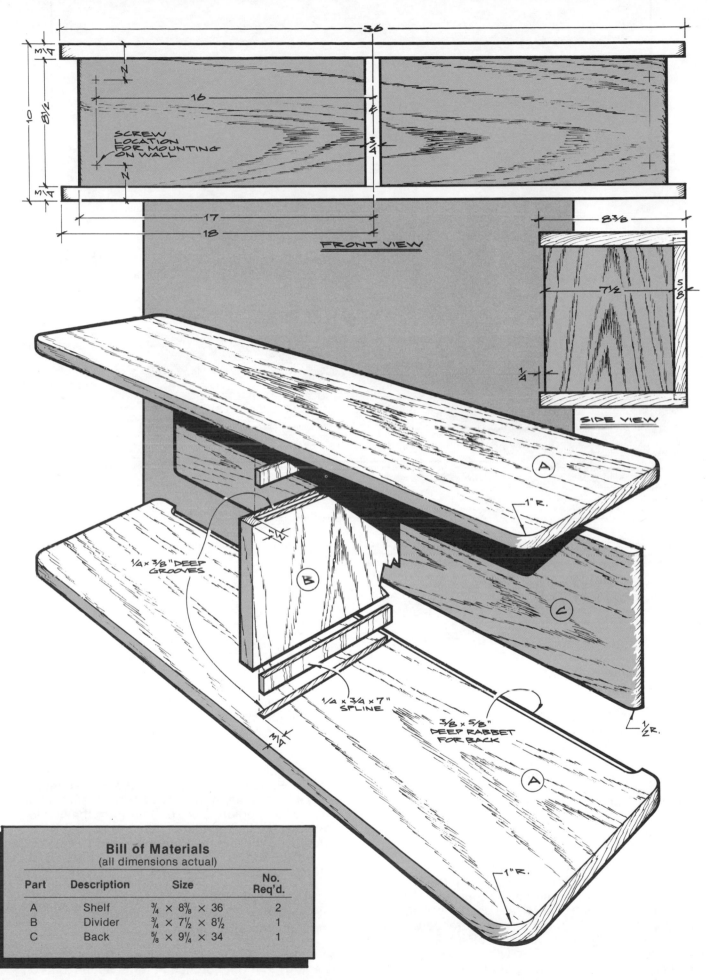

36

3/4

10
8 1/2
16

SCREW
LOCATION
FOR MOUNTING
ON WALL

3/4

3/4

17
18

FRONT VIEW

8 3/8

7 1/2

5/8

1/4

SIDE VIEW

A

1" R.

1/4 × 3/8" DEEP
GROOVES

B

C

1/4 × 3/4 × 7"
SPLINE

3/8 × 5/8"
DEEP RABBET
FOR BACK

1/2 R.

3/4

A

1" R.

Bill of Materials
(all dimensions actual)

Part	Description	Size	No. Req'd.
A	Shelf	3/4 × 8 3/8 × 36	2
B	Divider	3/4 × 7 1/2 × 8 1/2	1
C	Back	5/8 × 9 1/4 × 34	1

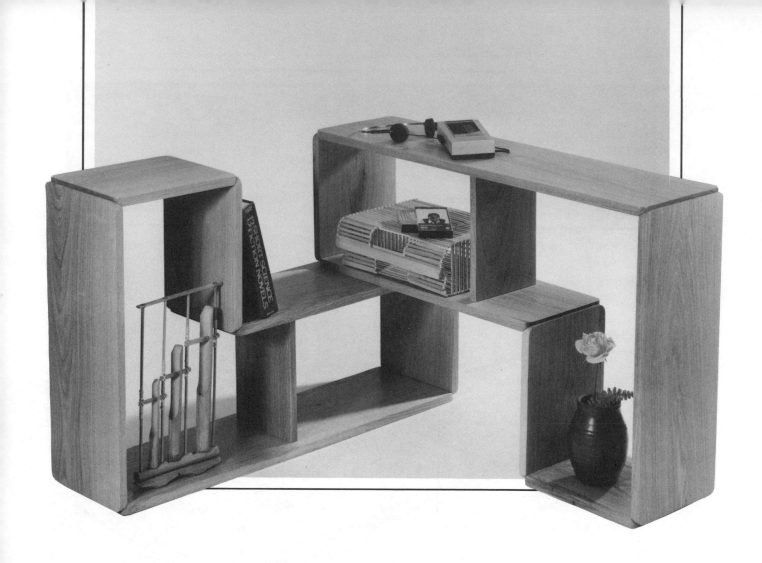

modular shelf

the modular shelf system is a design based on a 3-to-2-to-1 geometric relationship of the various shelves. As you can see in the front view, the overall dimensions of the shelves are 12 in., 24 in., and 36 in. This modularity permits the use of these shelf units in any number of different configurations, as illustrated. The photos show some of the possibilities with two shelf modules, but by making three or even four units, you can create a whole new realm of creative arrangements. The fact that these shelves can be used in so many configurations makes them an extraordinarily versatile project, and one that I'm certain will be a favorite.

Although these shelves are crafted in oak to coordinate with the various projects in the bedroom group, other woods could be used as well. In fact, the stock width of 9¼ in. for the shelf parts was selected to simplify construction for those who work in pine. A 1 in. by 10 in. common pine board will measure ¾ in. thick by 9¼ in. wide, meaning that no thickness planing or jointing should be required if

you decide to make the shelf units from pine. The various modular dimensions can also be increased, if you prefer to make these units larger. I have constructed similar modules from 1 in. thick material, using a 15 in. to 30 in. to 45 in. length relationship for the sides.

Start by getting out stock for the shelves, parts A through E. As you will note in the bill of materials, and as illustrated in the front view, the short shelf (D) and the medium shelf (E) that form the inside corner of the L-shaped modules are each ¾ in. longer respectively than the other short and medium shelves (C and B). This extra length is needed to establish the 12 in. depth and 24 in. length dimensions of the inside corner, without which the shelves would not be truly modular and could not be used in the various interlocking arrangements.

Referring to the step-by-step instructions on pages 60 and 61, cut the notched mitered spline joint on

Bill of Materials
(all dimensions actual)

Part	Description	Size	No. Req'd.
A	Long Shelf	¾ × 9¼ × 35⅜	1
B	Medium Shelf	¾ × 9¼ × 23⅜	1
C	Short Shelf	¾ × 9¼ × 11⅜	2
D	Short Shelf (inside corner)	¾ × 9¼ × 12⅛	1
E	Medium Shelf (inside corner)	¾ × 9¼ × 24⅛	1
F	Divider	¾ × 7¼ × 11¼*	1

*Length includes tenons.

Note: The bill of materials shows number required for one shelf module.

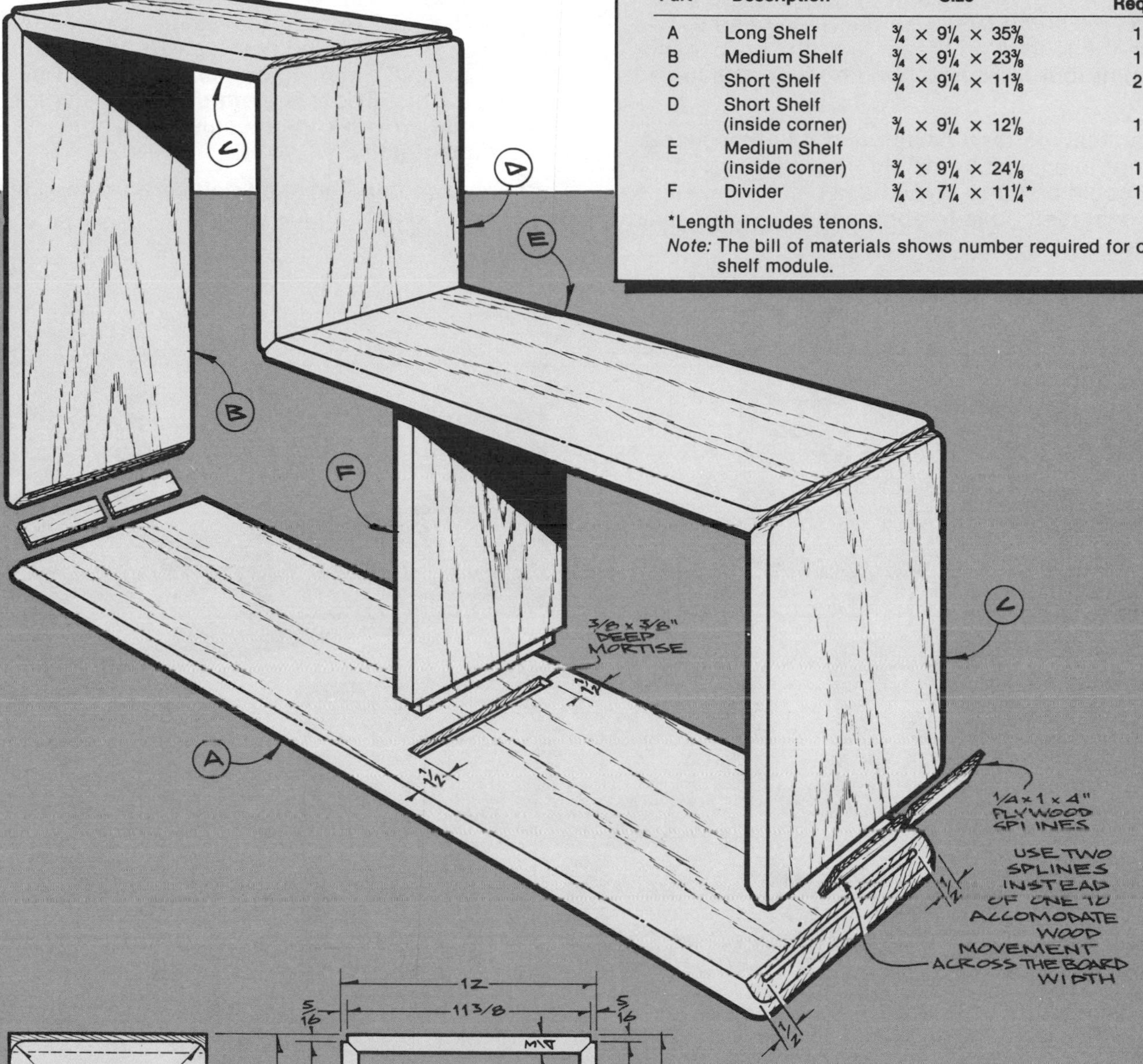
C
D
E
B
F
C
A
3/8 x 3/8" DEEP MORTISE
1/2
1/4 x 1 x 4" PLYWOOD SPLINES
USE TWO SPLINES INSTEAD OF ONE TO ACCOMODATE WOOD MOVEMENT ACROSS THE BOARD WIDTH

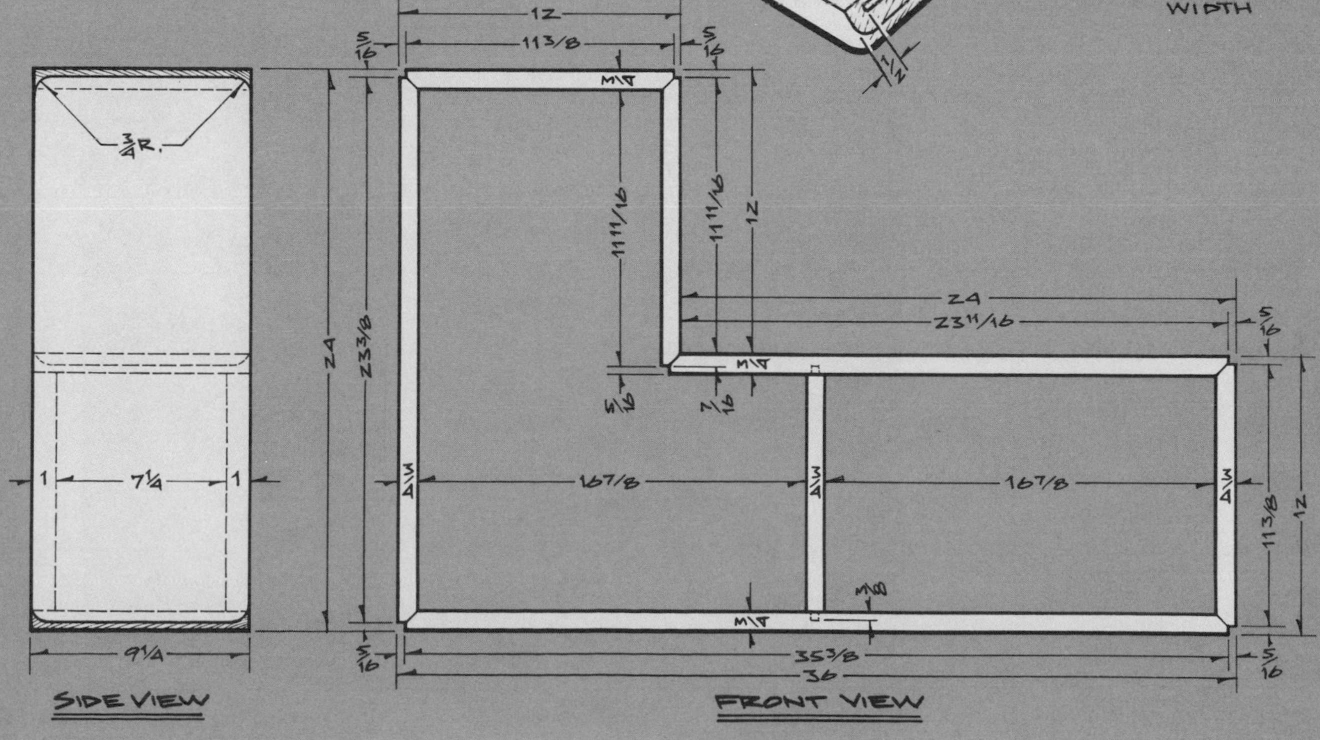
3/4 R.
1
7¼
1
9¼
24
23 3/8
12
11 3/8
5/16
24
23 11/16
16 7/8
3/4
11 3/8
35 3/8
36
M/T
SIDE VIEW
FRONT VIEW

(continued on next page)

the ends of all the shelf parts except the divider (F). Remember that the notched mitered spline joints on the ends of parts D and E are cut on opposite sides, while the joint on the ends of parts A, B, and C are all cut on the same side. Use the dado head to machine the tenons on the ends of the divider and chop out or rout the corresponding mortises in parts A and E.

As a practical matter, I have found it unreasonable to attempt to assemble the shelf modules all at once. It could be done if you have plenty of clamps, but the best method is to approach the assembly in sections.

Start with a dry test-fitting of all the parts with the splines in place to insure that all your miters are accurate and that the corners meet up as intended. Glue and clamp parts A and B to form one corner, and parts D and E to form the inside corner. Then join these pre-assembled corners with the short shelf sections (C), making certain that the divider (F) is in place. This divider is an important structural element that provides the modules with both support and rigidity.

After final sanding, the shelf units are finished with two coats of Watco Danish Oil. □

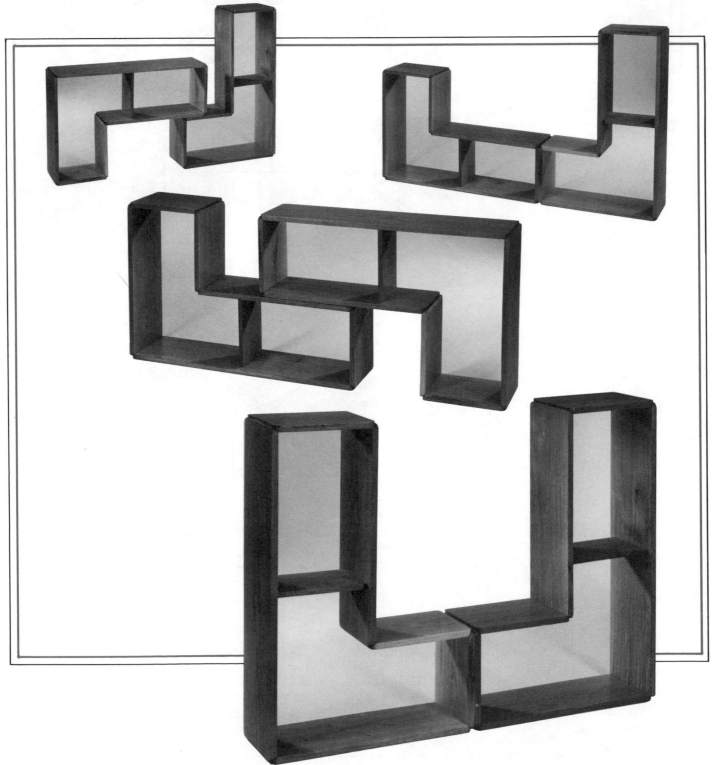

children's toys and things

jigsaw puzzle

my opinion may be biased, but I confess to thinking that anything made with wood has a unique appeal. For example, a jigsaw puzzle doesn't ordinarily make much of a decorative item, yet make one from an attractive piece of wood, like the one shown, and it becomes something special.

This project makes a great gift item that can be easily produced for sale at craft shows and fairs. My puzzle is made from oak, but most any wood can be used. Remember though that the selection of a choice piece of stock is essential to the project's looking good.

The small frame box is a nice feature and can be made first. About 30 inches of ⅜ by ¹³⁄₁₆ stock will provide enough material to make the outer frame. The cove detail is added using a router equipped with a ½ in. core box bit. Note that the depth of the cove is ³⁄₁₆ in. and that the cove is slightly offset, leaving a wider lip on the bottom than on

the top of the frame sides. The ¼ in. wide by ⅛ in. deep groove to accept the ¼ in. plywood bottom may now be cut with the table saw.

Next, cut the 6 in. square plywood bottom and miter the four frame pieces, which will each be 6½ in. long. Glue and assemble the frame around the plywood bottom, using either a web clamp or large rubber bands to provide clamp pressure.

The puzzle pattern is shown full size. Transfer it to the 1 in. thick stock you have selected for the piece, and cut the pattern out carefully with a jigsaw. The saw kerfs will slightly reduce the puzzle size so it will fit within the 5¾ in. square box opening.

Fine sand all surfaces, keeping in mind that a nice finish will add considerably to the appearance. Rub in several coats of penetrating oil to bring out the grain and character of the wood. ☐

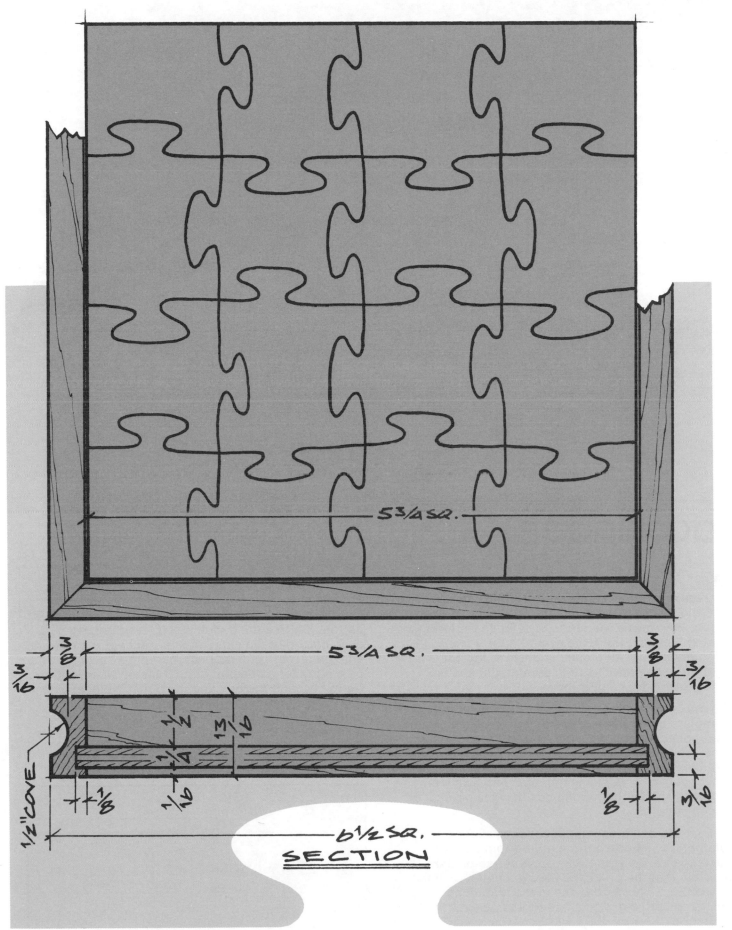

5³/₄ SQ.

3/8

3/16

5³/₄ SQ.

3/8

3/16

1/2

13/16

1/2

1/16

1/8

1/2"COVE

1/8

3/16

6¹/₂ SQ.

SECTION

dominoes

this is a great little gift idea that can be completed in several hours. To make the 28 playing pieces (A), first rip 1⁹⁄₁₆ in. wide strips of birch, then resaw the strips to ⁹⁄₁₆ in. thick. Next use a stop block on the table saw to cut off the 3⅛ in. long dominoes. All these dimensions include a little extra for sanding. The final domino dimensions should be ½ by 1½ by 3 in.

To make the dimples, fashion a cardboard or brass template using the full-size pattern provided. Brass is recommended if you intend to make more than one set of dominoes. Punch through each of the dimple spots in the template. Then lay the template over each domino blank and, using an awl, mark the appropriate number of dimples that the particular piece requires.

Adjust the drill press depth collar so that a ⁵⁄₁₆ in. diameter twist drill cutting a V-bottom hole will establish a ¹⁄₁₆ in. shoulder, as illustrated. Make certain that the drill bit is always centered on the awl marks. The divider line in the dominoes is a ¹⁄₁₆ in. deep kerf, cut with a fine-tooth backsaw in the miter box.

The domino box is made of ¼ in. thick cherry sides (B) and ends (C), a ½ in. thick resawn and book-matched walnut top (E), and a ¼ in. thick plywood bottom (D). Use the dado head to cut the ¼ by ⅛ in. deep groove in the sides that will accept the bottom, and cut a ¼ by ¼ in. rabbet around the top. Glue and clamp the four sides up around the plywood bottom. Carefully sand the box and the domino pieces, rounding all corners and edges. Finish with penetrating oil and butcher's wax. More information on dominoes can be found in the book *Dominoes* by Dominic C. Armanino, published by the David McKay Co., Dunmore, Pennsylvania. □

Bill of Materials
(all dimensions actual)

Part	Description	Size	No. Req'd.
A	Dominoes	½ × 1½ × 3	28
B	Side	¼ × 2¼ × 8¼	2
C	End	¼ × 2¼ × 7	2
D	Bottom	¼ × 6¾ × 8	1
E	Top	½ × 7 × 8¼	1

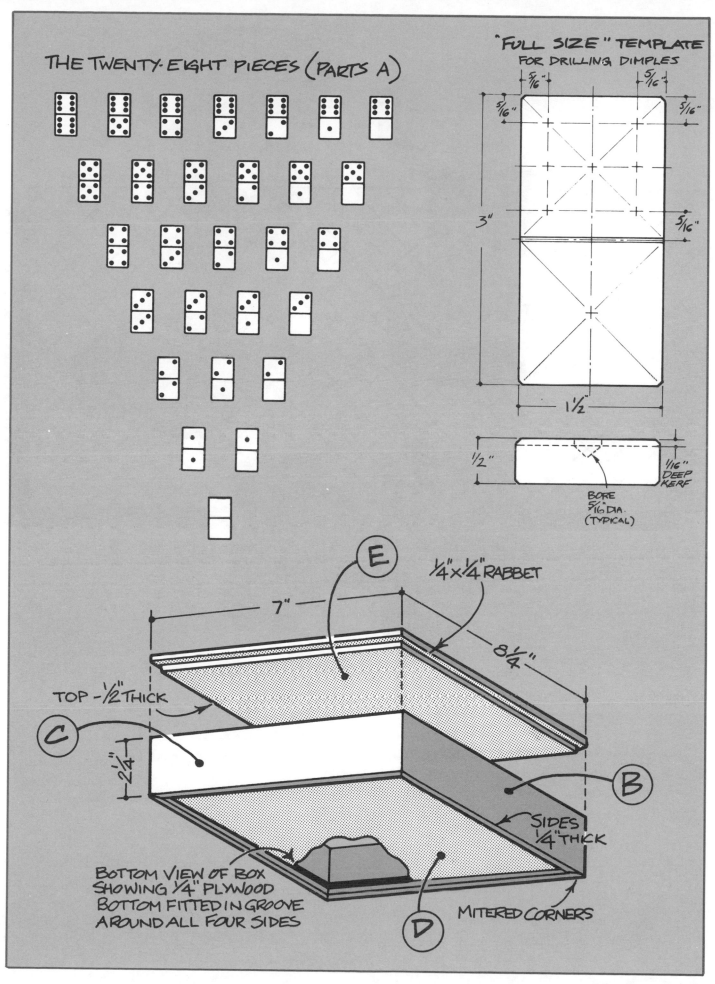

THE TWENTY-EIGHT PIECES (PARTS A)

"FULL SIZE" TEMPLATE
FOR DRILLING DIMPLES

5/16"   5/16"

5/16"   5/16"

3"   5/16"

1½"

½"   1/16" DEEP KERF

BORE 5/16" DIA. (TYPICAL)

E

¼" x ¼" RABBET

7"

8¼"

TOP - ½" THICK

C

2¼"

B

SIDES ¼" THICK

BOTTOM VIEW OF BOX SHOWING ¼" PLYWOOD BOTTOM FITTED IN GROOVE AROUND ALL FOUR SIDES

MITERED CORNERS

D

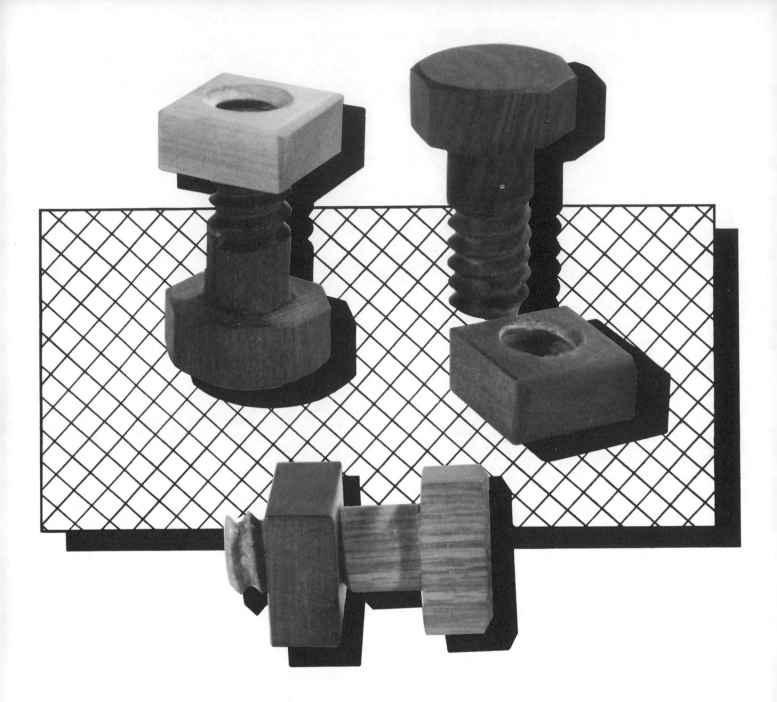

nut & bolt toy

t hese nuts and bolts are fun to play with, even for those who aren't in their "formative years". A lawyer I know, who has them on his coffee table, claims his clients can't put them down. They're also helpful in developing eye/hand coordination and motor skills in youngsters.

Most any wood can be used for this project, but if you have some scraps of exotic woods such as padouk, rosewood, or zebrawood, the nuts and bolts will look even better. To make the bolt, start with stock 1¾ in. square by at least 3½ in. long. You may wish to add a little extra length for trimming waste. Mount the stock in a lathe, measure for the $\frac{7}{8}$ in. bolt head, mark the shoulder point, and turn the 1 in. diameter by $2\frac{5}{8}$ in. long shank section.

After removing the stock from the lathe, trim the ends and sand the bolt head corners to create an octagon. Now use a 1 in. thread box device to cut the threads in the shank. Tap and die wood threading kits are available from Conover Woodcraft Specialties, Inc., 18125 Madison Road, Parkman, OH 44080.

The nut is made from a $\frac{3}{4}$ in. thick piece of scrap. Start with the stock slightly oversize, drill through with a $\frac{3}{4}$ in. drill, then use the tap to cut the 1 in. threads. The nut is trimmed to the final $1\frac{1}{2}$ in. square dimension *after* the threads are cut to minimize any chance of splitting.

I recommend letting the nut and bolt sit for a few days, and then recutting the threads. They will operate much more smoothly.

Wipe on a generous coat of Watco Danish Oil to finish this project.
Production Tips: The bolts can be turned back-to-back, then cut apart before threading. The nuts can be laid out on a long strip, bored, threaded and cut apart after. □

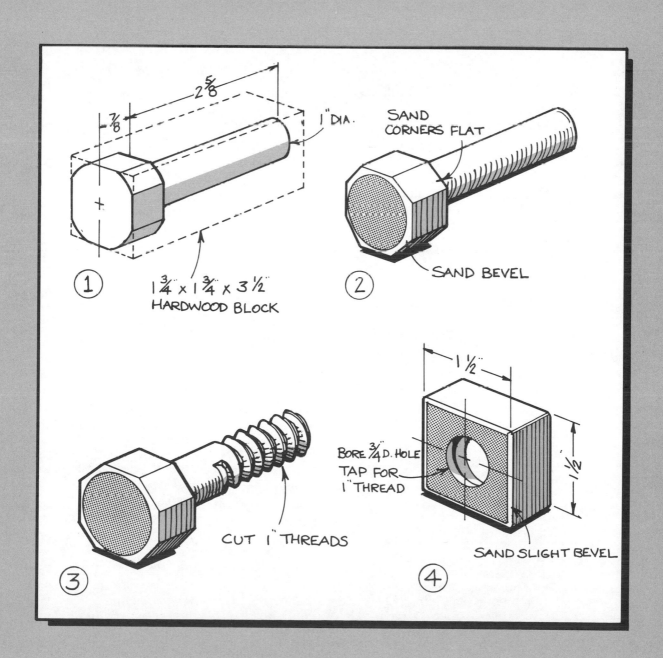

① $1\frac{3}{4}'' \times 1\frac{3}{4}'' \times 3\frac{1}{2}''$ HARDWOOD BLOCK — $2\frac{5}{8}''$ — $\frac{7}{8}''$ — 1" DIA.

② SAND CORNERS FLAT — SAND BEVEL

③ CUT 1" THREADS

④ BORE $\frac{3}{4}''$ D. HOLE TAP FOR 1" THREAD — $1\frac{1}{2}''$ — $1\frac{1}{2}''$ — SAND SLIGHT BEVEL

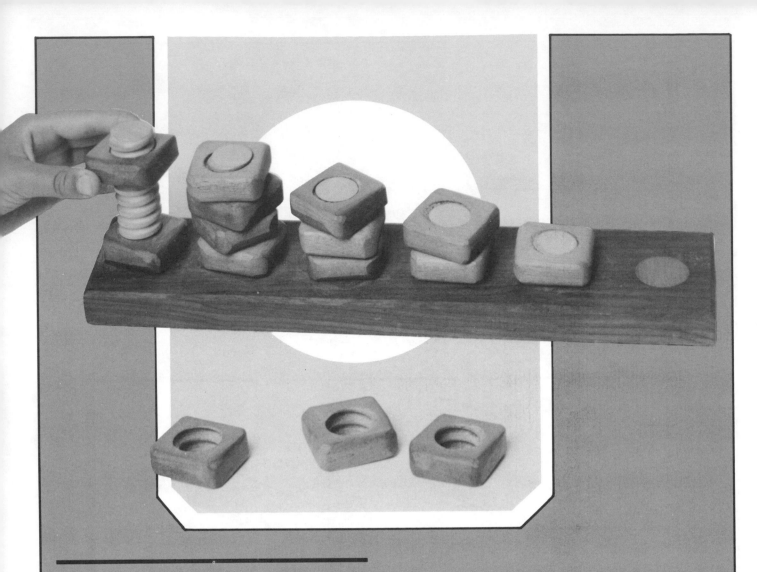

counting toy

educational toys are very popular and always in demand. Here's a toy that not only has educational value, but is easy to build and should prove to be an ideal item to make for resale. It does an excellent job helping pre-schoolers' (ages 2-6) counting and motor skills.

To cut a 1 in. thread you'll need a threadbox and tap. Conover Woodcraft Specialties, Inc., 18125 Madison Road, Parkman, OH 44080, sells both a 1 in. tap and die set, and the same set in kit form at a considerable savings.

Begin by cutting the base to size from 3/4 in. hardwood stock, bevelling the edge as shown. Select a wood that will contrast with the light color of the birch spindles, or else apply a dark stain. The first spindle is set flush with the base and is used for counting zero. It's made by gluing a short length of 1 in. birch dowel into a 1 in. diameter hole. Cut the spindle a little longer than necessary so that it can be sanded flush. Now, lay out and mark the location of the other five

threaded spindle holes, then drill and tap all the way through.

You'll need about a 15 in. length of 1 in. birch dowel to make the spindles. Most dowel stock carried by lumber yards is out-of-round, and this sometimes can cause threading problems. You may want to lathe-turn your own, or you can purchase high quality birch dowel stock for threading from Conover. After threading, cut each spindle to length, then glue and screw to the base as shown.

To make the nuts, cut a piece of 1/2 in. hardwood stock to 2 3/4 in. wide by 25 in. long. The extra width is needed to prevent splitting when tapping the holes. Lay out the location of the 15 nuts, drill and tap the holes, then cut into the 1 1/2 in. square finished nuts.

Sand the ends of the spindle and oil or wax the entire piece. A piece of felt glued to the bottom will protect any surface on which the toy is placed. □

WOOD NUT ACTUAL SIZE 15 REQ'D

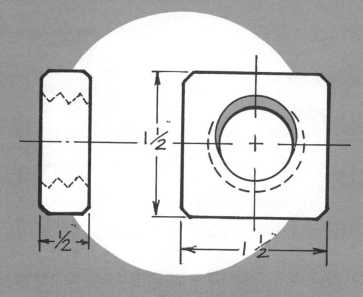

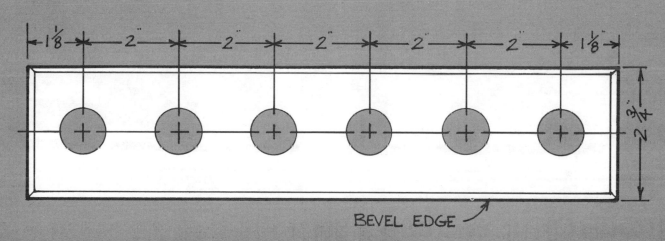

BEVEL EDGE

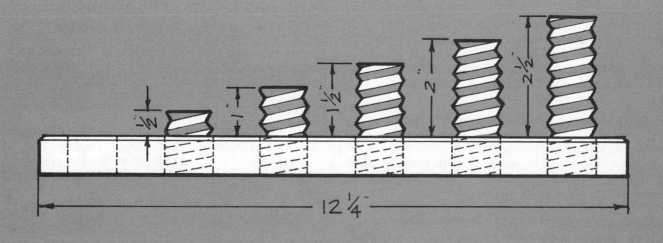

Design by Martin Bloomenthal, AIA, Princeton, N.J.

storage seats

Storage has always been a problem for me. All the closets in our house are bulging, and only one car fits in our two-car garage. Whatever the cause of this plague, these storage seats will offer extra storage space anywhere you decide to locate them. They are especially handy for children's toys, to which my two daughters can well attest. Make at least one for each child.

The basic box is constructed of 1 by 12 clear pine, which measures $\frac{3}{4}$ in. thick by $11\frac{1}{4}$ in. wide. Miter the sides (A) to establish their length, then use the dado-head to cut the $\frac{1}{4}$ in. deep by $\frac{1}{2}$ in. wide groove to accept the $\frac{1}{2}$ in. thick plywood bottom (B), and the $\frac{1}{4}$ in. deep by $\frac{3}{4}$ in. wide groove to accept the $\frac{3}{4}$ in. thick seat support cleats (C). Next, use the router, guide, and a $\frac{1}{4}$ straight cutter to cut the $\frac{1}{4}$ in. thick by $\frac{1}{4}$ in. deep spline grooves. As shown in the spline groove cutting detail, the sides (A) are clamped back-to-back with a router support piece in place to help support the router. You will need to make two $\frac{1}{8}$

in. deep passes to achieve the full $\frac{1}{4}$ in. spline groove depth. Note from the spline detail that these grooves are located $\frac{1}{8}$ in. from the inside face of the sides. Next, make the $\frac{1}{4}$ in. by $\frac{1}{2}$ in. by $11\frac{1}{4}$ in. long splines (D) from $\frac{1}{4}$ in. thick plywood. Also cut the four base pieces (E) from $\frac{3}{4}$ in. by 2 in. pine, mitering the ends to achieve the $14\frac{1}{2}$ in. length. As shown in the side section, the base is sized to fit flush inside the box.

Now make the $\frac{1}{4}$ in. thick hardboard template that is used to rout the incised numerals. Transfer the numerals from the grid pattern to the template material, then cut out with the jig or saber saw and smooth to the line. I used a $\frac{1}{4}$ in. straight bit for the routing, and made the template $\frac{3}{32}$ in. larger than the finished numeral for use with a $\frac{7}{16}$ in. guide bushing (Figs. 1 and 2). The grid pattern numerals are sized for the $\frac{7}{16}$ in. guide bushing. The template can be temporarily secured with brads. As shown in the front elevation, the finished numerals will be $9\frac{3}{4}$ in.

high. The numeral 1 is located 1⅛ in. from the edge, while numerals 2 through 9 are located ⅞ in. at their closest points from the edge. Set the bit depth at ⅝ in., which when taking the ¼ in. thick hardboard into account, will result in a ⅜ in. numeral depth. After the routing is complete, use a chisel to square any rounded corners and to scrape the numeral bottom flat. Unless you prefer otherwise, the numeral is only routed into one side of the box.

Next, make the ½ in. by 15 in. plywood bottom and the ¾ in. by ¾ in. by 15 in. mitered seat support cleats. Note that both these cleats and the bottom must be cut back ¼ in. at the four corners, so they do not interfere with the splines. Assemble the box around the bottom with the cleats and splines in place, then add the base, using white or yellow glue throughout.

After final sanding, paint the numerals and the base.

I chose black for the base and a rust color for the numerals. Varnish all the remaining unpainted surfaces.

The seat is a covered cushion which sits on a ½ in. thick by 14¼ in. by 14¼ in. plywood bottom (F). Drill a ¾ in. finger hole through the seat bottom to facilitate lifting out. The seat bottom should also be sanded and varnished. The seat cushion (G) is 2 in. thick by 14¼ in. square foam rubber with a removable zippered fabric slip cover (H). Foam rubber is available at upholstery shops and suppliers. I recommend an easy-care, washable slip cover material that will simplify cleanup of spills, stains, and dirt.

In addition to providing useful and quickly accessible storage, groupings of these storage seats make great extra seating, especially for parties and large gatherings. □

(continued on next page)

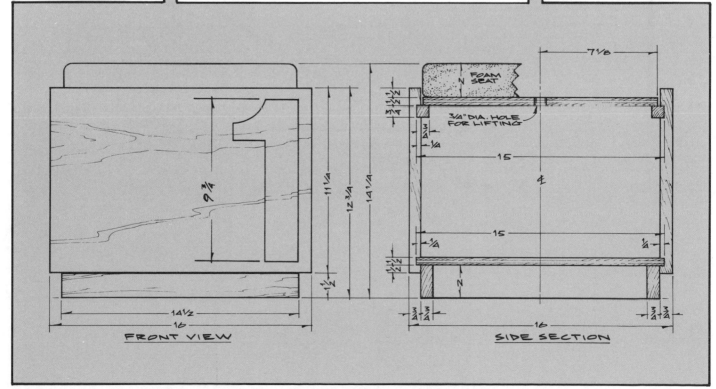

Bill of Materials
(all dimensions actual)

Part	Description	Size	No. Req'd.
A	Side	¾ × 11¼ × 16	4
B	Bottom	½ × 15 × 15	1
C	Seat Support Cleat	¾ × ¾ × 15*	4
D	Spline	¼ × ½ × 11¼	4
E	Base	¾ × 2 × 14½	4
F	Seat Bottom	½ × 14¼ × 14¼	1
G	Foam Cushion	2 × 14¼ × 14¼	1
H	Slip Cover	To fit cushion	1

*Length before trimming to prevent interference with splines.

FRONT VIEW

SIDE SECTION

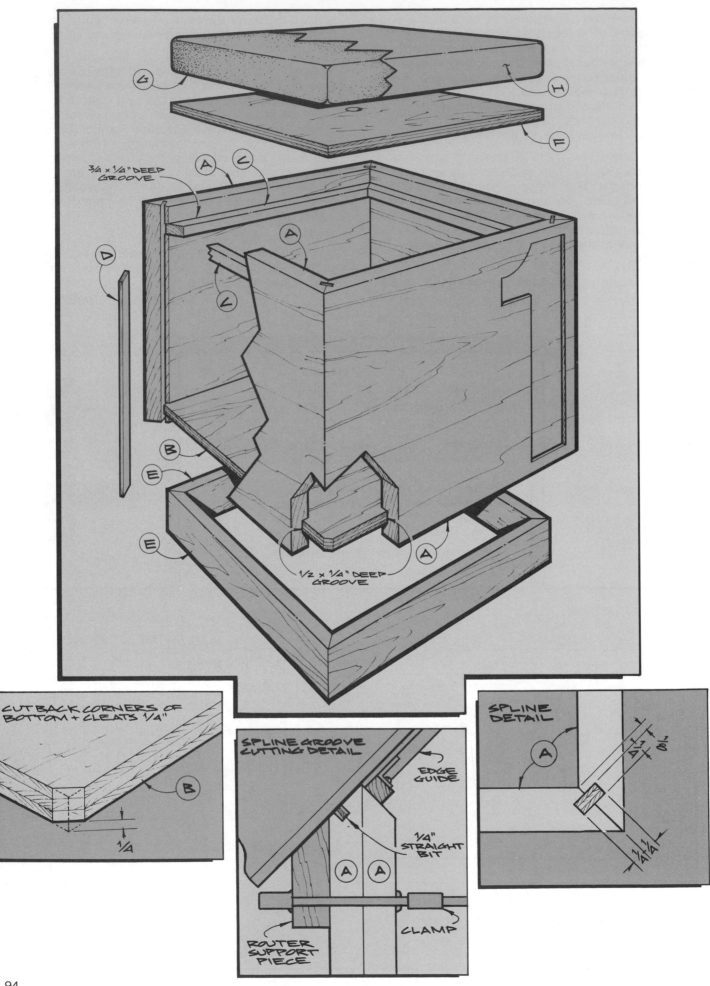

3/4 x 1/4" DEEP GROOVE

G

H

F

A

C

A

D

L

B

E

E

A

1/2 x 1/4" DEEP GROOVE

CUTBACK CORNERS OF BOTTOM + CLEATS 1/4"

B

1/4

SPLINE GROOVE CUTTING DETAIL

EDGE GUIDE

1/4" STRAIGHT BIT

A

A

ROUTER SUPPORT PIECE

CLAMP

SPLINE DETAIL

A

1/8

1/4

1/4
1/2

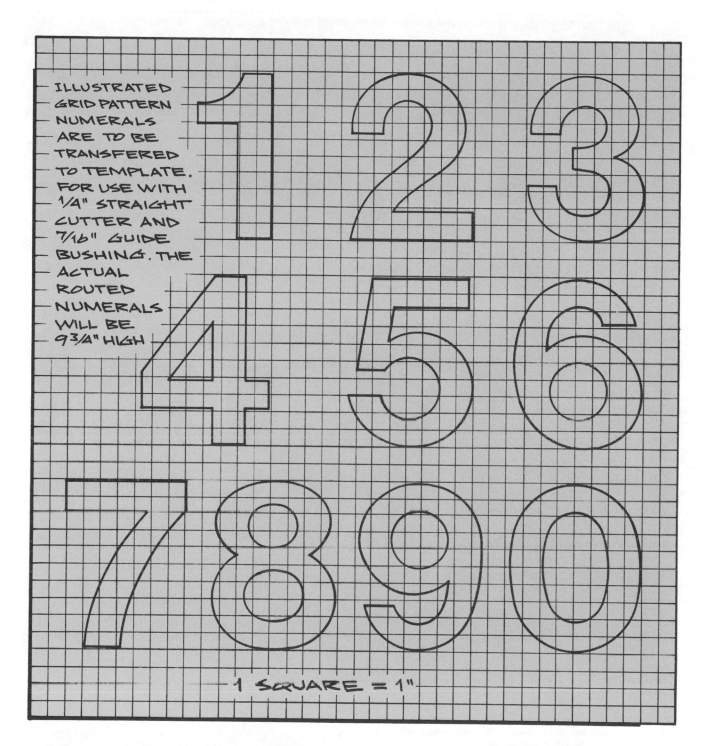

ILLUSTRATED GRID PATTERN NUMERALS ARE TO BE TRANSFERED TO TEMPLATE. FOR USE WITH 1/4" STRAIGHT CUTTER AND 7/16" GUIDE BUSHING. THE ACTUAL ROUTED NUMERALS WILL BE 9 3/4" HIGH

1 SQUARE = 1"

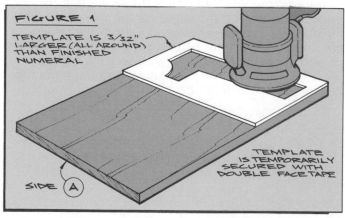

FIGURE 1

TEMPLATE IS 3/32" LARGER (ALL AROUND) THAN FINISHED NUMERAL

TEMPLATE IS TEMPORARILY SECURED WITH DOUBLE FACE TAPE

SIDE A

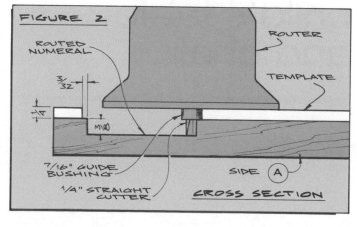

FIGURE 2

ROUTED NUMERAL

ROUTER

3/32

1/4

M100

TEMPLATE

7/16" GUIDE BUSHING

1/4" STRAIGHT CUTTER

SIDE A

CROSS SECTION

child's table and chair

t his child's matching set is not only pleasing to the eye, but you'll find it is sturdy enough to provide a work or play center for the most active of children for many years to come. Both the table and chair are crafted from hardwood. Oak, maple, cherry, or walnut are all ideal choices. The chair seat is woven from Hong Kong seagrass, and the table top is covered with a plastic laminate.

To make the table, first cut 1¾ in. square material for the legs (A), 20¼ in. long. Use a bearing-guided ¼ in. radius round-over bit to round all edges except the leg tops. Mortise the legs ½ in. by 2½ in. by 1¼ in. deep to accept the stretcher tenons. Note that the mortises start ½ in. from the front and side edges, and ½ in. down from the top. Next make the stretchers (B and C). Round the bottom edges and tenon the ends. The tenons, which have a ⅛ in. shoulder on both sides, are flush at the bottom and located ½ in. from the top edge. These can be cut with the dado head. As shown in the tenon detail, the tenons must be mitered where they meet. I recommend shaving the miters a hair short so they don't quite meet, since their butting could prevent the tenon shoulders from flushing with the legs. After sanding parts A, B, and C, use yellow glue to assemble the table frame. Remember to check for squareness.

To make the laminated top, cut both the ¾ in. thick plywood top core material (D) and the plastic laminate (E) (use whatever color you prefer) slightly oversize. After gluing up with contact cement, trim the laminated top assembly to the final 19½ in. by 28½ in. dimension on the table saw. Now make sufficient ¾ in. by 1½ in. edging for parts F and G, and cut to length. The ¾ in. radius is applied *after* the square edging has been glued up around the laminated top. You will need a ¾ in. bearing-guided round-over bit with the router to cut this radius. Turn the top assembly over, and cut the lower portion of the half-round by running the bearing off the edging perimeter. Then position the top assembly on edge, and again using the bearing-guided ¾ in. round-over bit and the router, cut the upper portion of the half-round ¾ in. radius. Note the bearing will gauge off

the laminate surface for this cut. The bullnose edged top assembly is now glued in place to the previously assembled table frame. Glue blocks can be added to help support the edging, as shown in the cross-section.

Note: Although we show the final table height as 21 in., the actual height will be about 1/16 in. more with the thickness that the plastic laminate adds to the top.

(continued on next page)

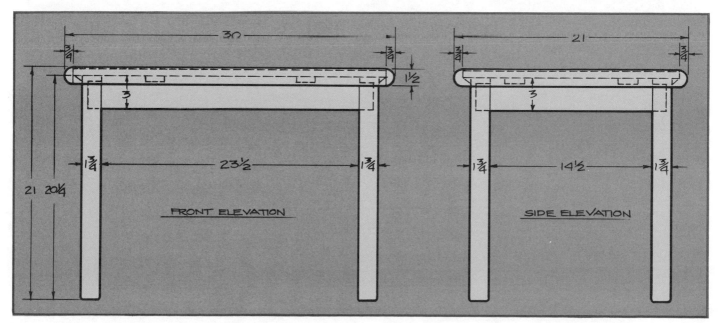

FRONT ELEVATION   SIDE ELEVATION

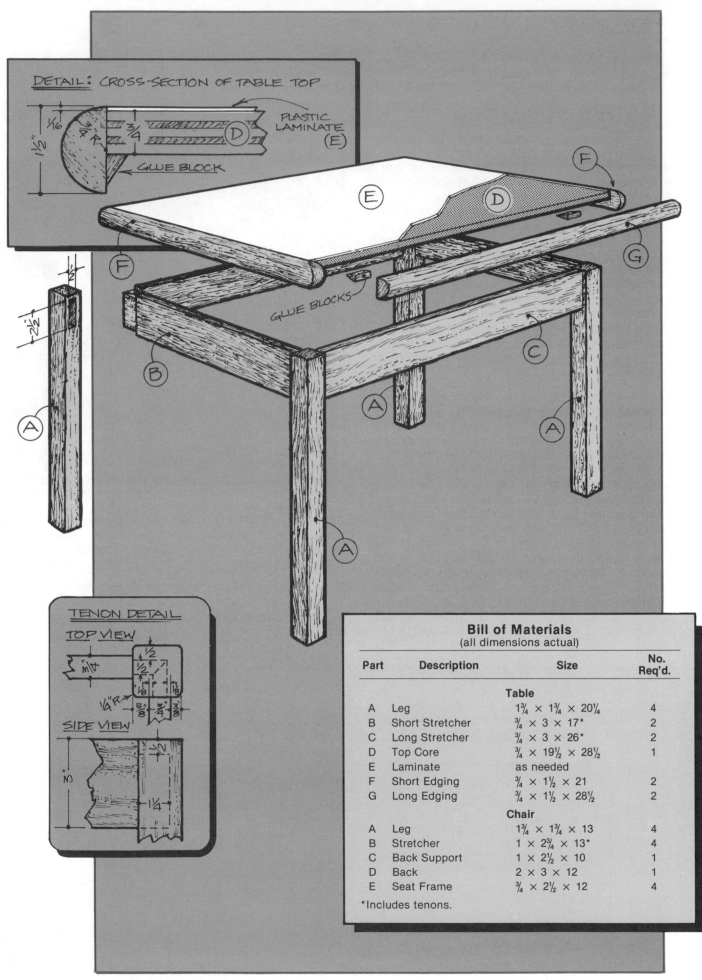

DETAIL: CROSS-SECTION OF TABLE TOP

1/16
3/4
1 1/2
3/4
D
PLASTIC LAMINATE (E)
GLUE BLOCK

E
D
F
G
F

2 1/2
1 1/2

GLUE BLOCKS

A
B
C
A
A
A

TENON DETAIL

TOP VIEW
1/2
1/2
1/2
1 1/4
1/8
1/8
1/4"R.
5/8
3/4
3/8

SIDE VIEW
3
1/2
1 1/4

Bill of Materials
(all dimensions actual)

Part	Description	Size	No. Req'd.
		Table	
A	Leg	1¾ × 1¾ × 20¼	4
B	Short Stretcher	¾ × 3 × 17*	2
C	Long Stretcher	¾ × 3 × 26*	2
D	Top Core	¾ × 19½ × 28½	1
E	Laminate	as needed	
F	Short Edging	¾ × 1½ × 21	2
G	Long Edging	¾ × 1½ × 28½	2
		Chair	
A	Leg	1¾ × 1¾ × 13	4
B	Stretcher	1 × 2¾ × 13*	4
C	Back Support	1 × 2½ × 10	1
D	Back	2 × 3 × 12	1
E	Seat Frame	¾ × 2½ × 12	4

*Includes tenons.

the chair frame is similar in construction to the table frame. Cut the legs (A) to length from 1¾ in. square stock, and use a bearing-guided ¼ in. round-over bit to radius all the edges. Next make the four stretchers (B). After cutting to length and width from 1 in. material, radius the edges with the same ¼ in. bearing-guided round-over bit used on the legs. Then use the dado head to cut the ½ in. by ¾ in. rabbet. Now tenon the ends of the stretchers, ½ in. by 2 in. by 1¼ in. long. Note that the tenon shoulders are ¼ in. on both sides and ¾ in. at the top edge. As with the table, the mitered tenon ends should be shaved back a little to prevent them from butting and possibly holding the tenon shoulders away from the legs. Next mortise the legs to accept the stretcher tenons. As shown in the mortise and tenon detail, the mortise starts 1½ in. down from the top of the legs. After cleaning out these mortises, dry assemble the legs and stretchers to check for fit. Adjust if necessary, and when satisfied, glue up and clamp, taking care to keep the assembly perfectly square.

Next, after cutting the back support (C) to length

and width from 1 in. stock, use the dado head to remove the ½ in. deep by 6 in. long waste area. Plane the top end to a blunt wedge and sand all edges. The back (D) is fashioned from a 2 in. by 3 in. by 12 in. block, as shown in the step-by-step detail. Use the band saw to first round the ends (step 1) and then cut the curved shape (step 2). Last, use a rasp to achieve the final form, as shown in the step 3 back cross-section. Final sand both the back support and back before assembling and mounting to the chair frame with several lag screws, as illustrated in the exploded view.

Make the seat frame by half-lapping the four seat frame parts (E). Note that the corners must be notched 1 in. by 1 in. to accommodate the chair legs (see seat frame detail). After these notches have been cut, use the ¼ in. bearing-guided round-over bit to round over *all* the exposed seat frame edges. All the seat frame dimensions allow for the installation of the woven Hong Kong seagrass, which is shown in the step-by-step weaving instructions. The woven seat is press-fit into the chair frame. Both the chair and table are finished with Watco Danish Oil. □

(continued on next page)

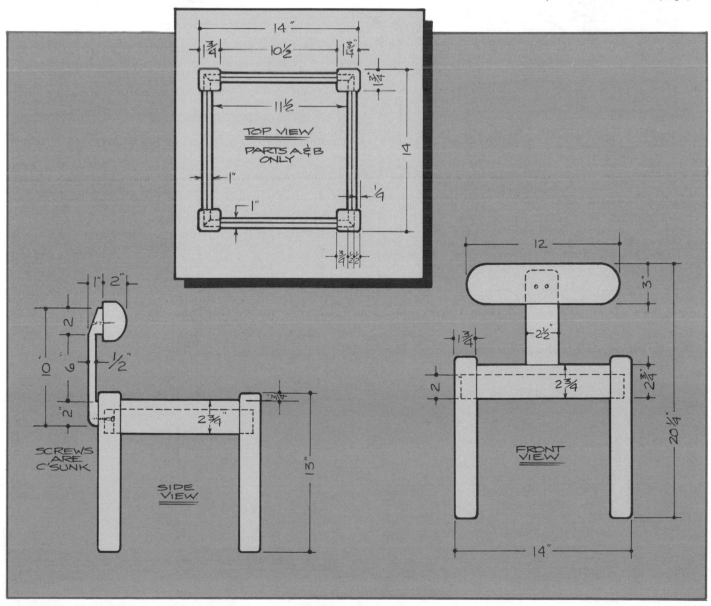

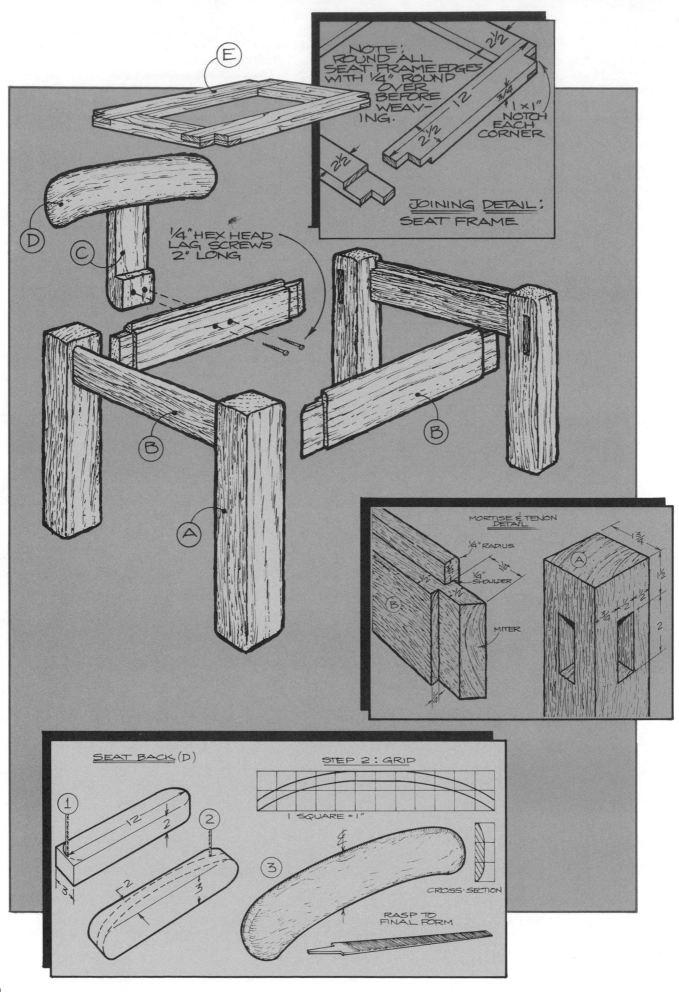

E

NOTE:
ROUND ALL
SEAT FRAME EDGES
WITH 1/4" ROUND
OVER
BEFORE
WEAV-
ING.

2½
12
¾
1 × 1"
NOTCH
EACH
CORNER
2½
2½

JOINING DETAIL:
SEAT FRAME

D

C

¼" HEX HEAD
LAG SCREWS
2" LONG

B

B

A

MORTISE & TENON
DETAIL

¼" RADIUS

¼
¼" SHOULDER
¼

MITER

B

A
1¾
1½
¼
½
½
¾
2
2

SEAT BACK (D)

STEP 2: GRID

1 SQUARE = 1"

1
12
2
3
2

2
3

3

CROSS-SECTION

RASP TO
FINAL FORM

weaving the seat

Hong Kong seagrass has a naturally waxy texture, is easy to work, strong and durable. Sold in 3 lb. rolls it is available from: Connecticut Cane & Reed Company, P.O. Box 1276, Manchester, CT 06040. I used the large size ($\frac{3}{16}$ in. diameter) seagrass. A 3 lb. roll provides enough material to make one seat.

Start by pre-wrapping the sides of the seat frame. As shown in Step 1, you will need to temporarily tack finishing nails at the corners to hold the seagrass in position. The bottom should face up, so that all staples will be located on the underside of the seat. Pre-wrap both sides, then the front and back.

Step 2 shows how to accomplish the actual weaving. Staple the end, carry the seagrass over and then under the top frame, then over itself, over and back under the left side frame, over and under the right side frame, over itself, over and under the top frame again, over and under the bottom frame, over itself, over and under the right side frame, over and under the left side frame, over itself, and over and under the bottom frame and voila! You have completed one cycle. Repeat the process until the entire seat is covered (Step 3). The weaving process is really quite simple. Once you try it, you may be surprised at how quickly you'll have this seemingly complicated procedure mastered. *Note:* Since a single long piece of seagrass is too cumbersome to weave, use manageable lengths, tying them together with the splice knot, as shown in Step 3. Be sure to locate the splices on the bottom of the seat. □

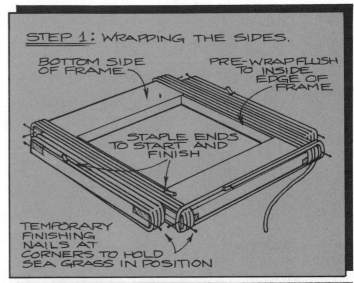

STEP 1: WRAPPING THE SIDES.

BOTTOM SIDE OF FRAME

PRE-WRAP FLUSH TO INSIDE EDGE OF FRAME

STAPLE ENDS TO START AND FINISH

TEMPORARY FINISHING NAILS AT CORNERS TO HOLD SEA GRASS IN POSITION

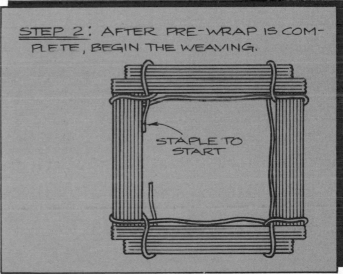

STEP 2: AFTER PRE-WRAP IS COMPLETE, BEGIN THE WEAVING.

STAPLE TO START

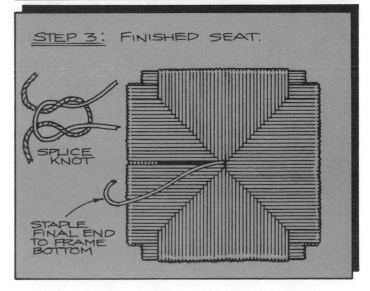

STEP 3: FINISHED SEAT.

SPLICE KNOT

STAPLE FINAL END TO FRAME BOTTOM

indoor/outdoor climber

althought I've constructed a variety of climbers and playhouses for my two daughters over the years, this indoor/outdoor climber is by far and away the best liked and most used. Perhaps the secret lies in the three movable platforms that enable young imaginations to create their own play space. Altering the position of these platforms can transform the climber into a desk, a jail, a fort, a loft, an observation post, a play gym . . . the possibilities are endless. The construction is simple, and by pulling the hinge (F) pins from two diagonal corners, the climber can be folded into two sections for easy storage or transport.

Begin by making the 16 posts (A). I used poplar, but most any hardwood will suffice. Be sure to apply a $\frac{1}{4}$ in. radius to all edges. Locate for and drill the $1\frac{1}{8}$ in. diameter by $\frac{3}{4}$ in. deep dowel holes, leaving the

space for the doorway. Mortise for the hinges, and after making the oak saddle (B), chop out the corresponding mortises in the doorway posts. When making the saddle, note the generous chamfer (see saddle detail) which can either be made with the router and a chamfering bit, or be cut by hand with a drawknife.

After cutting the 68 dowels (C) to their $13\frac{1}{2}$ in. length ($1\frac{1}{8}$ in. diameter hardwood dowel stock is available at most building supply stores and lumberyards), assemble the climber. The dowels are all glued in place. You will probably need pipe clamps to force the dowels all the way into the posts. Work on one section at a time. The saddle is both glued and screwed in place as shown. Mount the hinges to fasten the four climber sides together.

Now make the three oak platforms. After cutting the

(continued on next page)

slats (D) to length and width from ¾ in. thick stock, notch the outside corners of the two outside slats of each platform so they fit around the posts (see platform assembly detail). Make the cleats (E), also from oak, and sand all edges and corners before assembling with countersunk 1¼ in. by no. 8 brass flathead wood screws. Check the fit of the platforms carefully in multiple positions. They should fit snugly for safe use. Be sure to apply a ¼ in. radius to all exposed edges and corners.

Once the children discover the different play areas they can make by rearranging the platforms, this climber may just become their favorite recreation place. If you intend to use the climber exclusively indoors, no finish is needed. For outdoor use, however, an exterior grade polyurethane finish is recommended to seal and protect the wood against moisture and weather. ☐

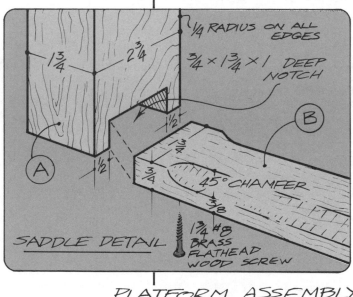

SADDLE DETAIL

Bill of Materials
(all dimensions actual)

Part	Description	Size	No. Req'd.
A	Post	1¾ × 2¾ × 48	16
B	Saddle	¾ × 1¾ × 14	1
C	Dowel	1⅛ diameter × 13½	68
D	Slat	¾ × 3¾ × 48	9
E	Cleat	¾ × 1½ × 13	6
F	Hinge	3½ × 3½ brass plated	4/pair

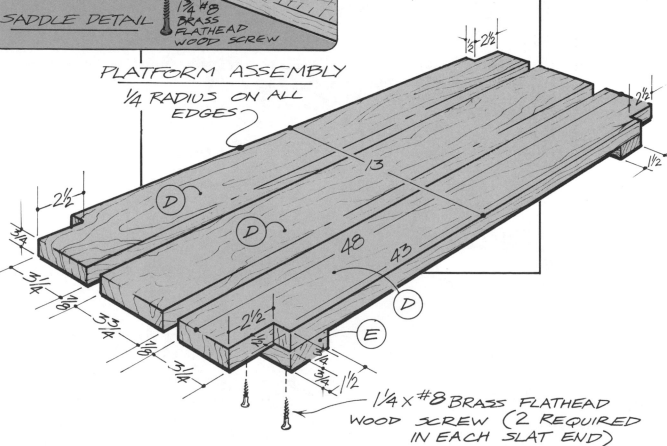

PLATFORM ASSEMBLY
¼ RADIUS ON ALL EDGES

1¼ × #8 BRASS FLATHEAD WOOD SCREW (2 REQUIRED IN EACH SLAT END)

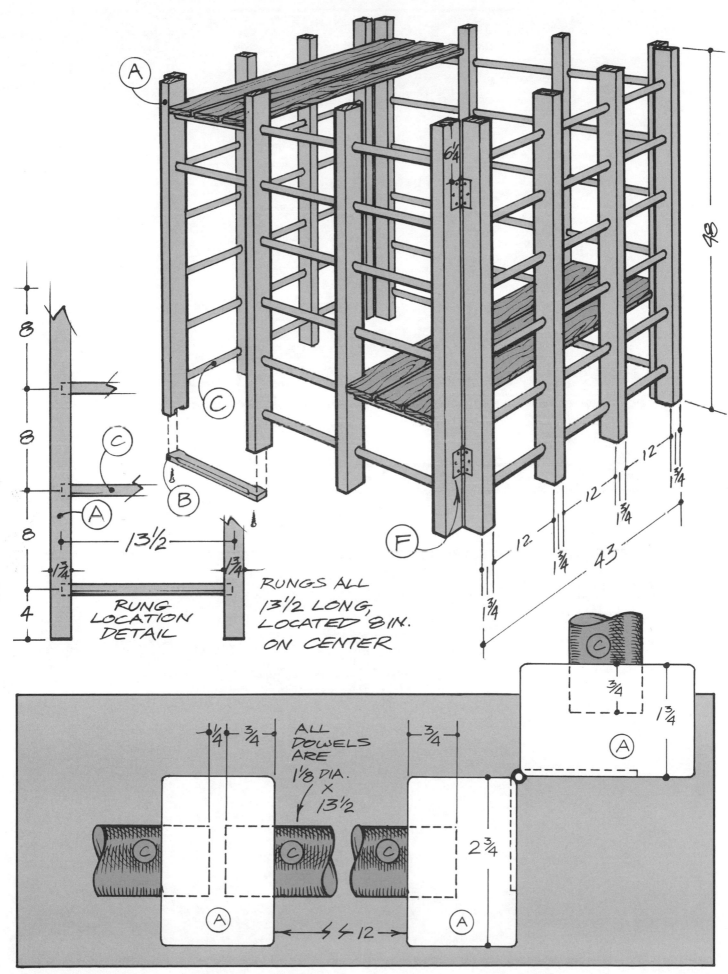

A

8

8

C

A

8

4

C

B

13½

1¾

1¾

RUNG
LOCATION
DETAIL

6¼

F

48

12   12   12   ¾
¾   ¾   ¾
¾
43

RUNGS ALL
13½ LONG,
LOCATED 8 IN.
ON CENTER

C

3/4

1¾

A

¼   ¾

ALL
DOWELS
ARE
1⅛ DIA.
X
13½

¾

C   C   C

A

2¾

A

12

accessories

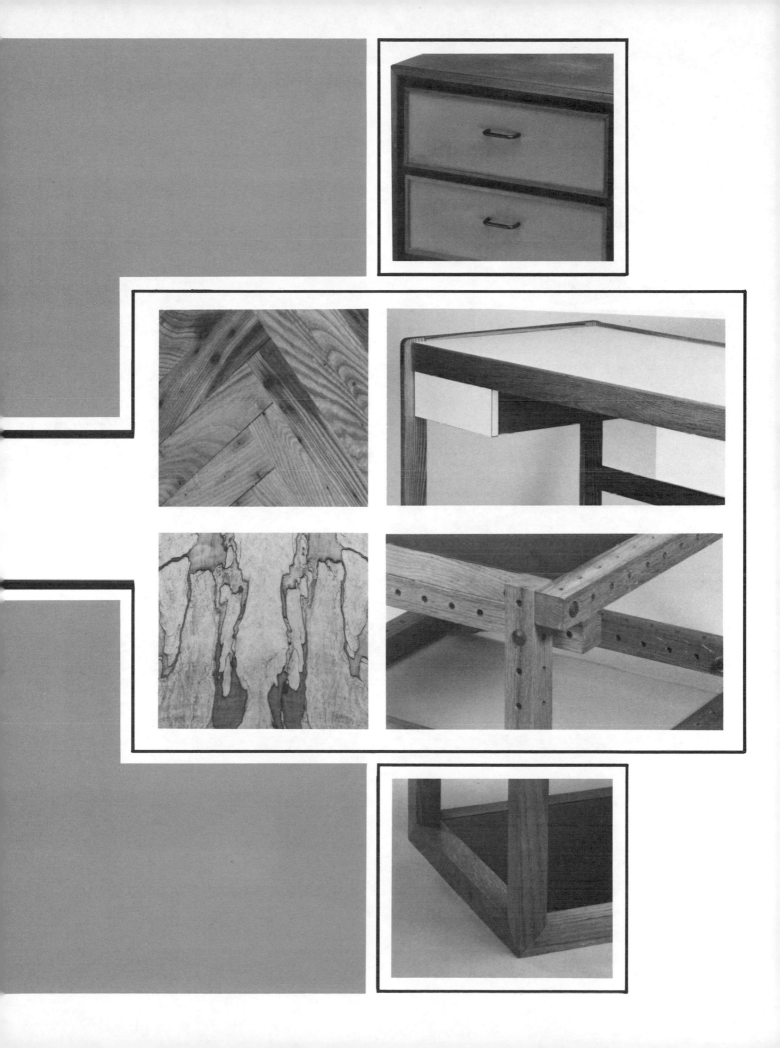

spalted wood boxes

If you have access to a woodlot or even a good pile of well-seasoned firewood, you may have the opportunity to obtain some spalted or partially rotted wood. When cut into longitudinal slices and/or book-matched, this spalted wood can produce some exquisite small panels for box lids, small frame and panel doors, and even jewelry.

Spalting is caused by moisture and fungus and can be recognized by intricate patterns of black or dark brown lines and sometimes zones of varying colors within the wood. The lines, which look as if they had been drawn with a fine pen and India ink, mark the advance of various fungi responsible for rot. When wood is left in contact with warm moist earth, fungus attack is likely. If left alone under the right conditions, the wood will eventually decompose entirely. However, if you dry the wood out, the decaying process is halted. The trick is to find the right kind of wood at the right time . . . when the decay process is far enough advanced to produce spalted patterns, but before the wood reaches the "punky" or soft rotted stage.

pale color such as the maples, various birches and fruitwoods. Oak will sometimes display spalting, though most of the time it will start getting rotted and soft in the outer layers without any appreciable spalting advancing into the heartwood. Some fruitwoods, particularly apple, will spalt though generally not in as colorful a way as maple.

To determine if spalting exists within a piece of wood, examine the end grain. If the ends haven't blackened, the irregular patterns may be apparent. A good clue for firewood, standing or felled dead trees is fungus growths on the ends of logs or anywhere along the trunk. Smaller parts, such as limbs, may display more advanced spalting than the trunk or very large limbs.

Once you've located a piece of spalted wood, you have to decide how to cut it to achieve the most interesting figures. I recommend consecutive slices book-matched to form intriguing "pictures" which, like Rorschach ink blots, are limited only by the imagination of the viewer. End grain and long grain cuts will produce entirely different patterns. For

A chunk of spalted maple and two book-matched slices cut lengthwise with the grain.

Harvesting spalted wood may be easier than you think. In a pile of well-seasoned firewood, chances are that some of it may be spalted. Generally, firewood cut in short lengths and left in open uncovered piles for a few months will be moderately spalted. Not all species display beautiful and complex spalting patterns though. The best examples will be found in hardwoods of normally

small boxes 4 or 5 inches long, even a short chunk of spalted maple will provide enough material for you to experiment with different types of cuts. It's fascinating to make consecutive cuts along different planes and see what kind of interesting designs can be achieved, particularly in view of the fact that the spalting patterns may vary depending on the thickness of the slices.

(continued on next page)

End grain cuts are made straight down just like cutting a loaf of bread, or they may be made at a slant. End grain cuts made perpendicular to a small log or limb are sometimes referred to as oysters. When the cuts are made at a slant, the sectional slices are more elliptical in shape and do, in fact, resemble oyster shells. Oyster shell veneering is an interesting method of decorating small boxes. Thin cross sections of a limb are cut and dried. These sectional wafers are then cut into various shapes such as squares or polygons and glued together to form panels which are then glued to the surfaces of a box. Cuts made lengthwise with the grain will produce equally interesting designs and result in longer slices which can be book-matched to form larger panels.

The easiest way to make either long or end grain cuts is with a bandsaw, but a bow saw will also do the job nicely. An ordinary panel saw can be used though its kerf is a bit wide and the cut surface will require more sanding. The sections or lengths are usually small so the rough cutting takes little time. The only difficulty is in cutting the slices very thin. I generally cut mine to $\frac{3}{16}$ in. thickness; final sanding brings them down to $\frac{1}{8}$ in. If thicker slices are used, remember to allow more drying time.

After cutting either end or long grain sections, keep

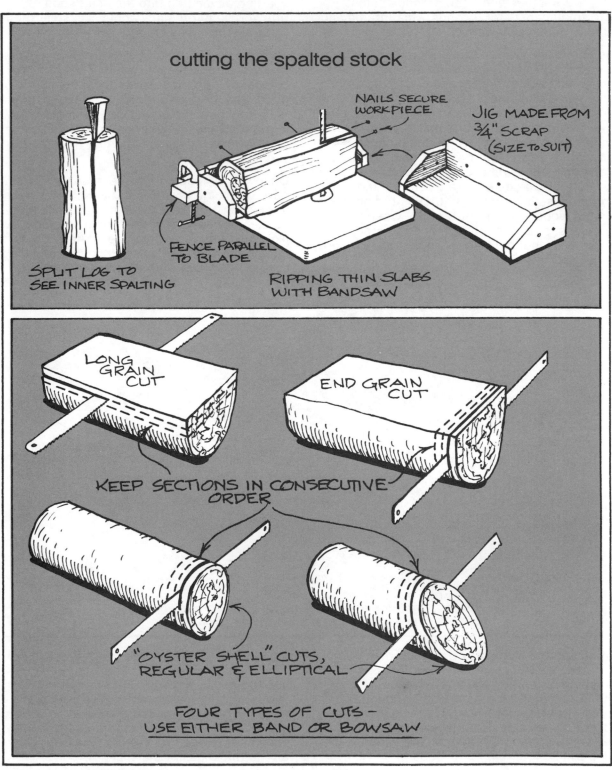

cutting the spalted stock

NAILS SECURE WORKPIECE

JIG MADE FROM ¾" SCRAP (SIZE TO SUIT)

FENCE PARALLEL TO BLADE

SPLIT LOG TO SEE INNER SPALTING

RIPPING THIN SLABS WITH BANDSAW

LONG GRAIN CUT

END GRAIN CUT

KEEP SECTIONS IN CONSECUTIVE ORDER

"OYSTER SHELL" CUTS, REGULAR & ELLIPTICAL

FOUR TYPES OF CUTS — USE EITHER BAND OR BOWSAW

them in consecutive order and stack them with paper towels or other absorbent material interleaved. The stack should then be covered top and bottom with a piece of plywood and pressed under heavy weights or put in a press or vise (step 1). Kept dry and warm they will be ready for use in a few days. Drying time will vary depending on species, amount of moisture present and the drying environment, but don't try to rush the process with excessive heat as a lot of cracking will occur.

When the sections are dry, choose consecutive pieces with a potentially interesting picture and book-match them. To do this, tape them together and, using a sharp x-acto or utility knife and straight edge, make two parallel cuts, each being about $\frac{1}{4}$ in. from each long side (step 2). This will give you your gluing edge plus parallel straight edges to clamp against. Place the book-matched pieces on wax paper, or some other surface where glue will not adhere, and clamp the pieces together using only light pressure to prevent buckling (step 3). The assembly is left in the clamps just long enough for a good glue bond. In a dry shop at about 65 degrees, twenty-five minutes using yellow glue is sufficient. With only one side of the panel exposed, it doesn't take long for warping to occur; hence the clamping time should be kept to a minimum.

After removing the clamps, stand the assembled panel on end so both sides are free to dry evenly, and keep the panel this way until the glue has completely dried. The panel can then be cut and sanded to the desired dimensions and stored on end until needed.

Of course you don't have to make a box; you can use this spalted material in any way you wish. If you do choose to make a box, instead of providing a book-matched panel just for the lid, you can completely veneer the box with matched pieces cut either along the grain or as oysters cut from end grain. Incidentally, you don't have to use only spalted wood for oyster veneering. Cross sections cut from unspalted limbs of many species, particularly those which have great contrast between sapwood and heartwood, will provide a striking effect when bookmatched and used to cover small boxes.

making boxes

To make boxes of the type shown, select a book-matched spalted panel and measure the sides to determine the dimensions of the box sides. The height of the boxes shown, including the lids, runs between 1½ in. and 2 in. For the sides and box bottom, select a wood that will compliment the spalted top. You really can't go too far wrong here. The top will steal the show no matter what you choose.

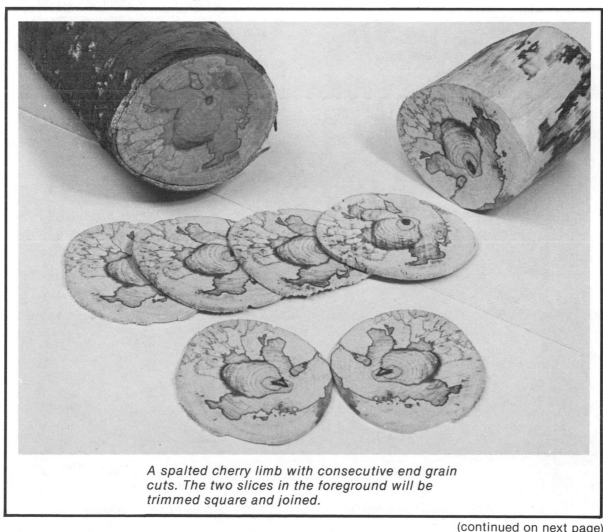

A spalted cherry limb with consecutive end grain cuts. The two slices in the foreground will be trimmed square and joined.

(continued on next page)

Resaw the wood for the sides to $\frac{3}{16}$ in. or $\frac{1}{4}$ in. thickness. Thinner is better for me. I like the light and delicate feel of a thin box, but you must decide for yourself what you prefer and what your ability can handle. The resawed pieces are ripped to a width equal to the depth of the box. The ends of these strips are then crosscut at 45 degrees to form miter joints at the box corners. I use a miter trimmer (sold by Pootatuck Corp., Box 24, Windsor, VT 05089) for these cuts, but you can also use a miter box and an x-acto razor saw, which looks like a small dovetail saw.

The strips, after being mitered, should be $\frac{1}{4}$ in. longer respectively than the sides and ends of the top panel. The inside faces must then be grooved near the top and bottom edges to receive the top panel and box bottom. Because very small amounts of material are being removed, handling these small pieces can be tricky and great care must be taken while machining them. If proper push sticks are used, the work can be done easily and safely. I used a table saw, after first fitting the table with an auxiliary blade insert.

The insert is made from plywood and shimmed, if necessary, so that it will sit flush with the table top. After cutting the insert to fit the shape of the opening, start the saw and raise the blade to a height of $\frac{1}{16}$ in. while holding the insert down with a clamp or a push stick. This insert will prevent the thin piece being worked from slipping down alongside the blade.

Set the fence so that the first cut will be made $\frac{1}{8}$ in. from the edge of a side strip. Make a test cut on scrap using push sticks. If the test cut is correct, make the two grooving cuts on the inside face of each side. These grooves can also be cut with a router mounted in a table. *Note:* The two grooves in the four sides of each box are located about $\frac{1}{8}$ in. from the top and bottom edges respectively. The depth of the grooves can be between $\frac{1}{16}$ in. and $\frac{1}{8}$ in., depending on the thickness of the box sides.

If you have cut your top panel so that after sanding it is about $\frac{1}{8}$ in. thick, and you have a carbide blade that cuts a $\frac{1}{8}$ in. kerf, the box will be ready for test assembly. If your top is a bit thicker than $\frac{1}{8}$ in. or your saw blade cuts a narrow kerf, you will have to reset the fence for another series of cuts to widen the grooves. Again, make test cuts first. The top panel should fit snugly in the side grooves, and the joints at the corners should be tight. If the joints don't quite close, pare the top down until they do.

When the top and four sides fit together properly, make a bottom exactly the same size as the top. I usually use the same species of wood as for the box sides. Depending on the size of the box, this bottom panel can either be resawed in one piece from thicker wood, or glued up from two pieces as was the top.

When you are ready for final assembly, dry test the fitting once more. If everything looks good, use yellow glue sparingly at the mitered corners and add one small dot of glue in the grooves, on the center of each end, to secure the top and bottom panels. Try to use as little glue as possible to prevent squeeze-out, particularly on the inside of the box. Hold the assembly tight with hand pressure for about three minutes and then set down to dry completely.

After drying, give the outside surfaces a final sanding. I generally finish with 220 grit paper. The

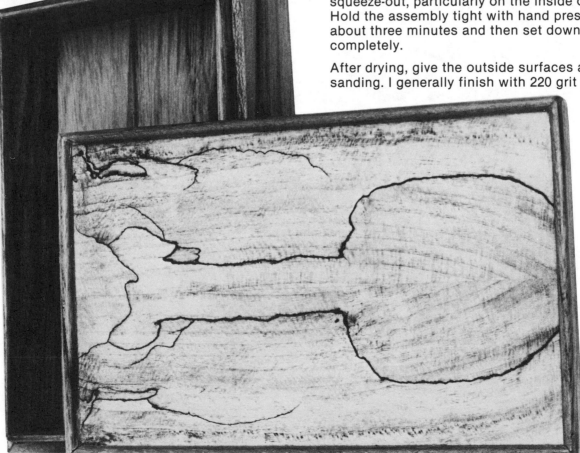

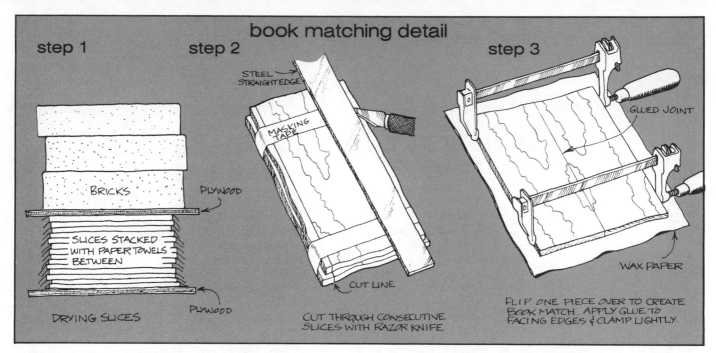

book matching detail

step 1

step 2

step 3

BRICKS

PLYWOOD

SLICES STACKED
WITH PAPER TOWELS
BETWEEN

DRYING SLICES

PLYWOOD

STEEL
STRAIGHTEDGE

MASKING
TAPE

CUT LINE

CUT THROUGH CONSECUTIVE
SLICES WITH RAZOR KNIFE

GLUED JOINT

WAX PAPER

FLIP ONE PIECE OVER TO CREATE
BOOK MATCH. APPLY GLUE TO
FACING EDGES & CLAMP LIGHTLY.

lid must now be cut from the box. This cut is located about one-third of the way down from the top of the box. I recommend using the band saw with a fence as a guide for this cut. The top may also be cut off with the table saw. Use a plywood blade and the same insert used earlier for the groove cuts. Raise the blade slightly higher than the thickness of the box sides, and cut through the four sides. Take care with the final cut which frees the top.

I rarely hinge my box lids, but instead fit a thin liner in place on the inside. This liner forms a lip which locates and holds the lid. The liner can be resawed from the same wood as the box sides, or you may prefer a contrasting wood. The thickness of the liner is slightly less than the thickness of the box sides. After measuring the depth of the box without the lid, I add $\frac{3}{16}$ in. to this measurement and rip the liner

strips to that width. These are then mitered at the ends for a snug press fit around the inside of the box. A dab of glue on each piece secures the liner, and the edges of the protruding lip are rounded slightly with fine sandpaper.

Most of my boxes are finished with Watco Danish Oil and wax. You can use any finish you prefer, but if you use an oil finish and intend to sell the boxes, remind your customers that the finish will have to be renewed from time to time.

In closing I'd like to add that I sell these boxes just about as fast as I can make them. They make great gifts, and are always a hot-selling item at craft fairs, shows, galleries and shops. In fact, over the years I would have to say that these spalted wood boxes have been my most popular creation. □

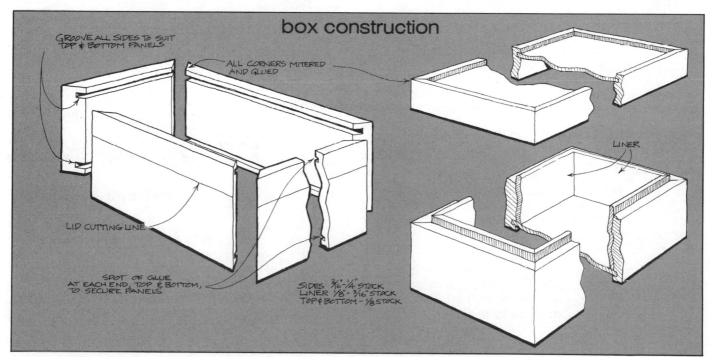

box construction

GROOVE ALL SIDES TO SUIT
TOP & BOTTOM PANELS

ALL CORNERS MITERED
AND GLUED

LINER

LID CUTTING LINE

SPOT OF GLUE
AT EACH END, TOP & BOTTOM,
TO SECURE PANELS.

SIDES 3/16"-1/4" STOCK
LINER 1/8"-3/16" STOCK
TOP & BOTTOM - 1/8 STOCK

oak writing desk

t hose with a flair for contemporary styling will like this nicely proportioned desk. Solid oak stock is used for all visible wood surfaces. The top core (G), false front core (O), box top and bottom (J) and drawer bottom (N) are plywood. Parts G and O are covered with white plastic laminate.

Begin by cutting the four legs (A) to size. On one end, a ⅜ in. thick by 1½ in. wide by 2½ in. long tenon is made, while the other end is cut to form a ⅜ in. wide by 2½ in. deep open mortise. With this completed, set up the dado head cutter to cut the ¾ by 2½ in. notch in the two back legs. Now the end rail (B) tenons can be cut to fit the leg mortises. To look best, this joint must have a good tight fit, so use special care here.

The foot (C) is cut to length and width from ¾ in. thick stock. Note that the front and rear mortises are made to accept the leg tenons. Parts A, B, and C can now be glued together to form the side frames. Apply sufficient glue and clamp securely. When dry, round the top corners and the top front end of the

feet to a ¾ in. radius, as shown.

Using stock that measures a full 1 in. thick, now cut the front rail (D) and rear rail (E) to size. In order to accept the laminated top, a ⅝ by ⅞ in. rabbet is applied to part D, and a ⅝ by 1¼ in. rabbet is applied to part E. It's best to cut the front rail slightly wider than 2½ in. and make the rabbet about 1 in. deep, however. Later, after the top is added, you'll be able to lightly plane the front rail perfectly flush with the laminate.

The ¾ in. thick plywood top core (G) is covered with white plastic laminate (H), although other colors can also be used if you prefer. It is important to laminate both sides of the top to equalize tensions. After the top has been laminated (with contact cement) and trimmed, it can be glued and clamped to the front rail (D) and rear rail (E). Lightly plane the front rail flush with the plastic laminate top, then round off the front edge with a router and ¼ in. rounding-over bit.

The side frames can now be joined to the top

assembly (parts D, E, G, and H) with glue and woodscrews. As shown, the screws are counterbored and plugged. Plated screws are suggested because oak will sometimes corrode unplated steel. To support the top while the side frames were being attached, I clamped auxiliary legs (made from ¾ in. scrap pine) to the inside of all four legs. The length of the auxiliary legs was such that when the front and rear rails rested on them, the top was properly located in relation to the side frames. Two 5 ft. pipe clamps were spanned across the top, clamping the top assembly between the side frames and temporarily holding things together while the screws were drilled and secured. The stretcher (F) was also attached at this point.

Now make the two drawer box assemblies, consisting of parts I, J, and K, as shown in the drawer box detail. After rabbeting the back, make the ¼ by ¼ in. tongues on the top and bottom, and the corresponding ¼ by ¼ in. grooves in the sides. Note that the 5/16 in. deep by 1 in. wide drawer guide groove in the sides must be cut before the box is assembled. Pilot holes for the 1¼ in. long screws must also be located and drilled before assembly. To facilitate drilling these holes, turn the desk over and temporarily assemble and clamp in place one side, the top and the back. Repeat the process for the box on the other side of the desk.

Glue and assemble the boxes (make sure they are square) and mount them with the lag screws. We chose lag screws so a socket wrench could be used.

The drawers can now be constructed. Note the ⅜ in. deep by ⅛ in. wide tongue and groove joint (see drawer joint detail) with which the drawer front and back (L) are joined to the sides (M). The 3/16 in. deep by 1 in. wide grooves in the sides to accept the guides (P), and the ¼ in. deep by ¼ in. wide grooves in the front, back, and sides to accept the plywood drawer bottom (N) must also be cut before assembly. The bottom is rabbetted on all four sides to create the ¼ by ¼ in. tongue.

The false front core material (O) can be cut to size next. I used ½ in. thick plywood. Using the laminate (H), cover both sides, the edges and the ends. Note the bevel applied to create the black line detail around the false drawer fronts. Mount the fronts to the assembled drawers using ¼ in. threaded inserts and screws. I recommend drilling oversize ⅜ in. diameter holes through the drawer carcase front, which will allow some adjustment in the false fronts. Lastly, glue the drawer guides into the drawer guide grooves on the drawer sides. The drawer guide additional length will allow the drawers to be fully extended. *Note:* The false front is sized 12⁷⁄₁₆ in. long to allow some clearance at the desk sides. The 4⅜ in. width of the false front provides a small finger grip along the bottom edge with which to pull the drawer out. After sanding, I finished the desk with two coats of Watco Danish Oil. □

Bill of Materials
(all dimensions actual)

Part	Description	Size	No. Req'd.
A	Leg	¾ × 2½ × 28⅞*	4
B	End Rail	¾ × 2½ × 24*	2
C	Foot	¾ × 2½ × 24¾	2
D	Front Rail	1 × 2½ × 46½	1
E	Rear Rail	1 × 2⅞ × 46½	1
F	Stretcher	¾ × 2½ × 48	1
G	Top Core	¾ × 21¾ × 46½	1
H	Laminate	as needed	
I	Box Side	¾ × 5⅞ × 20⅛	4
J	Box Top & Bottom	½ × 11½ × 20⅛*	4
K	Box Back	¾ × 5⅞ × 12½	2
L	Drawer Front & Back	½ × 3½ × 10¾*	4
M	Drawer Side	½ × 3½ × 13	4
N	Drawer Bottom	½ × 10½ × 12½*	2
O	False Front Core	½ × 4¼ × 12⁵⁄₁₆	2
P	Drawer Guide	½ × 1 × 19	4

*Includes tenon or tongue.

(continued on next page)

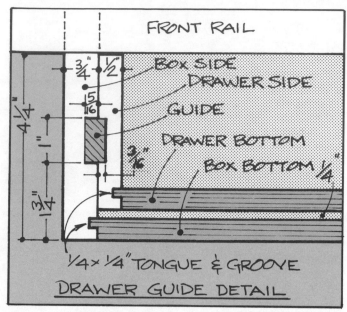

FRONT RAIL

Box SIDE
DRAWER SIDE
GUIDE
DRAWER BOTTOM
BOX BOTTOM ¼"

¾" ½"
5/16
4 ¼"
1"
3 ¼"
3/16"

¼ × ¼" TONGUE & GROOVE

<u>DRAWER GUIDE DETAIL</u>

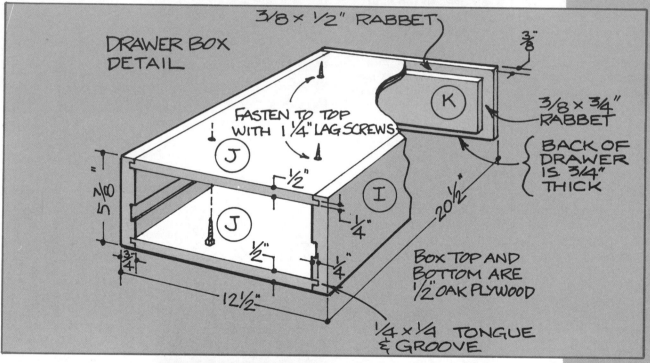

DRAWER BOX DETAIL

3/8 × ½" RABBET
3/8"

FASTEN TO TOP WITH 1 ¼" LAG SCREWS

K
J
J
I

3/8 × ¾" RABBET

BACK OF DRAWER IS ¾" THICK

5 7/8"
½"
¼"
½"
¼"
3/4"
12½"
20½"

BOX TOP AND BOTTOM ARE ½" OAK PLYWOOD

¼ × ¼ TONGUE & GROOVE

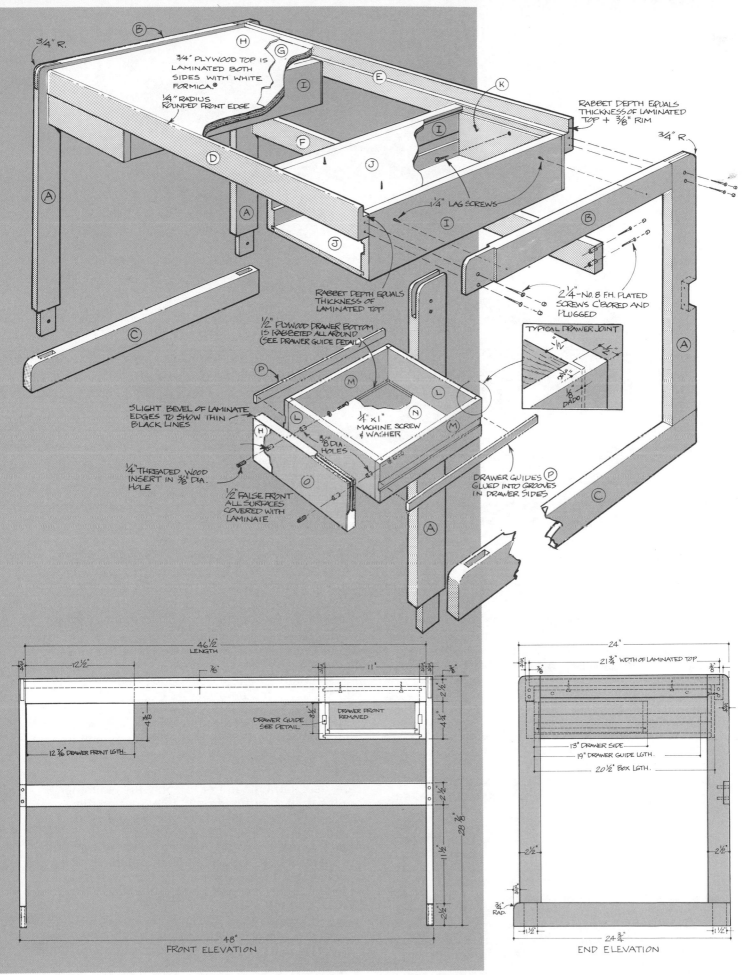

3/4" R.

3/4" PLYWOOD TOP IS
LAMINATED BOTH
SIDES WITH WHITE
FORMICA.®

1/4" RADIUS
ROUNDED FRONT EDGE

RABBET DEPTH EQUALS
THICKNESS OF LAMINATED
TOP + 3/8" RIM

3/4" R.

1/4" LAG SCREWS

RABBET DEPTH EQUALS
THICKNESS OF
LAMINATED TOP

2 1/4"-No. 8 F.H. PLATED
SCREWS C'BORED AND
PLUGGED

1/2" PLYWOOD DRAWER BOTTOM
IS RABBETED ALL AROUND
(SEE DRAWER GUIDE DETAIL)

TYPICAL DRAWER JOINT

1/8" DADO

SLIGHT BEVEL OF LAMINATE
EDGES TO SHOW THIN
BLACK LINES

1/4" x 1"
MACHINE SCREW
& WASHER

3/8" DIA.
HOLES

1/4" THREADED WOOD
INSERT IN 3/8" DIA.
HOLE

1/2" FALSE FRONT
ALL SURFACES
COVERED WITH
LAMINATE

DRAWER GUIDES
GLUED INTO GROOVES
IN DRAWER SIDES

46 1/2"
LENGTH

12 1/2"

7/8"

11"

3/4"

DRAWER FRONT
REMOVED

DRAWER GUIDE
SEE DETAIL

12 3/16" DRAWER FRONT LGTH.

2 1/2"

4 1/4"

2 1/2"

28 7/8"

11 1/2"

2 1/2"

48"

FRONT ELEVATION

24"

21 3/4" WIDTH OF LAMINATED TOP

13" DRAWER SIDE
19" DRAWER GUIDE LGTH.
20 1/2" BOX LGTH.

2 1/2"

2 1/2"

3/4"
RAD.

1 1/2"

24 3/4"

1 1/2"

END ELEVATION

117

bolt-together table

t he bolt-together concept of this table can be used in building a great variety of furniture. Much like an erector set, the pieces are easily disassembled, and parts used for one piece can often be used to build something else. The bolt-together approach produces pieces that have exceptional strength and a unique contemporary look.

To build the table you will need sufficient 1¾ in. square stock for parts A and B, ¾ in. thick stock for parts C, and a quarter sheet each of ¾ in. thick plywood for part D and plastic laminate for part E. Cherry, walnut, maple, birch, pine, or oak would all be fine for this project.

After cutting to length parts A and B, mark for the ⅜ in. diameter bolt holes on two adjacent faces of each piece. Starting ⅞ in. from the end, lay out the holes on center 1¾ in. apart. Use either the drill press or a drill guide to insure that the ⅜ in. holes are all bored through straight and true. Sand lightly to soften all sharp edges and corners. The stretchers and legs are finished with penetrating oil, and then assembled with ⅜ by 4 in. long carriage bolts, nuts, and washers, as shown.

To make the drop-in table top, first cut down the quarter sheet of ¾ in. thick plywood to a 20¼ in. by 20¼ in. square. Next miter the ends of the four frame pieces (C), and cut a ⅜ in. deep by ¾ in. wide rabbet (Fig. 1) around the top inside edge of each. If you intend the laminate surface to be perfectly flush with the table perimeter, the width of part C must be 1¾ in. minus the laminate thickness. Assemble the frame and plywood with glue. The frame can be reinforced by gluing and screwing corner blocks to the inside corners (Fig. 2).

Now use contact cement to apply the laminate across the top of the drop-in frame. Although we used black plastic laminate, you may wish to coordinate with your decor by using another color. The laminate is laid up oversize and then trimmed back with a flush cutting laminate trimmer bit. Lastly, use a file to apply a slight bevel to the laminate edge. The oak frame is finished with penetrating oil.

Note: Since the top frame is sized for a perfect fit, loosening the table bolts may be necessary to permit the top to drop in. Retightening the bolts should lock the top firmly in place. ☐

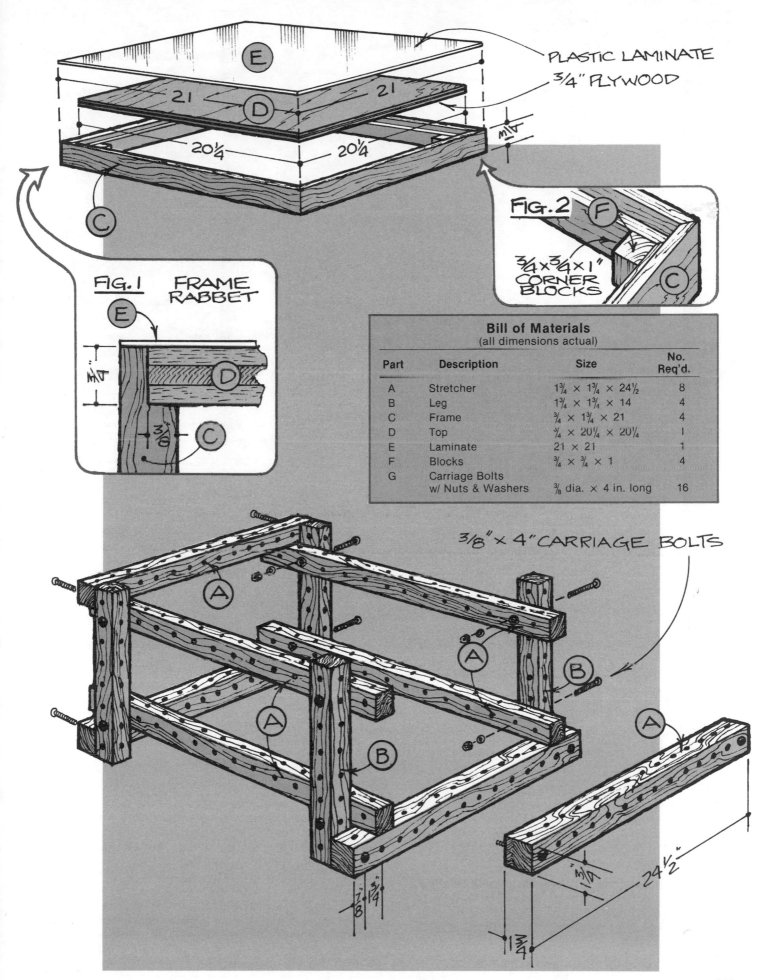

PLASTIC LAMINATE

3/4" PLYWOOD

E

21 — D — 21

20¼ — 20¼

C

FIG.2 F

3/4 x 3/4 x 1"
CORNER
BLOCKS

C

FIG.1 FRAME
RABBET

E

D

3/8 C

Bill of Materials
(all dimensions actual)

Part	Description	Size	No. Req'd.
A	Stretcher	$1\frac{3}{4} \times 1\frac{3}{4} \times 24\frac{1}{2}$	8
B	Leg	$1\frac{3}{4} \times 1\frac{3}{4} \times 14$	4
C	Frame	$\frac{3}{4} \times 1\frac{3}{4} \times 21$	4
D	Top	$\frac{3}{4} \times 20\frac{1}{4} \times 20\frac{1}{4}$	1
E	Laminate	21×21	1
F	Blocks	$\frac{3}{4} \times \frac{3}{4} \times 1$	4
G	Carriage Bolts w/ Nuts & Washers	$\frac{3}{8}$ dia. $\times$ 4 in. long	16

3/8" x 4" CARRIAGE BOLTS

A

A

B

A

B

A

A

1/8 1 3/4

1 3/4 24 ½"

multipurpose cabinet

the most reliable construction for cabinets of this type makes use of plywood, which is much more stable than solid wood. Using plywood is also a lot easier than forming wide surfaces from a lot of edge-joined narrow boards.

In addition to plywood, I often use plastic laminates in contemporary style cabinet work. The ease with which laminated surfaces can be cleaned plus the relatively low cost of the material makes it ideal for cabinet construction.

Given these realities, I wanted to develop a practical

design that would also emphasize the beauty of natural wood. Using plywood construction for the carcase, covering it with a laminate, and then adding a distinctive solid wood front and edgings, I feel I've achieved a compromise which combines practical materials with the appeal of solid wood.

I made two of these cabinets to serve as nightstands flanking a bed, but they will also serve nicely as end or lamp tables in a contemporary setting. Since I wanted wood to dominate the design, wormy chestnut with its distinctive color, grain and worm holes was chosen for the doorframes, herringbone panel, front trim and edging strips. Almost any fine cabinet wood can be substituted, however.

Birch plywood of ¾ in. thickness was used for the box sides (A), bottom (B), and top (C), while ¼ in. birch plywood was used for the back (D). The drawings show how the five parts of the box are joined. After the box was glued up, the top and sides were covered with 1/16 in. plastic laminate (P) using contact cement and plenty of pressure with a rubber roller to achieve a good bond. I used a deep rust-brown laminate which harmonizes with the chestnut.

The four corners of the box were then rabbeted with a router to take the square edging strips (E) which break up the plastic surfaces and help keep the chestnut as a dominant material. I used a router with a ⅜ in. carbide straight bit and an edge-guide to cut the rabbet, taking care to move the router from right to left to prevent chipping of the laminate. After the first pass you can then run the router from left to right to clean up. The wood edging strips are cut 5/16 in. square and glued into the rabbets, then carefully planed flush and rounded off.

The face frame (parts I and J), which is cut from ¾ in. stock, mitered and then butt joined, is sized to slightly overhang the outside edges of the box. This slight overhang is later planed flush with the laminate. Mount the face frame by pre-drilling and counterboring the four members for screws. First fasten the bottom piece with glue and screws, keeping its top edge flush with the inside of the box bottom. Then hold the next piece of frame along an adjacent edge and use a sharp pencil to mark the screw holes on the box edge. A small drill bit is then used to bore the pilot holes very slightly closer to the piece already fastened. This method will help draw the pieces tightly together at the corners when the screws are driven in. Do the other adjacent edge, using this same technique and the top piece last. In order to pull the top piece miter joints tight, bore the screw holes slightly toward the inside of the cabinet.

To bring the face frame flush with the laminated surface, use a sharp plane to shave the frame while resting the plane flat on the plastic. When setting the plane iron, bury the corner of the iron that will rest on the plastic. This will prevent gouging.

Don't wipe off glue that has squeezed out of the joints while fastening. This will drive glue into the face of the frame and inhibit the finish. Instead, let the squeeze out form beads and dry. The beads will be easy to scrape or plane off later.

The cabinet base (parts G and H) can be made up of ordinary ¾ in. pine, the corners being joined with splined miters. The base can be painted flat black or covered with the black plastic trim sold especially for kitchen counter bases. I do not feel that it's necessary to screw the base to the box; a good glue bond should be sufficient.

The doorframe, parts K and L, is joined with mortises and tenons. A ⅜ by ⅜ in. rabbet is routed around the frame inside after assembly to hold the door panel (M). The panel can be handled in a wide variety of ways. The method I chose was to make up an oversize panel of chestnut boards planed to ⅜ in. thickness and lap joined at the sides and ends. This permits the direct glue-joining of both halves of a herringbone pattern without splines. The glued up panel is weighted to keep it flat and, when dry, is cut to 14⅞ in. square, allowing ⅛ in. all around for expansion in the doorframe.

The panel is held in place on the back of the door with four battens or retainers (N) which are simply butted and screwed in place. These retainers should be cut and located after the hinges have been temporarily mounted. The door is hinged to glued-in hinge blocks (Q) inside the case which bring the hinges out flush with the face frame. The concealed European style hinges (O) are full-overlay, self-

Cabinet base consists of four pieces of pine with ends mitered and grooved for splines.

The completed box and base assembly ready to be covered with plastic laminate.

121

The four corners are routed for the strips which are glued in place and rounded off.

¼ in. quarter rounding bit. Run the bit all around the frame except where the cove cut was made.

Set the router against the frame edge near where the pull is to be, and mark where the router base lies when the bit guide bearing is against the side of the frame. Clamp a straightedge 3/16 in. away from this mark and rout the part of the frame face in line with the cove on the back.

The final step is the screw mounting of ¼ in. by 1 in. mitered back trim strips (F) around the sides and top back of the cabinet. These add to the design and cover the exposed dadoes. They are also handy for clamping on a nice adjustable reading lamp. The cabinet (and much of my other work) is finished with several coats of Watco Danish Oil. □

closing, and fully adjustable after installation. These hinges are available from The Woodworkers' Store, (see source index) and through other mail-order firms that carry cabinetmaker's supplies. Instructions for mounting are usually included with the hinges.

The batten (N) adjacent to the hinges will have to be located and notched to provide clearance for the hinge arms when the door is closed. Also, the door frame must be mortised with a Forstner bit, as shown in the hinge detail, to take the hinge cups.

To form the door pull, rout the back of the door frame starting 2½ in. from the top with a ½ in. cove bit. This cut can be made to suit or 3½ in. long as shown. Next, round the face of the doorframe with a

Rear view of door showing battens (N) holding panel. Note notches in batten for hinge arm.

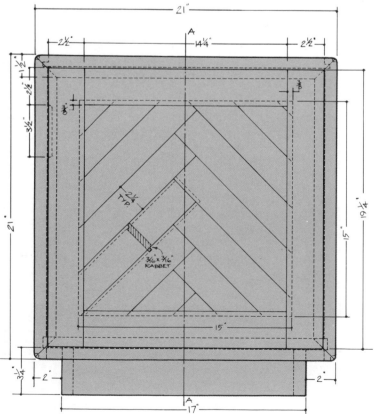

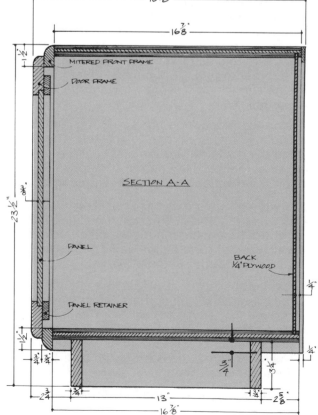

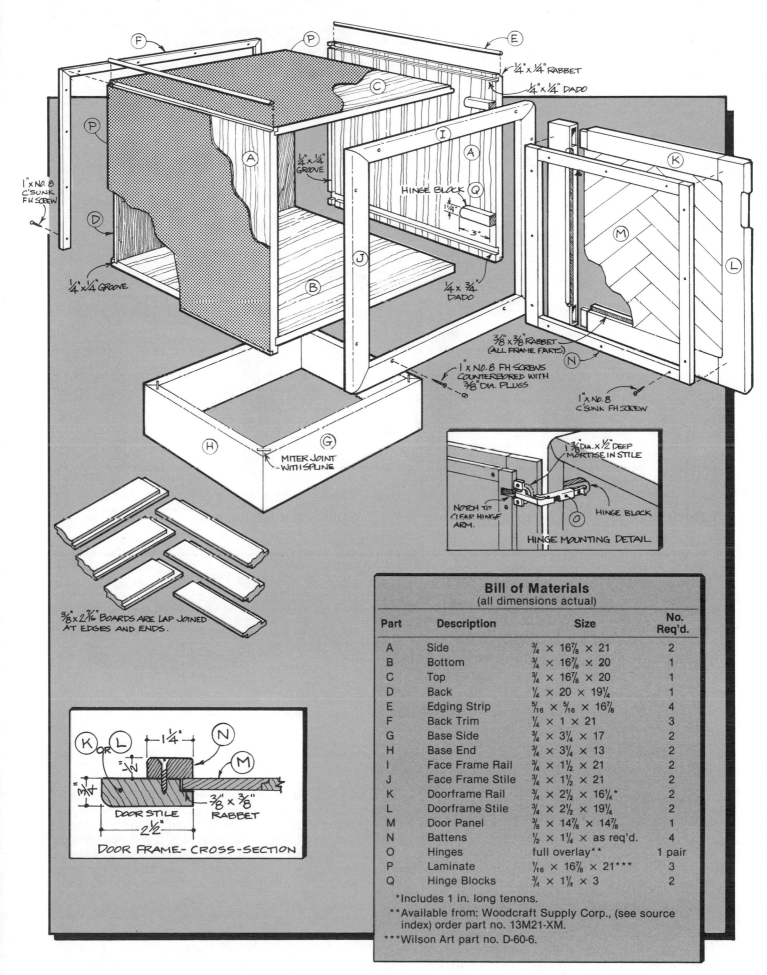

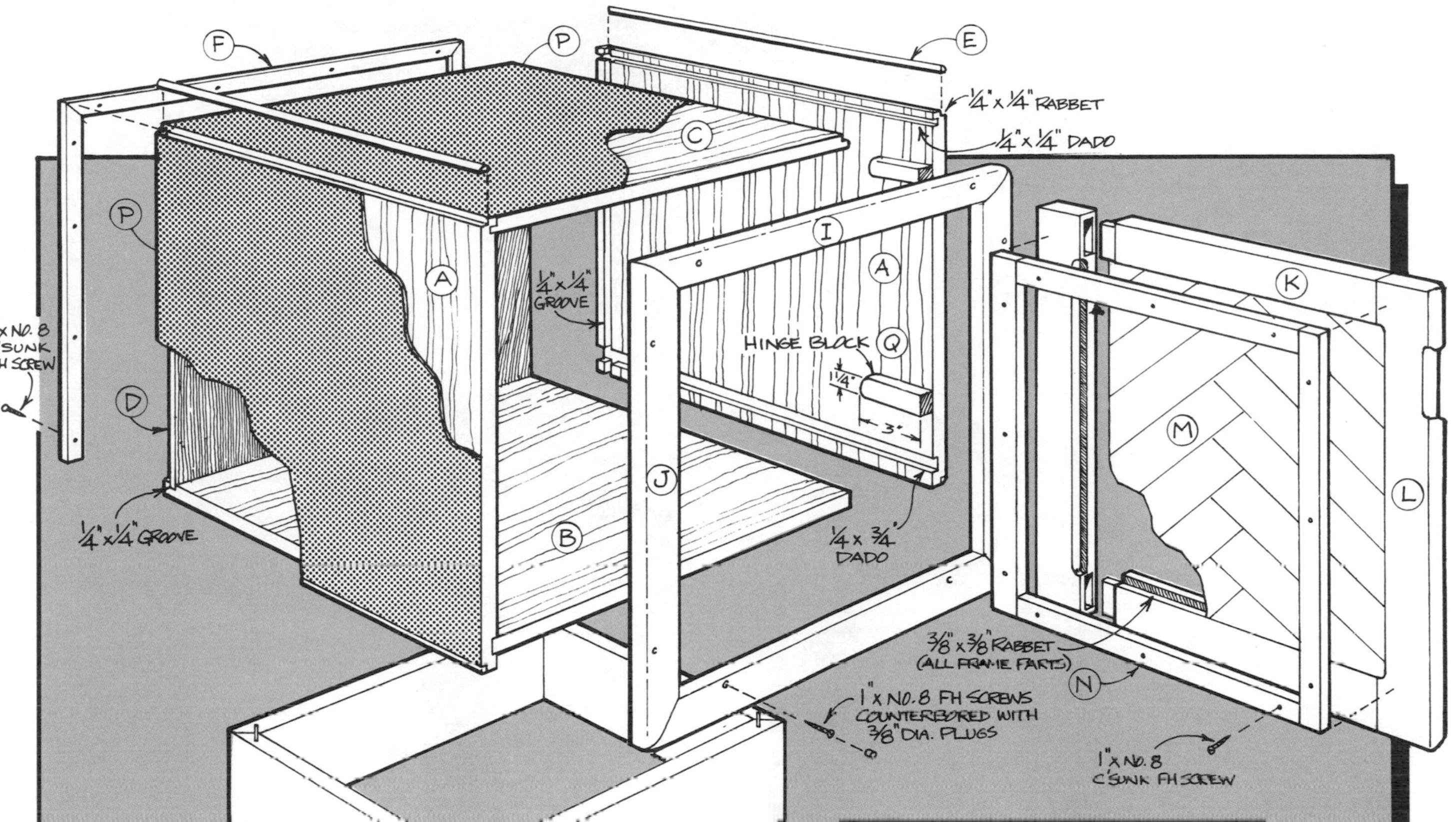
F
P
E
1/4" x 1/4" RABBET
1/4" x 1/4" DADO
C
P
A
1/4" x 1/4" GROOVE
I
A
K
1" x No. 8 C'SUNK FH SCREW
HINGE BLOCK Q
1 1/4"
3"
D
J
M
L
1/4" x 1/4" GROOVE
1/4 x 3/4 DADO
B
3/8" x 3/8" RABBET (ALL FRAME PARTS)
N
1" x No. 8 FH SCREWS COUNTERBORED WITH 3/8" DIA. PLUGS
1" x No. 8 C'SUNK FH SCREW
H
G
MITER JOINT WITH SPLINE

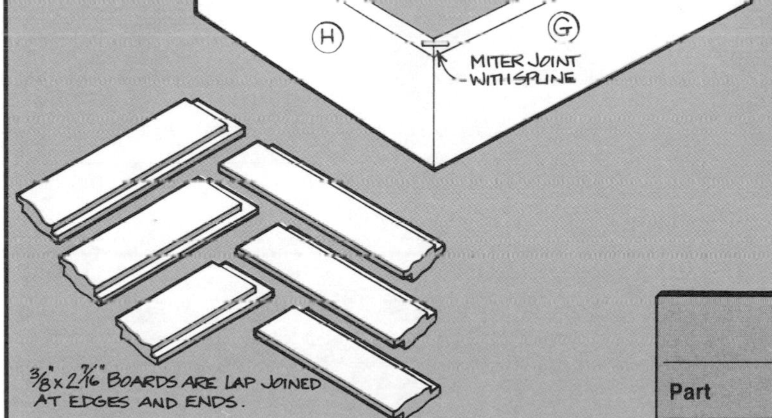
3/8" x 2 7/16" BOARDS ARE LAP JOINED AT EDGES AND ENDS.

1 3/8" DIA. x 1/2" DEEP MORTISE IN STILE
NOTCH TO CLEAR HINGE ARM.
O
HINGE BLOCK
HINGE MOUNTING DETAIL

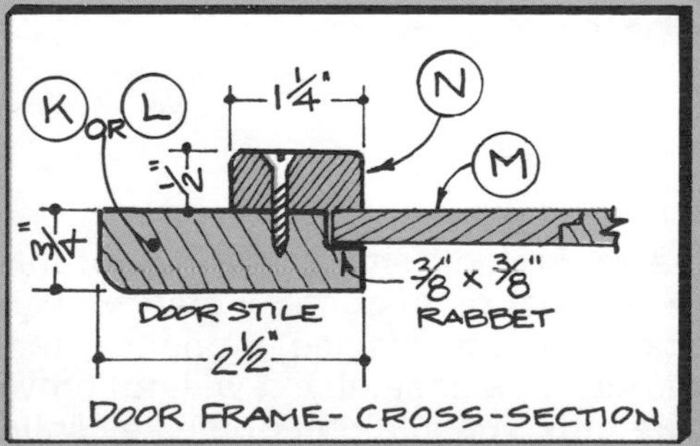
K OR L
1 1/4"
N
M
1/4"
3/4"
DOOR STILE
3/8" x 3/8" RABBET
2 1/2"
DOOR FRAME- CROSS-SECTION

Bill of Materials
(all dimensions actual)

Part	Description	Size	No. Req'd.
A	Side	3/4 × 16 7/8 × 21	2
B	Bottom	3/4 × 16 7/8 × 20	1
C	Top	3/4 × 16 7/8 × 20	1
D	Back	1/4 × 20 × 19 1/4	1
E	Edging Strip	5/16 × 5/16 × 16 7/8	4
F	Back Trim	1/4 × 1 × 21	3
G	Base Side	3/4 × 3 1/4 × 17	2
H	Base End	3/4 × 3 1/4 × 13	2
I	Face Frame Rail	3/4 × 1 1/2 × 21	2
J	Face Frame Stile	3/4 × 1 1/2 × 21	2
K	Doorframe Rail	3/4 × 2 1/2 × 16 1/4*	2
L	Doorframe Stile	3/4 × 2 1/2 × 19 1/4	2
M	Door Panel	3/8 × 14 7/8 × 14 7/8	1
N	Battens	1/2 × 1 1/4 × as req'd.	4
O	Hinges	full overlay**	1 pair
P	Laminate	1/16 × 16 7/8 × 21***	3
Q	Hinge Blocks	3/4 × 1 1/4 × 3	2

*Includes 1 in. long tenons.

**Available from: Woodcraft Supply Corp., (see source index) order part no. 13M21-XM.

***Wilson Art part no. D-60-6.

cube table

this cube table represents just about the most elementary table design possible. Except for the groove cut into the eight frame members (A) to accept the top and bottom tongue, both parts A and the four legs (B) are identical. The key splines in each corner locate the frames and legs, and simplify the assembly process.

As its name implies, the table is in fact a cube. Although the table I show here is 20 in. square, by altering the length of the frame and leg pieces, and correspondingly the size of the laminated plywood top and bottom, the table could be made either

larger or smaller. I might remind you that for this project, as with most other contemporary work, all cuts and joinery must be precise. A poorly fitted joint will not only look unsightly, it will not provide maximum strength. The addition of the key spline in all the corners reinforces the joint and serves as a valuable aid in the glue-up and assembly process.

Begin by making parts A and B. I used oak, but most any hardwood would be fine. Start with 1¾ in. square stock about 22 in. long. The extra length allows for waste when cutting the miters. All the parts A and B ends are cut in the same manner with adjacent 45 degree miters. With the table saw miter gauge in the right hand slot, cut the first 45 degree miter (see mitering detail, Step 1), then flip the piece to the adjacent face (Step 2) and cut the second 45 degree miter (Step 3). Reverse the workpiece (keeping face A up) and cut the first 45 degree miter on the opposite end (Step 4). Flip the piece so face A is away from you (Step 5), and cut the last miter (Step 6). Repeat this procedure on all ends of parts A and B.

Next, cut the identical $\frac{1}{8}$ in. wide key spline grooves in the ends of parts A and B, as shown in the key spline detail. Note that the spline groove location is $1\frac{1}{4}$ in. from the tip. Make a simple V-groove block as

illustrated in the key spline groove cutting detail. An auxiliary rip fence (needed for the Sear's table saw) is clamped to the table, and the workpiece (parts A or B) is then clamped to the V-block. A V-clamp cleat will protect the workpiece edge. Set the saw blade at a 55 degree angle to the table, and adjust the height to $1\frac{1}{8}$ in. (measure from table to point of high tooth), which will result in a $\frac{3}{8}$ in. deep kerf being cut into parts A and B. Repeat on each end until all the key spline grooves have been cut.

The triangular splines, which are cut from $\frac{1}{8}$ in. plywood, will measure about $1\frac{3}{8}$ in. on all three sides. Size the splines a little bit under, however, to insure that they do not prevent the miters from

(continued on next page)

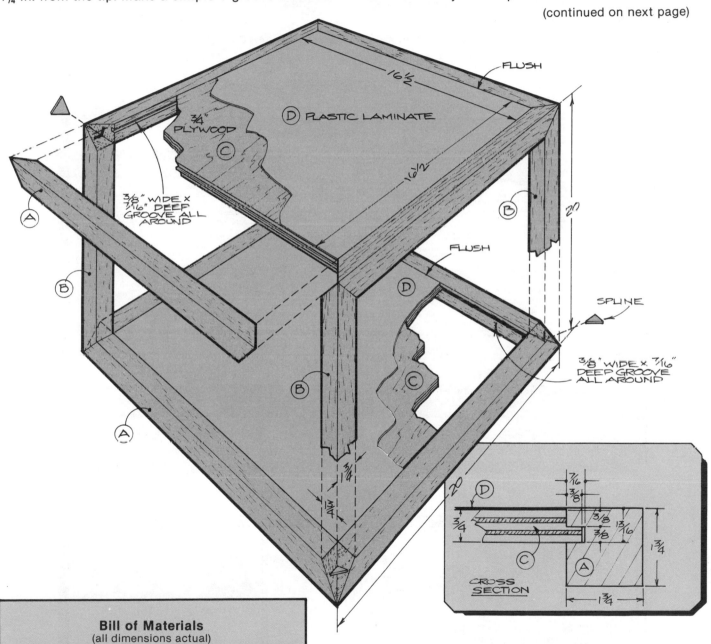

Part	Description	Size	No. Req'd.
A	Frame	$1\frac{3}{4} \times 1\frac{3}{4} \times 20$	8
B	Leg	$1\frac{3}{4} \times 1\frac{3}{4} \times 20$	4
C	Top & Bottom Core	$\frac{3}{4} \times 17\frac{1}{4} \times 17\frac{1}{4}$	2
D	Laminate	as needed	

Bill of Materials
(all dimensions actual)

meeting at the corner pieces during assembly. A dry assembly of the table will permit any adjustments that might be needed so that all parts fit up properly. Remember, accuracy is very important!

Now use the table saw dado head to cut the ⅜ in. by ⁷⁄₁₆ in. deep grooves on the inside face of the eight frame parts. Note that on the four frame parts that will form the top of the table, this groove location is ⅜ in. plus the laminate thickness from what will be the top edge, while with the four frame pieces around the table bottom, the groove is located ⅜ in. plus the laminate thickness from the *opposite* edge. The ¹⁄₁₆ in. extra depth in the dado will prevent the ⅜ in. long tongue on the top and bottom from bottoming, which could in turn prevent the shoulder from flushing with the frame.

The ¾ in. thick top and bottom core stock (C) is cut

next. Apply the laminate (D) to the core stock with contact cement. Then use the router and a rabbeting bit to cut the rabbet, resulting in the ⅜ in. by ⅜ in. tongue all around.

Assemble the frame members around the laminated top and bottom, using glue on the miters and in the tongue and grooves. Then add the key splines and the legs, applying glue to the miters and the splines. Strap clamps, located top and bottom and around the legs will provide a little clamping pressure. Only moderate pressure is needed since the key splines serve to hold the frame and leg parts in their proper position. As noted earlier, a dry run assembly of the completed table will insure that all parts fit as intended.

When dry, final sand the table, then finish with Watco Danish Oil. □

cutting the miters

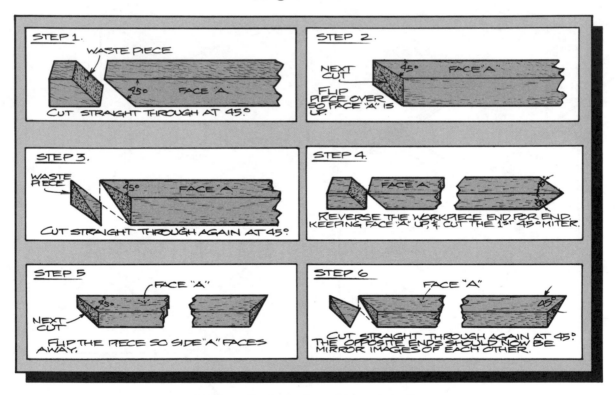

key spline and cutting details

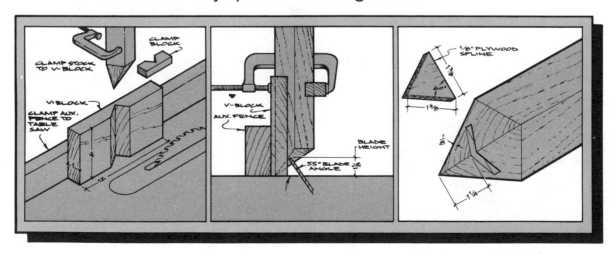

walnut chest

Placed at the foot of my bed, this walnut and laminate chest has withstood years as a dressing bench, in addition to its function as a chest, all the while looking every bit as good as the day I applied the original Danish Oil finish.

Begin by constructing the carcase. Cut parts A and B to width from ¾ in. thick walnut plywood, which is available from Constantine's, (see source index on page 161). Leave extra length on parts A and B since the ends are mitered *after* the ¼ in. by ¾ in. walnut edging is applied. Cut the ¼ in. deep by ¾ in. wide grooves that will accept the front and back frames, and rout the ¼ in. by ⅜ in. by 14¾ in. spline grooves. The location of these frame and spline grooves is illustrated in Fig. 1. Now make and assemble the front and back frames consisting of parts E, F, G, and H. The lap joint frame construction is shown in the lap joint detail. The front frame is solid walnut, although the back frame can be a secondary wood since it is not visible.

Parts A and B are assembled around the pre-assembled front and back frames, which are glued

into their respective grooves. The splines (D) used in the carcase assembly are ¼ in. by ¾ in. by 14¾ in. plywood. When dry, apply the ¼ in. radius around the front edge (see Fig. 1 "section").

Now cut the base front, back, and sides (parts I and J) to length and width from ¾ in. solid walnut stock, mitering the ends. Rout the ¼ in. by ⅜ in. by 2¾ in. spline grooves, and assemble the base using plywood splines, as illustrated in the base spline joint detail. The assembled base is simply glued to the chest carcase.

Now make the two interior end frames (parts K and L) and the one interior center frame (parts L and M), onto which the drawer guides will be mounted. All three interior frames, which like the back frame can be made of a secondary wood, are assembled *outside* the carcase using glue and screws. Take care that the length of parts L and M is exact, since if these parts are too long the assembled interior frames will not fit within the chest carcase. Mount the Accuride® drawer guides (N) to the interior frames, and tip the frames sideways to fit them into

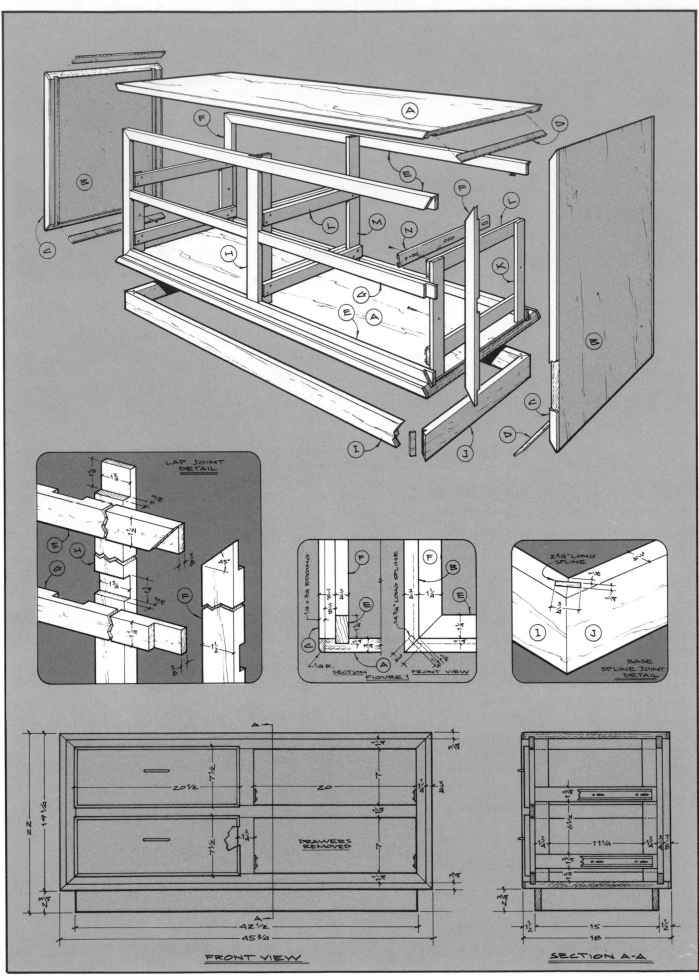

LAP JOINT DETAIL

BASE SPLINE JOINT DETAIL

2¾" LONG SPLINE

¼" x ¾ EDGING

14¾" LONG SPLINE

SECTION FIGURE 1

FRONT VIEW

DRAWERS REMOVED

FRONT VIEW

SECTION A-A

the chest. Screw the interior end frames in place, and glue the interior center frame along the front edge. This interior center frame is both glued and screwed at the back, inserting the screws through the back frame top and bottom (parts E).

Next, make the four drawers. The ½ in. thick plywood front (O) is laminated with both the plywood and the laminate (P) having been cut slightly oversize. I used a blue colored laminate, but you might prefer another color. Trim the laminated front to the final 7 in. by 20 in. size, then cut the ¼ in. by ½ in. dadoes to accept the sides, and the ¼ in. by ¼ in. groove to accept the bottom. Next, using solid ⅜ in. by ¾ in. walnut stock, make enough of the molding (Q), as shown in the drawer front detail top view, to trim all four drawer fronts. Miter the ends of this molding and glue it up around the drawer fronts. Also, pre-drill the fronts for the pull mounting screws. Next make the sides (R), grooving them for the bottom and back. Make the back (S), rabbeting the ends to accept the sides (see rabbet detail), and cutting the groove for the plywood bottom (T), which is cut to size next from ¼ in. thick plywood. The sides and back are also a secondary wood, since walnut is so costly. Assemble the drawers around the bottoms with glue.

For a satin smooth surface it is important to sand all wood surfaces thoroughly. I like to start with 100 grit, then follow with 150, 180, and 220. Once sanded, a coat of Watco Danish Oil (Natural) Finish is applied. I allow it to soak in for about 10 minutes before wiping off. When thoroughly dry (a day or two depending upon humidity), I add another coat of Watco, making sure the surfaces are well flooded. Now, using 220 grit sandpaper, I sand the wetted surfaces using a polishing motion. After sanding, it's wiped dry using the same motion. Allow several days for the piece to fully dry before adding two coats of paste (Butcher's) wax. □

Bill of Materials
(all dimensions actual)

Part	Description	Size	No. Req'd.
	Carcase		
A	Top & Bottom	¾ × 17½ × 45¾	2
B	Side	¾ × 17½ × 19¼	2
C	Edging	¼ × ¾ stock	as needed
D	Spline	¼ × ¾ × 14¾	4
E	Frame Top & Bottom	¾ × 1½ × 44¾	4
F	Frame Side	¾ × 1½ × 18¼	4
G	Frame Stretcher, Horizontal	¾ × 1¼ × 44¾	1
H	Frame Stretcher, Vertical	¾ × 1¾ × 18¼	1
I	Base Front & Back	¾ × 2¾ × 42½	2
J	Base Side	¾ × 2¾ × 15	2
K	Interior End Frame Stile	¾ × 1¾ × 11¾	4
L	Interior Frame Rail	¾ × 1¾ × 14¾	8
M	Interior Center Frame Stile	¾ × 1¾ × 17¾	2
N	Drawer Guide*	Accuride® 14 in. long	4 pair
	Drawer		
O	Front	½ × 7 × 20	4
P	Laminate	as needed	
Q	Molding	⅜ × ¾ corner	as needed
R	Side	½ × 7 × 15¾	8
S	Back	½ × 7 × 18	4
T	Bottom	¼ × 15½ × 18	4
U	Pull*	3 in. brass finish U-shaped	4

*Available from The Woodworkers' Store, (see source index on page 161).

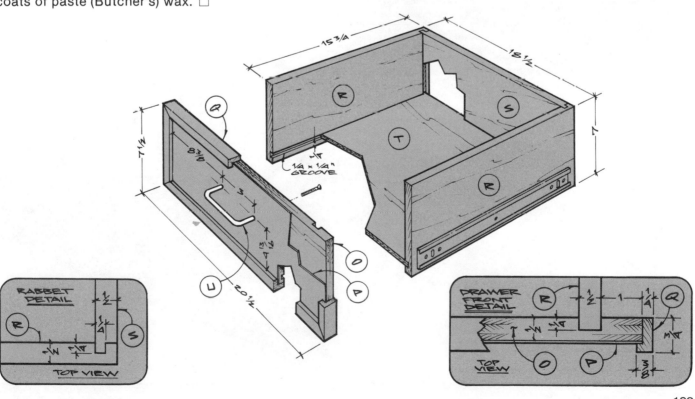

RABBET DETAIL — R — S — ½ — ¼ — TOP VIEW

DRAWER FRONT DETAIL — R — Q — ½ — 1 — 1¼ — TOP VIEW — O — P — ⅜

kitchen

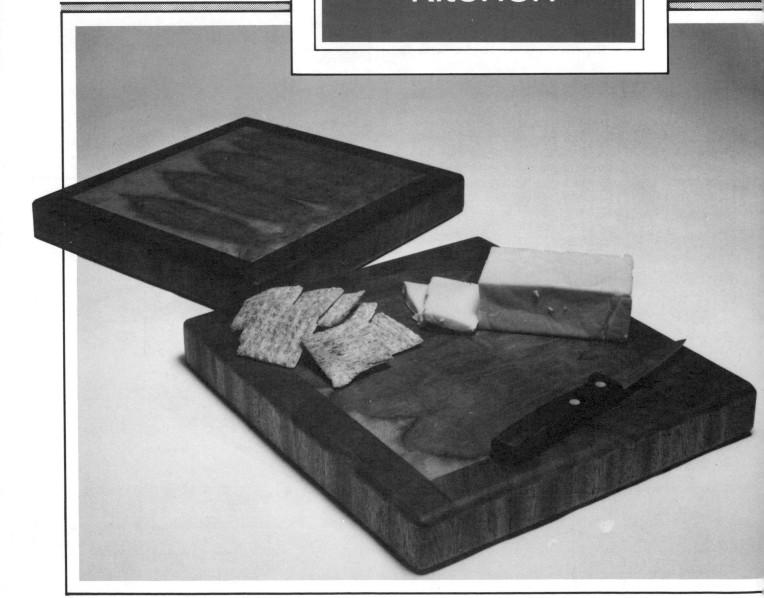

salt & pepper shakers

t hese salt and pepper shaker sets each have their own distinctive look, although the construction and assembly techniques are nearly identical. One set is crafted from alternating layers of oak and walnut, while the other set is made from stacked sections of ¾ in. thick Baltic birch plywood. Cork or rubber plugs serve as the stoppers.

Make the oak and walnut set as shown in steps one through five. I think you will agree that the contrast established by the light colored oak next to the dark walnut is quite attractive, however other combinations of contrasting woods can also be used.

The 1⅝ in. square oak base block is cut 4 in. long for the salt shaker and 2 in. long for the pepper shaker. Remember to align the grain of the ¼ and ¾ in. thick laminates so it all faces in the same direction. The ¼ in. thick top walnut section is added *after* the shakers have been centerbored. A Forstner bit will facilitate centerboring both sets of shakers, and is recommended for its clean and accurate cutting capability.

The second set of shakers is made by laminating 1⅝ in. square layers of ¾ in. thick Baltic birch plywood. I specify Baltic birch because it has no gaps or voids, and for the especially sharp contrast between the individual veneer plies. As you will note there are four layers for the pepper shaker and six layers for the salt shaker (see Baltic birch shaker illustration).

All the shakers are counterbored 1¼ in. by ½ in. deep at the bottom. This recess is to accommodate the stoppers, and should provide sufficient space for your fingers to grip them.

Sand all surfaces flush, round edges and corners and apply a non-toxic finish such as Behlen's Salad Bowl Finish (available from Woodcraft Supply Corp., see source index). □

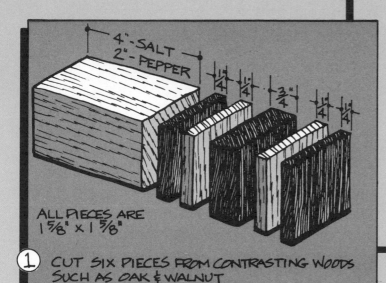

4" - SALT
2" - PEPPER

ALL PIECES ARE
1 5/8" × 1 5/8"

① CUT SIX PIECES FROM CONTRASTING WOODS
SUCH AS OAK & WALNUT

KEEP ALL END
GRAIN FACING
THE SAME WAY

② GLUE & CLAMP 5 PIECES AS SHOWN
(TOP PIECE IS ADDED LATER)

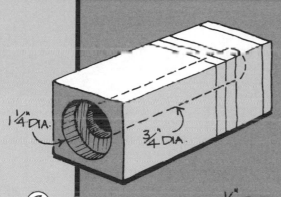

1 1/4" DIA.

3/4" DIA.

③ COUNTERBORE BOTTOM 1/2" DEEP,
THEN CENTERBORE COMPLETELY
THROUGH WITH 3/4" BIT

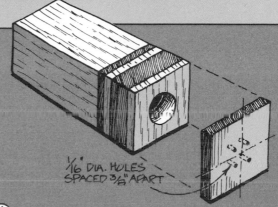

1/16" DIA. HOLES
SPACED 3/8" APART

④ GLUE AND CLAMP TOP PIECE. DRILL SMALL
HOLES THROUGH TOP INTO CENTRAL BORE

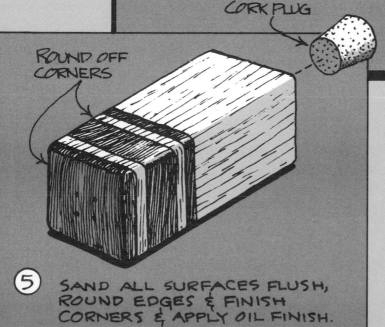

CORK PLUG

ROUND OFF
CORNERS

⑤ SAND ALL SURFACES FLUSH,
ROUND EDGES & FINISH
CORNERS & APPLY OIL FINISH.

1 5/8" × 1 5/8" PIECES OF
3/4" BALTIC BIRCH PLYWOOD

6 LAYERS - SALT
4 LAYERS - PEPPER

GLUE AND CLAMP 4 PIECES
FOR PEPPER, 6 PIECES
FOR SALT. COUNTER BORE
BOTTOM 1/2" DEEP × 1 1/4" DIA,
THEN USE 3/4" DIA FORST-
NER BIT TO CENTER BORE
TO WITHIN 1/4" OF TOP.
DRILL 4 HOLES; SAME
SPACING AS STEP 4.

133

cutting boards

I make these attractive cutting boards from scrap stock. Whether they are crafted from oak, walnut, maple, ash, or from some of the imported and exotic woods such as teak, purpleheart, and padouk, they are both easy and inexpensive to produce. They are perennial best sellers at fairs, shows and craft expos, and make great gifts.

To obtain the eight pieces for the bookmatched center, start with 1 in. thick stock 8 in. wide by 11¼ in. long. The extra length allows for the saw kerfs and a little scrap and the additional width provides for trimming after the first assembly step. Crosscut the stock into eight 1¼ in. wide strips, keeping them in consecutive order.

To create the bookmatches, flip the first, third, fifth and seventh pieces over one face, counter-clockwise, then flip the second, fourth, sixth, and eighth pieces over one face clockwise. You will now have all end grain facing up, with the eight pieces resulting in four bookmatches.

I recommend a contrasting wood for the 1⅛ in. by 1¼ in. end grain frame. I also bookmatched these frame pieces for an added detail.

Glue and assemble the eight bookmatched center pieces and the four end frame pieces. Then trim on the table saw, as illustrated, to 7½ in. Add the six side frame pieces and, when dry, belt sand all surfaces flush. A ¼ in. radius is then applied to the edges using a ¼ in. bearing-guided round-over bit.

After hand sanding with 320 grit paper, wipe on several coats of Salad Bowl Finish, available from Woodcraft Supply Corp., (see source index). □

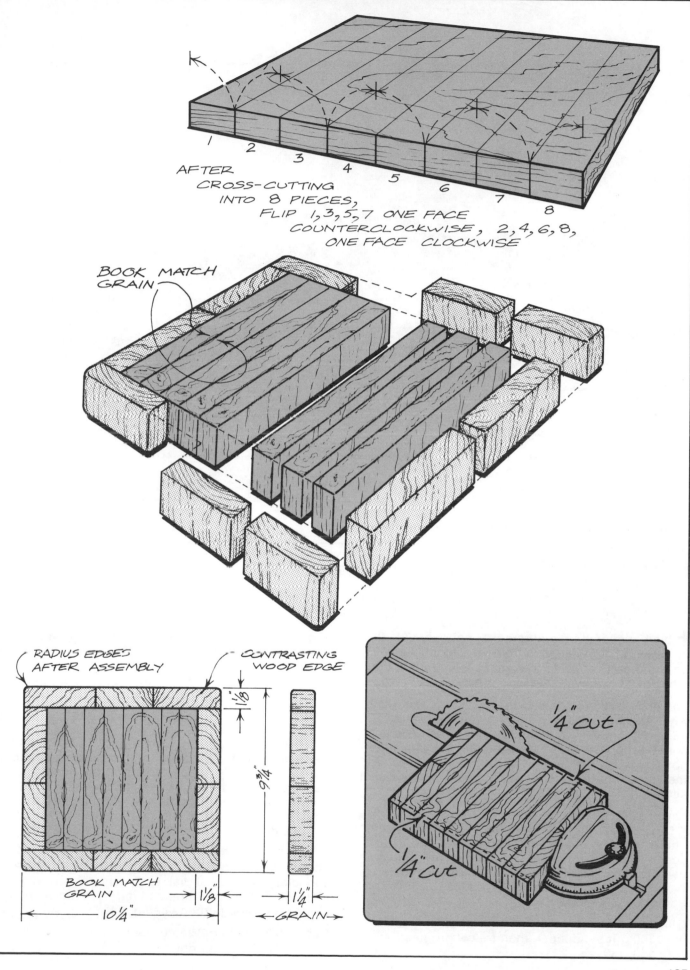

AFTER
CROSS-CUTTING
INTO 8 PIECES,
FLIP 1,3,5,7 ONE FACE
COUNTERCLOCKWISE, 2,4,6,8,
ONE FACE CLOCKWISE

1 2 3 4 5 6 7 8

BOOK MATCH
GRAIN

RADIUS EDGES
AFTER ASSEMBLY

CONTRASTING
WOOD EDGE

1 1/8"

9 3/4"

BOOK MATCH
GRAIN

1 1/8"

10 1/4"

1 1/4"

← GRAIN →

1/4" CUT

1/4" CUT

nutcracker

t his handsome little nutcracker not only gets the job done, it looks good doing it. The plywood bottom neatly collects the pieces, eliminating the mess usually associated with cracking nuts.

The ends of the box are crafted of $\frac{1}{2}$ in. thick walnut, while the sides are $\frac{1}{2}$ in. maple, and the bottom is $\frac{1}{4}$ in. by $1\frac{3}{4}$ in. by $2\frac{1}{2}$ in. birch plywood. The dovetailed construction is needed to withstand the strain the box will be subjected to when a nut is cracked, and the use of contrasting woods provides a nice visual accent.

Lay out and cut the dovetails as shown. Then drill a $\frac{1}{8}$ in. deep by $1\frac{1}{4}$ in. diameter recess on the inside of one end, and drill and tap the opposite end to accept the 1 in. threaded rod. The tap and threadbox used for this project are available from Conover Woodcraft Specialties, Inc., 18125 Madison Road, Parkman, OH 44080.

Glue and assemble the box and, when dry, sand with 100 grit sandpaper, then follow progressively with 150, 180, and 220 grit.

The threaded rod is made from a 5 in. length of $1\frac{1}{8}$ in. square maple. After turning to a 1 in. diameter, fashion the $\frac{1}{2}$ in. square by $\frac{3}{8}$ in. long tenon on one end. Use the threadbox to cut the 1 in. threads along the remaining rod, then trim to a final $3\frac{1}{2}$ in. length.

The handle is fashioned from a $\frac{3}{4}$ in. by 1 in. by 4 in. piece of mahogany. Referring to the full-size pattern, lay out the handle shape. Note that the handle narrows to $\frac{1}{2}$ in. thick at the middle when viewed from the side, and flares to 1 in. wide across the middle in the top view. After cutting the $\frac{1}{2}$ in. square by $\frac{3}{8}$ in. deep mortise, sand the handle and glue onto the tenoned end of the threaded rod.

Thread the rod into the box, and glue a $\frac{1}{4}$ in. thick by 1 in. diameter walnut disk to the end, as shown. This disk will prevent the threaded rod from unscrewing completely, and perhaps being lost.

Rub in two coats of Watco Danish Oil to achieve a soft, natural looking finish. □

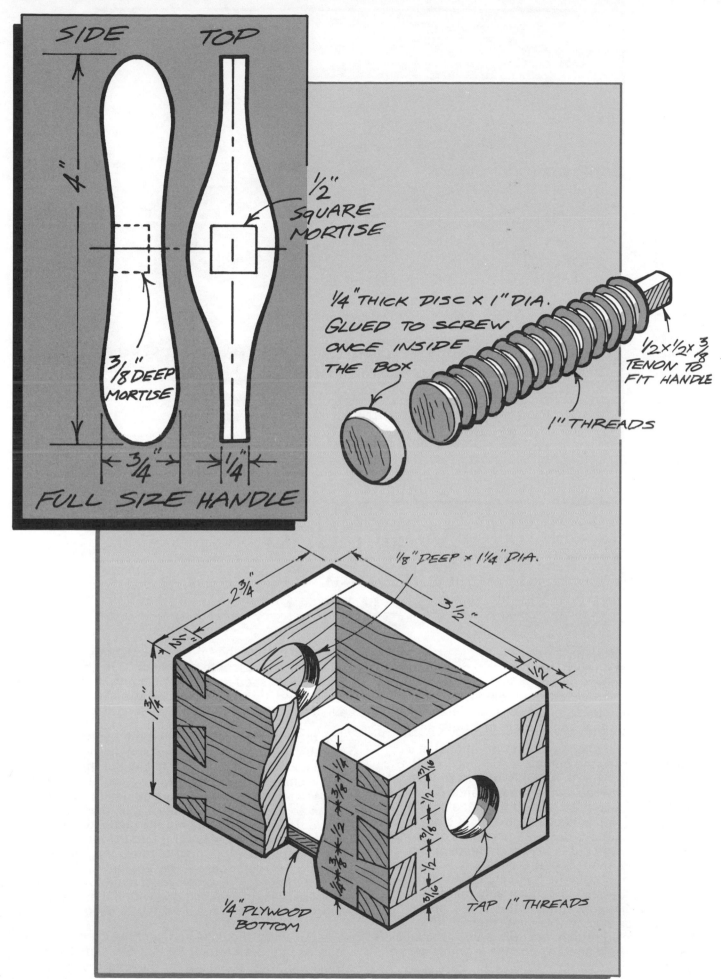

SIDE   TOP

4"

1/2" SQUARE MORTISE

3/8" DEEP MORTISE

3/4"   1/4"

FULL SIZE HANDLE

1/4" THICK DISC x 1" DIA. GLUED TO SCREW ONCE INSIDE THE BOX

1/2 x 1/2 x 3/8 TENON TO FIT HANDLE

1" THREADS

1/8" DEEP x 1 1/4" DIA.

2 3/4"

3 1/2"

1/2

3"

1/4
3/8
1/2
3/8
1/4

3/16
1/2
3/16
1/2
3/16

1/4" PLYWOOD BOTTOM

TAP 1" THREADS

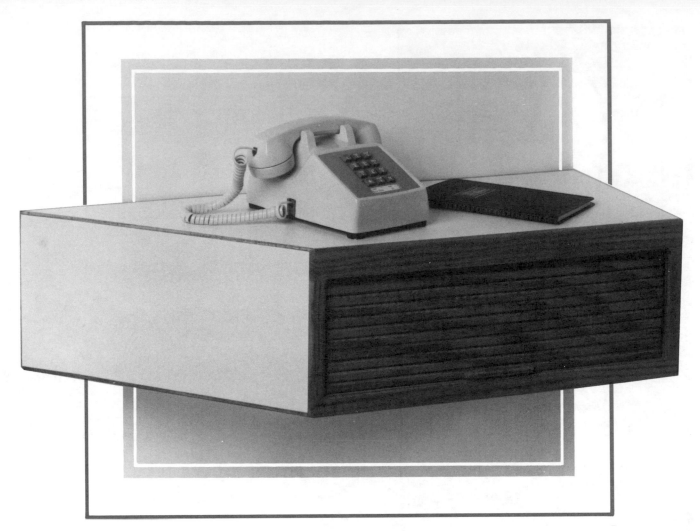

wall hung telephone cabinet

m ixing the warmth of oak with the practicality of plastic laminate, this multi-purpose shelf is a handy addition in the kitchen. Usable as a telephone shelf, mini-desk or counter surface, it can also conceal note paper, pencils, and many other odds and ends that accumulate in a busy kitchen.

The trapezoidal shape provides additional shelf space and gives the piece a less "boxy" look. The top and bottom (parts A and B) are made from ¾ in. thick birch plywood, while the box ends (C), the case end (D), the case back (E) and the false back (F) are made from ¾ in. solid oak stock. Solid stock was selected for parts C because tambours do not slide easily in grooves cut in plywood. Readers should keep in mind, though, that it generally is not good practice to apply plastic laminate directly to solid stock. With seasonal changes in humidity, solid stock will change width and this could cause warping. However, in this case, there is little likelihood of a problem occurring since the stock is relatively narrow and any change in width will be minimal.

Begin by cutting the top and the bottom to a width of 11½ in. and a length of around 33 in. (see Fig. 1). Trim one end square, then at a point 20 in. from the square end, crosscut the stock at a 45-degree angle as shown. The resulting overall length will be 31½ in.

The project is designed so that the tambour can be installed (or removed if necessary) through a slot in the back of part B (see Fig. 1). Lay out the location of the slot as shown, then equip a router with a ¾ in. diameter straight bit. Clamp a guidestrip to the stock and set the bit to make a ¼ in. deep cut. With the router base held against the guidestip, start the router, then carefully lower it into the stock. Move the router from left to right to make the cut, always holding the router base firmly against the guidestrip. To cut through ¾ in. stock you'll need to make two more passes; the second one with the bit set ½ in. deep, the third with the bit set ¾ in. deep.

The box ends, the case end, and the case back can now be cut to a width of 6⅜ in. from ¾ in. thick solid stock. Allow a little extra for the length of each piece. Lay the parts on the bottom (see Fig. 2), then mark and cut to the exact length. Miter both ends of the case end and one end of the case back as shown.

Next, the tambour groove is cut in each box end. You'll need a router equipped with a $\frac{1}{4}$ in. diameter straight bit and a $\frac{7}{16}$ in. guide bushing (available from Sears). To guide the router, you'll also need a template (see Fig. 3) made from $\frac{1}{4}$ in. hardboard. Once the template is made, locate it in its proper position (see Fig. 4), then tack it in place with three or four small brads driven flush with the surface of the template. Cut the groove in a counterclockwise direction with the router guide bushing held firmly against the template. *Note:* Parts C are not identical. Instead, the routed tambour grooves in the two parts C are mirror images of each other. Begin by marking the inside faces of both parts C. Figure 4 shows the template located $\frac{19}{32}$ in. from the *left* side or front edge (inside face up) of the left side part C, to rout the left side tambour groove. To rout the right side tambour groove, locate the template $\frac{19}{32}$ in. from the *right* or front edge of the right side part C, inside face up, of course.

Parts A, B, C, D, and E can now be assembled. Use glue and secure with countersunk flat-headed wood screws. Much of the case will be covered with plastic laminate, so work carefully to insure that the joints are flush with each other. Any unevenness at a joint will have to be trimmed flush before the laminate is applied. Since the tambours will be installed between parts C, it's important that these two ends be parallel to each other and at right angles to parts A and B.

The plastic laminate (parts N, O, and P) can now be applied. I chose a white matte finish laminate, although many readers will, no doubt, want to select other colors. To secure the laminate, apply two coats of solvent base contact cement to both the laminate and the wood. Cut the laminate slightly wider and longer than necessary, then apply to the case before trimming with a router equipped with a laminate trimmer. Use a hand plane to trim the mitered end.

Next, a $\frac{1}{4}$ in. by $\frac{1}{4}$ in. rabbet is cut on the side edges of the top to accept the right side (Q) and left side (R) edging. I used an edge-guided router with a $\frac{3}{8}$ in. straight bit to cut these rabbets, taking care to move the router from right to left to prevent chipping the laminate. After the first pass, I then ran the router from left to right to clean up the cut.

The right side and left side edging are cut to $\frac{5}{16}$ in. square and glued into the rabbets. Once dry, use a laminate trimmer or block plane to cut the edging flush to the surface of the laminate.

Parts K, L, and M can now be cut to size and joined to the front of the cabinet. It's best to cut the parts a little wider than necessary so that they can be trimmed flush to their mating surfaces. Assemble with glue and clamps.

Rip the $\frac{1}{4}$ in. thick trim stock (parts S, T, U, V, and W) a little wider than necessary, then glue in place as shown. Trim any overhang with a block plane.

Make the tambours (I) next. Try to select a piece of wood with an attractive grain pattern (I chose a piece of curly red oak), then surface plane the stock to a thickness of $\frac{3}{8}$ in. To minimize any tendency to warp, it's best to plane the same amount of material from each side of the stock. As soon as the tambours are ripped to width, though, a number of strips will probably warp to the point of being useless, so it's a good idea to allow for some extra stock.

Next, rip the stock into $\frac{1}{2}$ in. wide tambour strips. Keep the strips in the sequence they are ripped so that later, when they are glued to the canvas, the original grain pattern will be preserved. Once ripped, cull out any warped or twisted strips. (If too many strips warp, you may have to abandon the idea of keeping the grain pattern in sequence.) Then apply the 45-degree chamfer with a chamfering bit. A router table or shaper will come in handy here, although it can also be done using a hand plane.

Cut the tambours to final length, then lay out all 23 of them bevel side up on a piece of scrap plywood or particleboard. Next, form a supporting frame all around the 23 tambours by nailing batten strips in place (see Fig. 5). These batten strips should be

(continued on next page)

about 1½ in. wide and not any thicker than the ⅜ in. thick tambours. Make sure that the frame is square and that the tambours are held firmly in place.

With a guidestrip clamped to the tambours, use a router with a ⅜ in. diameter straight bit to cut the shoulder on each end of the tambours (see Fig. 6). Now each piece can be removed from the batten strip frame and given a good sanding. Once sanded, place them back in the frame. Make sure they are in sequence and facing bevel side down. Cut a piece of artist's canvas (available at art supply shops) to size. Apply a thin coat of yellow glue to the back of the tambours, then add the canvas (H). Gently stretch it out, pressing into the glue. Allow 24 hours to dry, then trim the canvas about ⅜ in. from each shouldered end.

At this point you should test fit the completed

tambours. Apply a coat of paraffin wax to the tambour ends for lubrication. If they fit properly and slide easily along the groove as intended, remove the tambours and mount the cabinet to the wall with four 2½ in. long by no. 10 wood screws. The 16 in. on center screw mounting holes (to accommodate conventional wood frame wall construction) should have been pre-drilled and countersunk through the back. With the cabinet in place on the wall, insert the tambours and add the two cleats (F) which serve to both support the false back (G) and act as stops for the tambours. Two small felt dots are glued to the top of each cleat to cushion the tambour when it hits. Screw the false back in place as shown, and last of all, add the pull (J) which is secured with a pair of small brass screws (see pull detail).

Several coats of Watco Danish Oil applied to all wood parts provide a good final finish. □

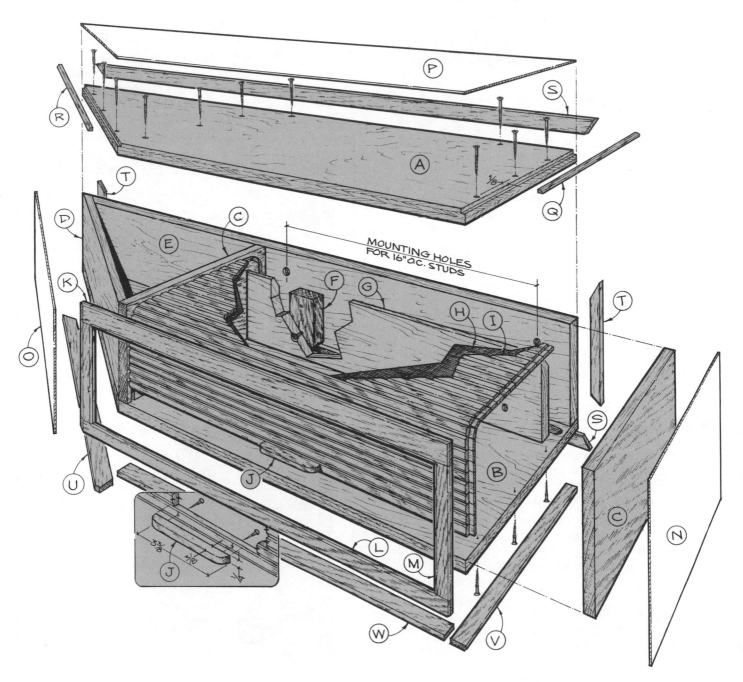

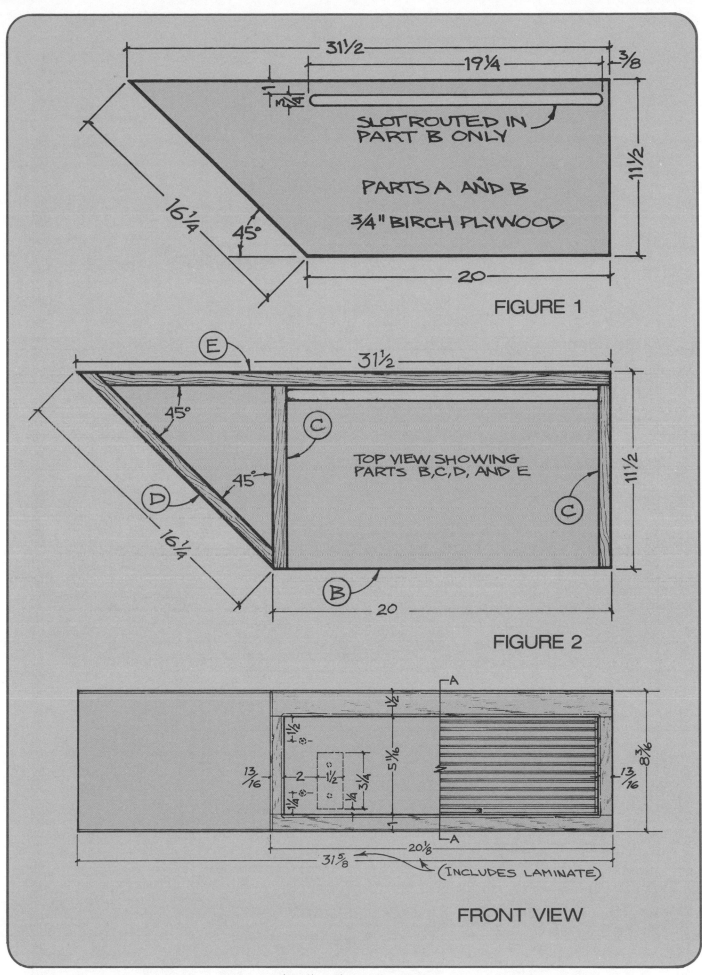

SLOT ROUTED IN
PART B ONLY

PARTS A AND B

3/4" BIRCH PLYWOOD

FIGURE 1

TOP VIEW SHOWING
PARTS B, C, D, AND E

FIGURE 2

(INCLUDES LAMINATE)

FRONT VIEW

(continued on next page)

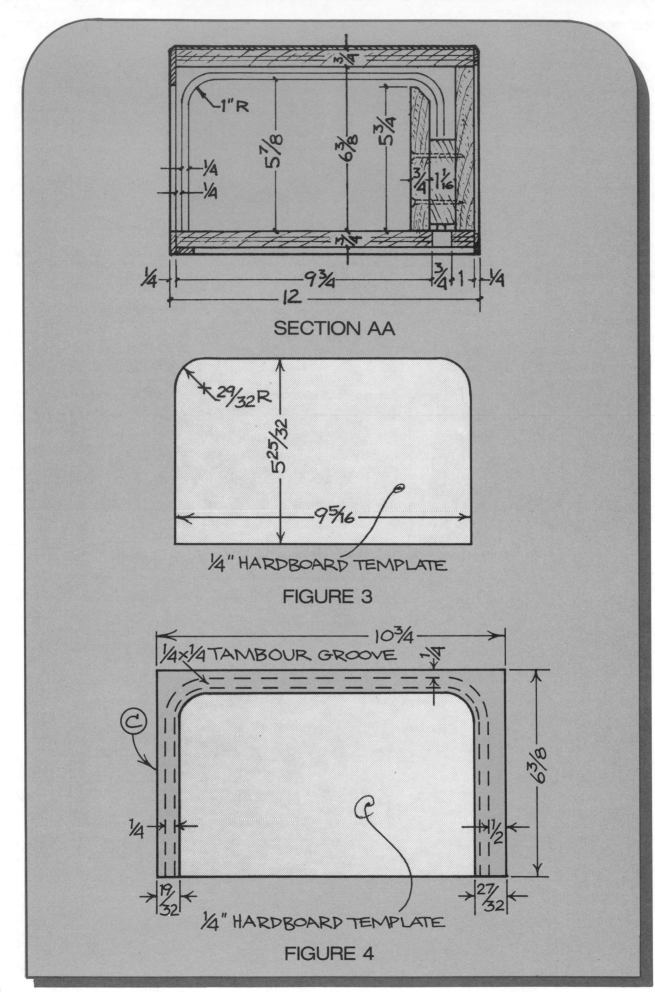

SECTION AA

¼" HARDBOARD TEMPLATE

FIGURE 3

¼ x ¼ TAMBOUR GROOVE

¼" HARDBOARD TEMPLATE

FIGURE 4

cutting tambour shoulders

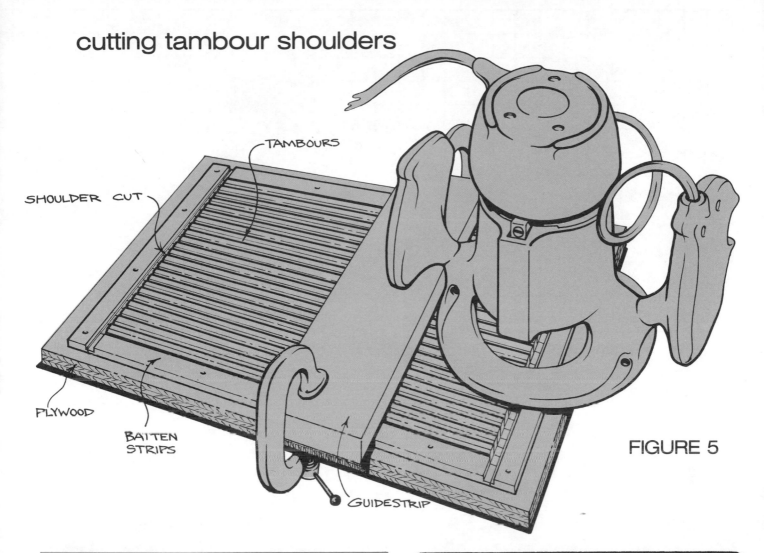

TAMBOURS

SHOULDER CUT

PLYWOOD

BATTEN STRIPS

GUIDESTRIP

FIGURE 5

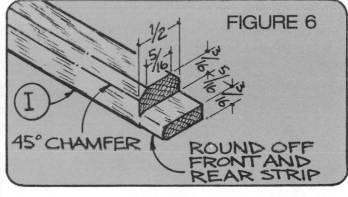

FIGURE 6

I

45° CHAMFER

ROUND OFF FRONT AND REAR STRIP

1/2

5/16

3/8

5/16

3/8

Bill of Materials
(all dimensions actual)

Part	Description	Size	No. Req'd.
A	Top	$\frac{3}{4} \times 11\frac{1}{2} \times 31\frac{1}{2}$	1
B	Bottom	$\frac{3}{4} \times 11\frac{1}{2} \times 31\frac{1}{2}$	1
C	Box End	$\frac{3}{4} \times 6\frac{3}{8} \times 10\frac{3}{4}$	2
D	Case End	$\frac{3}{4} \times 6\frac{3}{8} \times 16\frac{1}{4}$	1
E	Case Back	$\frac{3}{4} \times 6\frac{3}{8} \times 30\frac{1}{2}$	1
F	Cleat	$1\frac{1}{16} \times 1\frac{1}{2} \times 3\frac{1}{4}$	2
G	False Back	$\frac{3}{4} \times 5\frac{3}{4} \times 18\frac{1}{2}$	1
H	Canvas	$11\frac{1}{2} \times 17\frac{1}{2}$	1
I	Tambour	$\frac{3}{8} \times \frac{1}{2} \times 18\frac{7}{8}$	23
J	Pull	$\frac{1}{4} \times \frac{3}{8} \times 3\frac{3}{8}$	1
K	Top Front Edging	$\frac{1}{4} \times 1\frac{1}{2} \times 20\frac{1}{8}$	1
L	Bottom Front Edging	$\frac{1}{4} \times 1 \times 20\frac{1}{8}$	1
M	Front Side Edging	$\frac{1}{4} \times \frac{13}{16} \times 5\frac{11}{16}$	2
N	Right Side Laminate	as needed	1
O	Left Side Laminate	as needed	1
P	Top Laminate	as needed	1
Q	Right Side Edging	$\frac{1}{4} \times \frac{1}{4} \times 11\frac{1}{2}$	1
R	Left Side Edging	$\frac{1}{4} \times \frac{1}{4} \times 16\frac{1}{4}$	1
S	Top/Bottom Back Trim	$\frac{1}{4} \times \frac{3}{4} \times 31\frac{5}{8}$	2
T	Back End Trim	$\frac{1}{4} \times \frac{3}{4} \times 8\frac{3}{16}$	2
U	Left Bottom Trim	$\frac{1}{4} \times \frac{3}{4} \times 23\frac{1}{4}$	1
V	Right Bottom Trim	$\frac{1}{4} \times \frac{3}{4} \times 10\frac{3}{4}$	1
W	Front Bottom Trim	$\frac{1}{4} \times \frac{3}{4} \times 20\frac{1}{8}$	1

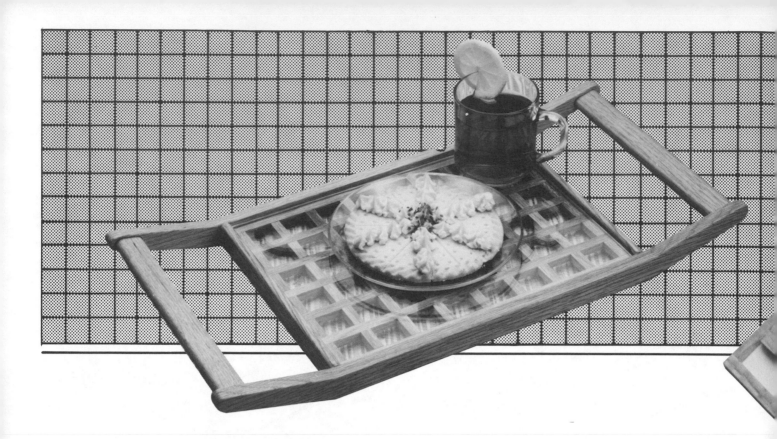

latticework

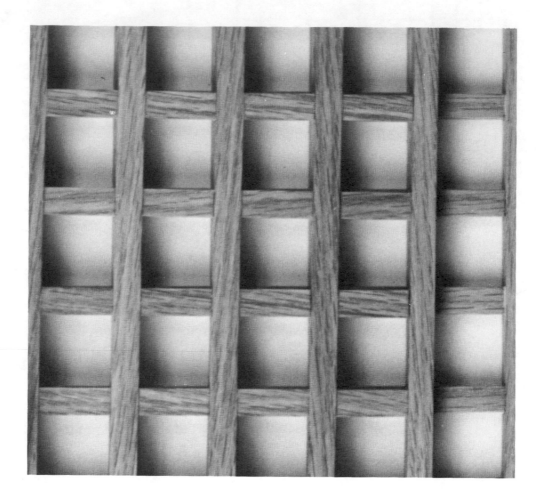

I used this lattice cutting technique to make the next five projects. Note that the first four projects use $\frac{3}{8}$ in. square stock for the lattice, while the shoji lamp features $\frac{1}{4}$ in. square material. You must make two separate jigs, one for the $\frac{3}{8}$ in. stock, and another for the $\frac{1}{4}$ in. stock. The technique and these jigs may come in handy with other woodworking projects.

Crisscross patterns require quite a few half-lap joints, and the purpose of this table saw jig is to simplify the task of cutting and locating all those joints. The design is fairly straightforward so the jig can be built in just a short time.

Radial arm saw owners can adapt this same basic idea to their saws. They need only to cut an identical hardwood index pin which is also glued to an auxiliary fence. The auxiliary fence is clamped to the radial saw's guide fence with the index pin oriented using the same basic idea as is used with the table saw jig.

When all dadoes have been cut, the jig is removed. Using the saw's fence, the workpiece is ripped into strips, each having a thickness equal to the dado groove width. *Assembly Notes:* The individual lattice or grid strips should be sanded to remove saw marks before assembly. The lattice is glued up with a drop of white or yellow glue at each half lap joint. Check the assembled lattice for squareness and place a layer of waxed paper on both sides. Then flatten and weigh the lattice down with books or some other flat, heavy object. □

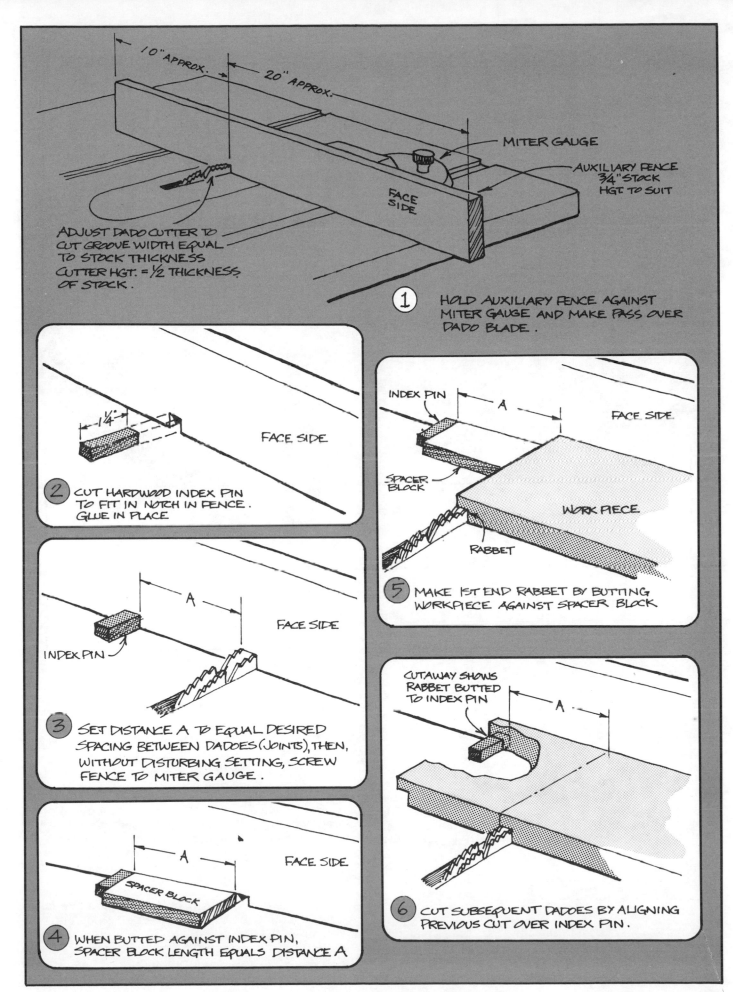

10" APPROX.

20" APPROX.

MITER GAUGE

AUXILIARY FENCE ¾" STOCK HGT TO SUIT

FACE SIDE

ADJUST DADO CUTTER TO CUT GROOVE WIDTH EQUAL TO STOCK THICKNESS CUTTER HGT. = ½ THICKNESS OF STOCK.

1 HOLD AUXILIARY FENCE AGAINST MITER GAUGE AND MAKE PASS OVER DADO BLADE.

1¼"

FACE SIDE

2 CUT HARDWOOD INDEX PIN TO FIT IN NOTCH IN FENCE. GLUE IN PLACE

A

FACE SIDE

INDEX PIN

3 SET DISTANCE A TO EQUAL DESIRED SPACING BETWEEN DADOES (JOINTS), THEN, WITHOUT DISTURBING SETTING, SCREW FENCE TO MITER GAUGE.

A

FACE SIDE

SPACER BLOCK

4 WHEN BUTTED AGAINST INDEX PIN, SPACER BLOCK LENGTH EQUALS DISTANCE A

INDEX PIN

A

FACE SIDE

SPACER BLOCK

WORK PIECE

RABBET

5 MAKE 1ST END RABBET BY BUTTING WORKPIECE AGAINST SPACER BLOCK

CUTAWAY SHOWS RABBET BUTTED TO INDEX PIN

A

6 CUT SUBSEQUENT DADOES BY ALIGNING PREVIOUS CUT OVER INDEX PIN.

napkin holder

this attractive napkin holder is constructed using the lattice cutting jig shown on page 146. Although I used red oak for the napkin holder, trivets (page 150), and coasters (page 152), most any hardwood can be used. Whether you use maple, ash, teak, or rosewood, remember that all three of these projects should be made from the same wood if you are to have a matching set.

The napkin holder features ⅜ by ⅜ in. grid, spaced 1 in. apart. After making the lattice (parts A and B), the retainer (C), and the edging (D), apply the plastic

laminate (E) to both sides of a piece of ¼ in. thick plywood (F). I used white or yellow glue instead of contact cement (which is usually used to apply laminates) since it reduced the work time. Start with both the plywood and laminate slightly oversized and trim the assembly to the final 6¼ in. square dimension on the table saw after the glue has set.

Assemble the grid work with a drop of glue at each dado joint and when dry, sand the grid sides and edges smooth. Glue and clamp the edging and the two grid assemblies around the laminated plywood. Finish the wood with penetrating oil. □

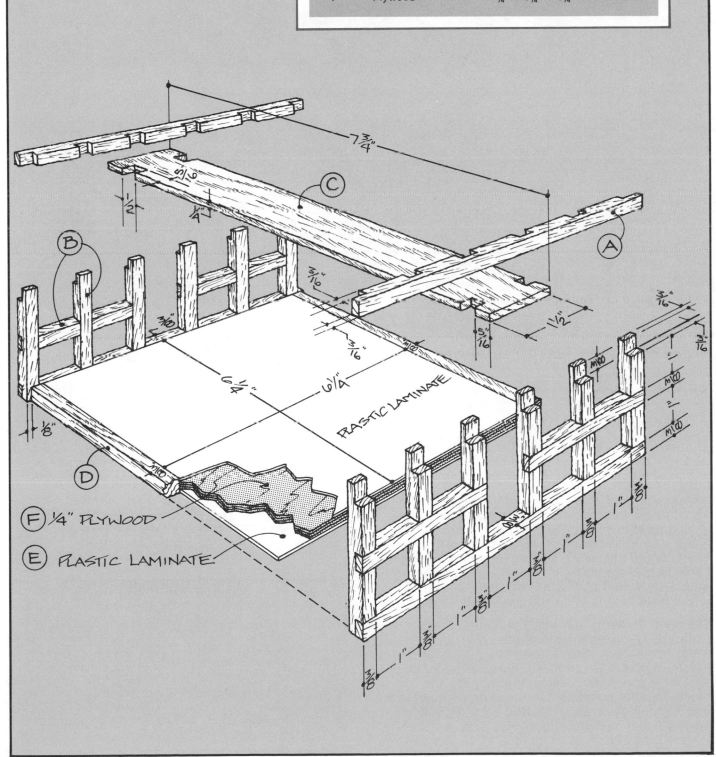

Bill of Materials
(all dimensions actual)

Part	Description	Size	No. Req'd.
A	Long Grid	$\frac{3}{8} \times \frac{3}{8} \times 7\frac{1}{4}$	4
B	Short Grid	$\frac{3}{8} \times \frac{3}{8} \times 3\frac{1}{8}$	16
C	Napkin Retainer	$\frac{1}{4} \times 1\frac{1}{2} \times 7\frac{3}{4}$	1
D	Edging	$\frac{3}{8} \times \frac{3}{8} \times 6\frac{1}{4}$	2
E	Laminate	$\frac{1}{16} \times 6\frac{1}{4} \times 6\frac{1}{4}$	2
F	Plywood	$\frac{1}{4} \times 6\frac{1}{4} \times 6\frac{1}{4}$	1

F ¼" PLYWOOD

E PLASTIC LAMINATE

PLASTIC LAMINATE

149

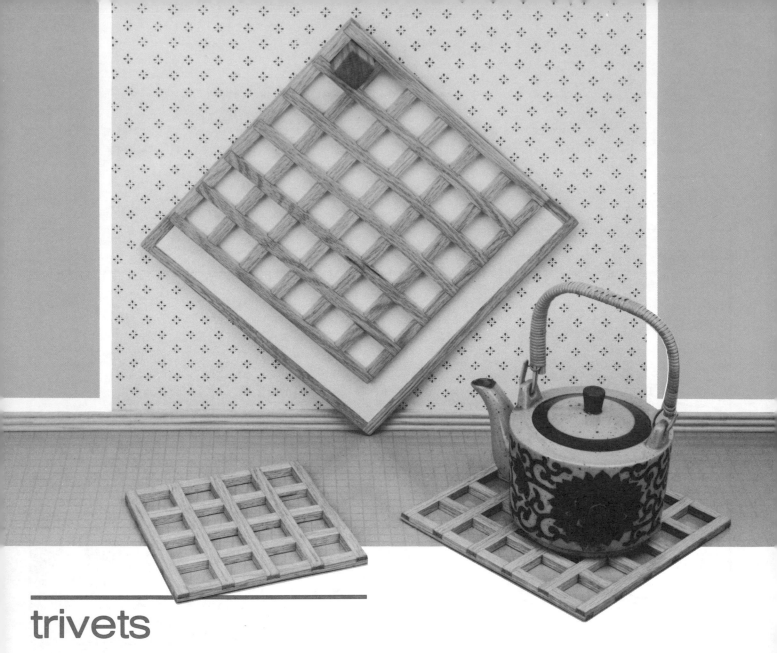

trivets

t hese trivets should be constructed from the same wood you used for the napkin holder and coasters if you intend to have a matching set.

As you will note, there are three trivets, each sized 1⅜ in. larger than the one before. Make the grid pieces as shown on page 146. For the small trivet make 10 grid pieces 5⅞ in. long (A), for the medium trivet 12 grid pieces 7¼ in. long (B), and for the large trivet 14 grid pieces 8⅝ in. long (C). Assemble the grids with a spot of glue at each half lap (see latticework detail), and sand the trivets smooth.

The trivet holder is made by first gluing the plastic laminate (G) on either side of the plywood (F). I used white laminate for the napkin holder, coaster, and trivet projects, but you may prefer a different color. Whatever your choice, remember to keep the laminate color consistent in these three projects for that matching set look. I started out with both the laminate and plywood slightly oversize, and then trimmed the assembly to its final 9¼ in. square

dimension on the table saw. Add the edging (D and E) as shown, and screw the block (H) in place at one corner to serve as an anchor for the three trivets.

Final sand and finish all the wood surfaces with the same penetrating oil you used for the napkin holder and coasters. The trivets may either be set on the table, or they can be hung on the wall. □

Bill of Materials (all dimensions actual)			
Part	Description	Size	No. Req'd.
A	Small Trivet Grid	⅜ × ⅜ × 5⅞	10
B	Medium Trivet Grid	⅜ × ⅜ × 7¼	12
C	Large Trivet Grid	⅜ × ⅜ × 8⅝	14
D	Side Edging	⅜ × ⅜ × 9¼	2
E	End Edging	⅜ × ⅜ × 10	2
F	Plywood	¼ × 9¼ × 9¼	1
G	Laminate	¹⁄₁₆ × 9¼ × 9¼	2
H	Block	¹⁵⁄₁₆ × ¹⁵⁄₁₆ × 1½	1

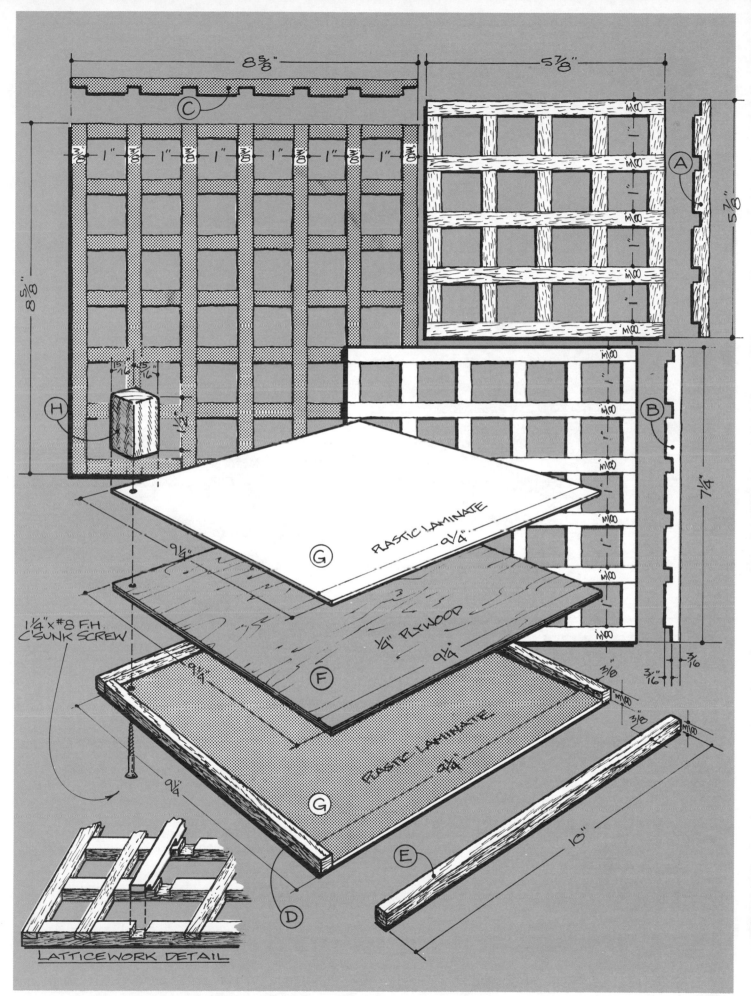

8⅝"

5⅞"

5⅞"

C

A

8⅝"

¾" 1" ¾" 1" ¾" 1" ¾" 1" ¾" 1" ¾"

7¼"

H

15/16" 15/16"

1½"

B

PLASTIC LAMINATE
9¼"

G

9¼"

½" PLYWOOD
9¼"

F

1¼" x #8 F.H.
C'SUNK SCREW

9¼"

PLASTIC LAMINATE
9¼"

G

3/8"

3/16"

3/16"

3/8"

10"

E

D

LATTICEWORK DETAIL

151

coasters

these coasters complete the three piece table setting that includes the rack of trivets and the napkin holder. Use the same hardwood and laminate combination that you selected for the other two projects.

As with the two previous projects, refer to page 146 for a step-by-step guide to cutting the coaster gridstock (A). The jig need not be altered since both the ⅜ in. square stock and the 1 in. grid spacing are the same as for the other projects. Assemble the eight coasters using a small dab of glue at each half lap, and sand them smooth.

The plywood base (D) and the laminate (E) are laid up slightly oversize using white or yellow glue, and then cut to the final 3¾ in. square size on the table saw. White or yellow glue is preferable to contact cement for small laminate projects, since there is no waiting time while the cement becomes tacky. Next, glue the side and end edging (B and C) in place. A bearing-guided flush trimming router bit can be used to flush the edging with the laminate surface.

To make the posts (F), cut about 7 in. of ¹⁵⁄₁₆ in. square stock, then crosscut to get two pieces, each one 3⅛ in. long.

The best way to position the posts is to use the coasters as a guide. Anchor each post with a number 8 flat head wood screw, as illustrated. The screwheads must be countersunk so the coaster base will sit flat on the table.

Final sand with 220 grit aluminum oxide paper and finish all wood surfaces with penetrating oil. □

Bill of Materials
(all dimensions actual)

Part	Description	Size	No. Req'd.
A	Grid	$\frac{3}{8} \times \frac{3}{8} \times 3\frac{5}{8}$	48
B	Side	$\frac{3}{8} \times \frac{3}{8} \times 3\frac{3}{4}$	2
C	End	$\frac{3}{8} \times \frac{3}{8} \times 4\frac{1}{2}$	2
D	Plywood	$\frac{1}{4} \times 3\frac{3}{4} \times 3\frac{3}{4}$	1
E	Laminate	$\frac{1}{16} \times 3\frac{3}{4} \times 3\frac{3}{4}$	2
F	Post	$\frac{15}{16} \times \frac{15}{16} \times 3\frac{1}{8}$	2

COASTER (8 REQ'D)

E PLASTIC LAMINATE

D ¼" PLYWOOD

E PLASTIC LAMINATE

1¼" × #8 F.H. C'SUNK SCREWS

serving tray

t his sturdy little serving tray is easy to make, and features the same grid common to the napkin holder, trivets, and coasters.

A good place to start is with the sides (A). Refer to the grid pattern for the side profile, and cut to shape with the band saw. Next, make the handles (B). Round the edges with the router, using a ³⁄₁₆ in. radius round over bit, or approximate a ³⁄₁₆ in. round over by hand sanding. Mortise the sides to accept the handles by using a ³⁄₈ in. Forstner bit to drill two side-by-side holes, ¼ in. apart and ¼ in. deep. Then clean the waste between the holes with a chisel (Fig. 1). The handle location is shown on the grid.

Now make the lattice (D and E), using the simple jig shown in the latticemaking section (page 146). Make the stretchers (C), tenoning the ends as shown in the tenon detail. Assemble the grid, and add the stretchers on either end (see Fig. 2). Mortise the sides to accept the stretcher tenons and, after assembling the tray, fine sand and finish with penetrating oil. You can have the ¼ in. thick acrylic surface (F) cut to size at your local glass shop. □

Bill of Materials
(all dimensions actual)

Part	Description	Size	No. Req'd.
A	Side	$\frac{1}{2} \times 1\frac{3}{4} \times 20\frac{1}{2}$	2
B	Handle	$\frac{3}{8} \times 1 \times 9\frac{1}{8}$	2
C	Stretcher	$\frac{3}{8} \times 1 \times 9\frac{1}{8}$	2
D	Long Lattice	$\frac{3}{8} \times \frac{3}{8} \times 11\frac{3}{8}$	7
E	Short Lattice	$\frac{3}{8} \times \frac{3}{8} \times 8\frac{5}{8}$	9
F	Acrylic	$\frac{1}{4} \times 8\frac{5}{8} \times 11\frac{3}{8}$	1

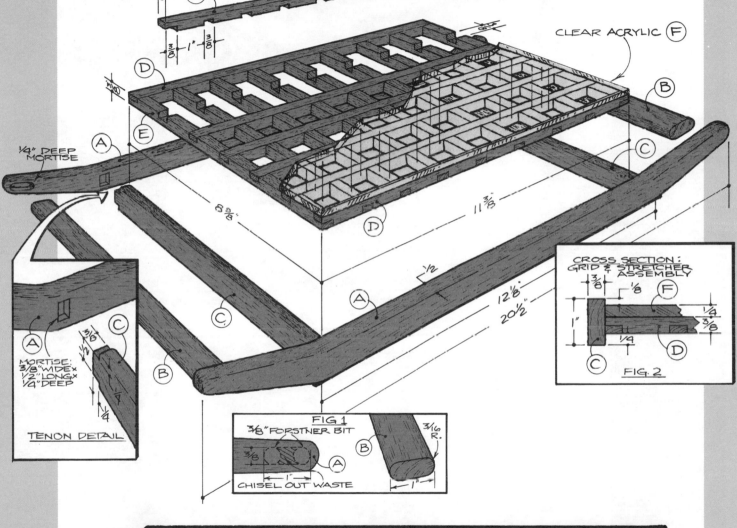

CLEAR ACRYLIC (F)

(D)

(D)

(E)

$\frac{3}{8}$ 1" $\frac{3}{8}$

(A)

¼" DEEP MORTISE

$8\frac{5}{8}$"

(D)

(C)

(B)

½

(A)

(C)

$11\frac{3}{8}$"

$12\frac{1}{8}$"

$20\frac{1}{2}$"

(B)

TENON DETAIL

(A)

(C)

MORTISE:
$\frac{3}{8}$"WIDE×
½"LONG×
¼"DEEP

$\frac{3}{8}$
½
¼
¼

CROSS SECTION:
GRID & STRETCHER
ASSEMBLY

$\frac{3}{8}$ $\frac{1}{8}$ (F)

1"   ¼   ¼ $\frac{3}{8}$

(C)   (D)

FIG. 2

FIG 1
$\frac{3}{8}$"FORSTNER BIT $\frac{3}{16}$ R.

(A)   (B)

$\frac{3}{8}$

1"   1"

CHISEL OUT WASTE

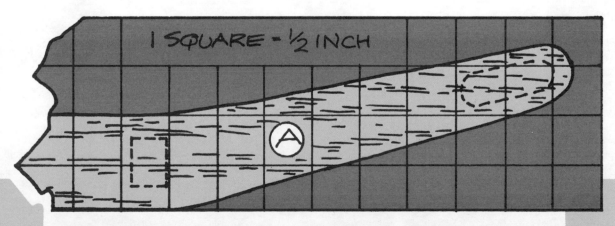

1 SQUARE = ½ INCH

(A)

shoji lamp

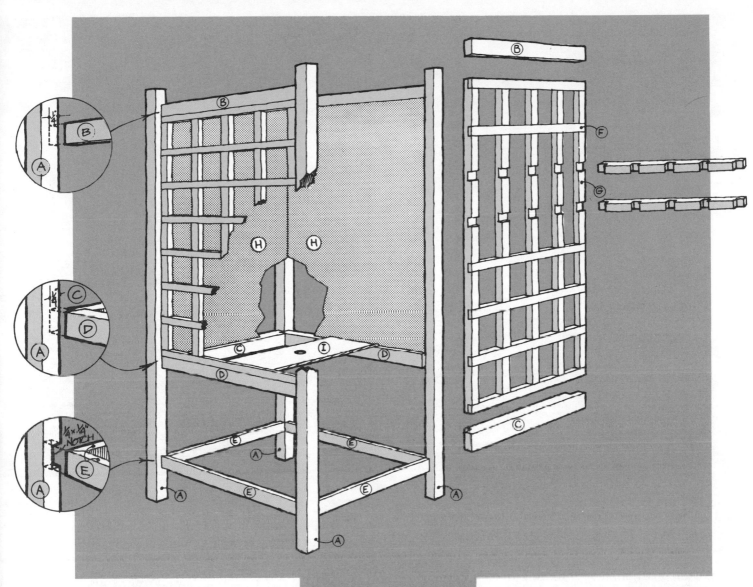

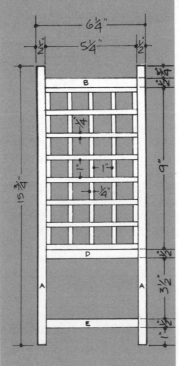

this particularly lovely accent piece was made using a combination of frosted glass, Brazilian rosewood, and walnut. Against glass, the crisscross latticework is very much reminiscent of shoji, the translucent paper screen partitions found in Japanese houses.

I used the rosewood for parts A, B, C, D, and E, and walnut for parts F and G. The result is very striking. However, keep in mind that just about any wood, even clear pine, can be used successfully.

Start by making the four posts (A). Select good straight stock and cut to the dimensions shown. Rip the posts slightly more than ½ in. square, then use a hand plane to shave them to size. Use a plane with a sharp blade, very little set, and cut with the grain. Removing a little from each of the four sides will result in a very smooth surface, eliminating the need for sanding later on.

Lay out the location of the notches for the lower stretchers (E). Use a sharp knife or hard, sharp pointed pencil to mark accurately, then chisel a ¼ in. deep by ¼ in. wide by ½ in. long notch in each post as shown. Chisel with care so that later, when the lower stretchers (E) are cut, they will fit snugly.

All the vertical grids (G) for one side can be made from a piece of stock measuring ¼ in. thick by 2 in. wide by 9½ in. long (these dimensions allow for some scrap). To get ¼ in. stock, start with a piece of ¾ in. stock measuring 2 in. wide by 9½ in.

(continued on next page)   157

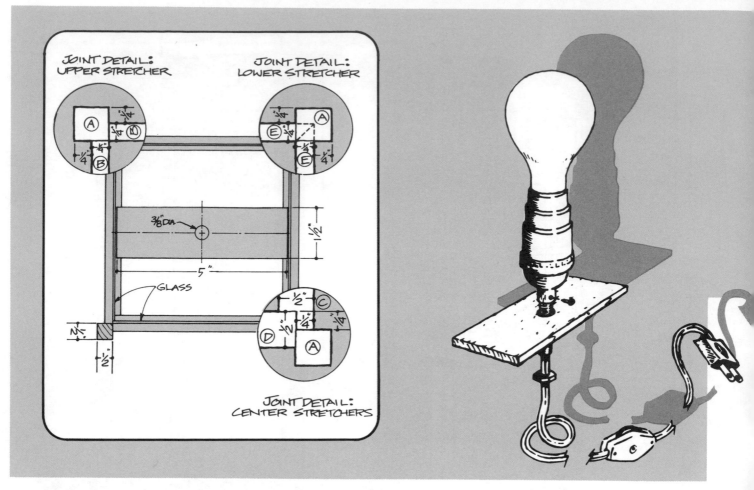

JOINT DETAIL:
UPPER STRETCHER

JOINT DETAIL:
LOWER STRETCHER

JOINT DETAIL:
CENTER STRETCHERS

long. Set the table saw blade to a height of $1\frac{1}{8}$ in. and adjust the rip fence to make a $\frac{1}{4}$ in. wide cut. Using a push stick, run the stock (on edge) through the blade, then flip over and make the same cut on the opposite edge. The result is a piece measuring $\frac{1}{4}$ in. × 2 in. × $9\frac{1}{2}$ in. If your sawblade cuts a reasonably narrow kerf, you should be able to cut one more piece from the original $\frac{3}{4}$ in. thick stock.

Probably the easiest way to make the notches is to use a lattice cutting jig. The cutting procedure is shown in the step-by-step drawings on page 146. After the notches have been cut, use the table saw to rip the stock into the required $\frac{1}{4}$ in. widths. (Before ripping, check the width of the notches, then rip the grid pieces so they are just slightly wider. Later, when the grids are sanded, the resulting fit should be near perfect.) A total of 20 vertical grids are needed. The horizontal grids (F) are made in the same way. Start with a piece of stock measuring $\frac{3}{4}$ in. thick by $1\frac{5}{8}$ in. wide by 11 in. long. When resawed, this should yield 16 pieces. The 11 in. length allows for two $5\frac{1}{4}$ in. lengths, thus yielding the necessary 32 horizontal grids.

Lay all the grid pieces on a flat surface, side by side. Using a medium sandpaper and a sanding block, lightly sand one side of the pieces until all noticeable saw marks are removed. Make sure you don't remove too much material or the pieces won't fit snugly in the notches. Final sand with fine sandpaper. Do this for all four sides of the grid pieces. When finished, check for a good fit-up in

the notches.

Assemble the grids using a dab of glue in each notch. With the grids laying on a flat surface, place a sheet of wax paper on top and add a few heavy books to provide clamping action. Make sure each grid is square before adding books. When the four grid assemblies have dried, cut parts B, C, and D to size and edge glue to the grids as shown. Note that parts C and D are the same except that parts C have a $\frac{1}{4}$ in. × $\frac{1}{4}$ in. notch on each end.

Cut parts E to size, mitering the ends. The grid assemblies are glued and clamped to the posts, and the lower stretchers are glued in place to provide additional rigidity. If the optional top grid is made, remember that it is not glued to the lamp. It must be removable to allow for bulb changing.

Four pieces of $\frac{1}{8}$ in. thick frosted glass (part H) are cut to fit the sides. Part I, the bulb socket support, also serves to contain the bottom of the glass. If necessary, a $\frac{1}{4}$ in. × $\frac{1}{4}$ in. × $5\frac{1}{4}$ in. strip (not shown) can be notched to fit over the glass to hold it in place at the top. Locate this strip against one of the upper stretchers so it will be unobtrusive.

A short nipple is now inserted into part I. The bulb socket is threaded into this and held in place with a locknut from underneath as shown. A line switch should be used in order to make it easy to turn the lamp on and off. Several coats of tung oil completes the project. □

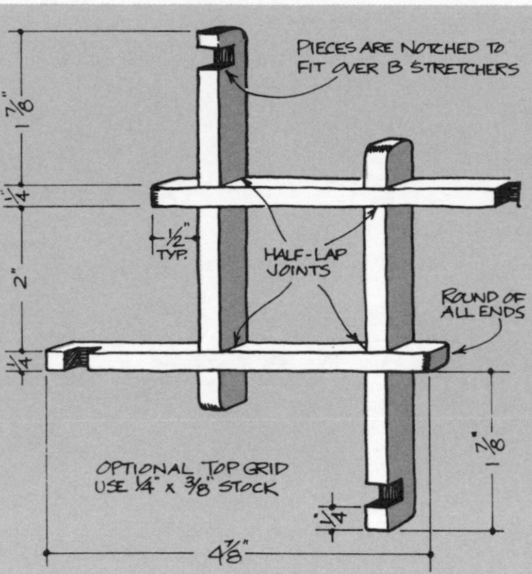
PIECES ARE NOTCHED TO FIT OVER B STRETCHERS
1 7/8"
1/4"
1/2" TYP.
HALF-LAP JOINTS
2"
ROUND OF ALL ENDS
1/4"
OPTIONAL TOP GRID USE 1/4" x 3/8" STOCK
1 7/8"
1/4"
4 7/8"

Bill of Materials
(all dimensions actual)

Part	Description	Size	No. Req'd.
A	Post	½ x ½ x 15¾	4
B	Upper Stretcher	¼ x ½ x 5¼	4
C	Center Stretcher (notched)	½ x ½ x 5¼	2
D	Center Stretcher	½ x ½ x 5¼	2
E	Lower Stretcher	¼ x ½ x 5¾	4
F	Horizontal Grid	¼ x ¼ x 5¼	32
G	Vertical Grid	¼ x ¼ x 9	20
H	Frosted Glass	⅛ thick	4
I	Socket Support	⅛ x 1½ x 5	1

sources of supply

united states

The following is a list of companies that specialize in mail-order sales of woodworking supplies. Write to them for the cost of their current catalog.

general woodworking suppliers

Constantine's
2050 Eastchester Rd.
Bronx, NY 10461

Craftsman Wood Service
1735 West Cortland Ct.
Addison, IL 60101

The Fine Tool Shops
20 Backus Ave.
Danbury, CT 06810

Frog Tool Co., Ltd.
700 W. Jackson Blvd.
Chicago, Il 60606

Garrett Wade
161 Avenue of the Americas
New York, NY 10013

Shopsmith, Inc.
6640 Poe Ave.
Dayton, OH 45414

Trend-Lines
375 Beacham St.
Chelsea, MA 02150-0999

Woodcraft Supply Corp.
41 Atlantic Ave.
Woburn, MA 01888

The Woodworkers' Store
21801 Industrial Blvd.
Rogers, MN 55374

Woodworker's Supply of New Mexico
5604 Alameda, N.E.
Alburquerque, NM 87113

hardware suppliers

Allen Specialty Hardware
332 W. Bruceton Rd.
Pittsburgh, PA 15236

Anglo-American Brass Co.
Box 9487
4146 Mitzi Drive
San Jose, CA 95157

Horton Brasses
Nooks Hill Rd.
P.O. Box 120
Cromwell, CT 06416

Imported European Hardware
3820 Schiff Dr.
Las Vegas, NV 89103

Paxton Hardware, Ltd.
7818 Bradshaw Rd.
Upper Falls, MD 21156

Period Furniture Hardware Co.
123 Charles St.
Box 314 Charles Street Station
Boston, MA 02114

Stanley Hardware
195 Lake Street
New Britain, CT 06050

The Wise Co.
6503 St. Claude
Arabi, LA 70032

hardwood suppliers

American Woodcrafters
905 S. Roosevelt Ave.
Piqua, OH 45356

Austin Hardwoods
2119 Goodrich
Austin, TX 78704

Craftwoods
109 21 York Rd.
Cockeysville, MD 21030

Croy-Marietta Hardwoods, Inc.
121 Pike St., Box 643
Marietta, OH 45750

General Woodcraft
531 Broad St.
New London, CT 06320

Hardwoods of Memphis
P.O. Box 12449
Memphis, TN 38182-0449

Kaymar Wood Products
4603 35th S.W.
Seattle, WA 98126

Kountry Kraft Hardwoods
R.R. No. 1
Lake City, IA 51449

Leonard Lumber Co.
P.O. Box 2396
Branford, CT 06405

Dimension Hardwood Inc.
113 Canal St.
Shelton, CT 06484

McFeely's Hardwoods & Lumber
43 Cabell St.
Lynchburg, VA 24505

Native American Hardwoods
Route 1
West Valley, NY 14171

Sterling Hardwoods, Inc.
412 Pine St.
Burlington, VT 05401

Wood World
1719 Chestnut
Glenview, IL 60025

wood finishing supplies

Finishing Products and Supply Co.
4611 Macklind Ave.
St. Louis, MO 63109

Industrial Finishing Products
465 Logan St.
Brooklyn, NY 11208

The Wise Co.
P.O. Box 118
6503 St. Claude
Arabie, LA 70032

WoodFinishing Enterprises
Box 10017
Milwaukee, WI 53210

Watco-Dennis Corp.
19610 Rancho Way
Rancho de Minguez, CA 90220

clock parts

Craft Products Co.
2200 Dean St.
St. Charles, IL 60174

Klockit, Inc.
P.O. Box 542
Lake Geneva, WI 53147

S. LaRose
234 Commerce Place
Greensboro, NC 27420

Mason & Sullivan Co.
586 Higgins Crowell Rd.
West Yarmouth, MA 02655

Newport Enterprises
2313 West Burbank Blvd.
Burbank, CA 91506

miscellaneous

Formica Corporation
1 Stanford Road
Piscataway, NJ 08854

Freud
218 Feld Ave.
High Point, NC 27264

Sears, Roebuck and Co.
925 S. Homan Ave.
Chicago, IL 60607

Wilson Art
600 General Bruce Drive
Temple, TX 76501

sources of supply

general woodworking suppliers

House of Tools Ltd.
131-12th Ave. S.E.
Calgary, Alberta T2G 0Z9

J. Philip Humfrey International
3241 Kennedy Rd., Unit 7
Scarborough, Ontario M1V 2J9

Lee Valley Tools
Unit 6, 5511 Steeles Ave. West
Weston, Ontario M9L 1S7

Stockade Woodworker's Supply
P.O. Box 1415
Salmon Arm, British Columbia V0E 2T0

Tool Trend Ltd.
3280 Steele's Ave. West
Concord, Ontario L4K 2Y2

Treen Heritage, Ltd.
P.O. Box 280
Merrickville, Ontario K0G 1N0

hardware suppliers

Home Workshop Supplies
RR 2
Arthur, Ontario N0G 1A0

Lee Valley Tools
Unit 6, 5511 Steeles Ave. West
Weston, Ontario M9L 1S7

Pacific Brass Hardware
1414 Monterey Ave.
Victoria, British Columbia V8S 4W1

Steve's Shop, Woodworking & Supplies
RR 3
Woodstock, Ontario M9V 5C3

hardwood suppliers

A & C Hutt Enterprises, Ltd.
15861 32nd Ave.
Surrey, British Columbia V4B 4Z5

Longstock Lumber & Veneer
440 Phillip St., Unit 21
Waterloo, Ontario N2L 5R9

Unicorn Universal Woods Ltd.
4190 Steeles Ave. West, Unit 4
Woodbridge, Ontario L4L 3S8

clock parts

Hurst Associates
151 Nashdene Rd., Unit 14
Scarborough, Ontario M1V 2T3

Kidder Klock
39 Glen Cameron Rd., Unit 3
Thornhill, Ontario L3T 1P1

Murray Clock Craft Ltd.
510 McNicoll Ave.
Willowdale, Ontario M2H 2E1

miscellaneous

Freud
100 Westmore Dr., Unit 10
Rexdale, Ontario M9V 5C3